1000
football
clubs

First published in the United States of America in 2016 by
Universe Publishing, a division of Rizzoli International Publications, Inc.
300 Park Avenue South, New York, NY 10010
www.rizzoliusa.com

Created by Copyright Éditions
www.copyrighteditions.com
104, boulevard Arago
75014 Paris – France

Editorial direction/ Nicolas Marçais
Art direction/ Philippe Marchand
Layout/ Emigreen and Thomas Hamel
Editor/ Zarko Telebak
Author/ Jean Damien Lesay

Acknowledgements
Copyright Éditions would like to thank all of the trademark holders (clubs, national associations, manufacturers, sponsors etc.) for the emblems reproduced in this work.

The honours listed are accurate as of November 9, 2015.

Library of Congress Control Number: 2015957351
ISBN-13: 978-0-7893-3110-6

2016 2017 2018 2019 / 10 9 8 7 6 5 4 3 2 1

Printed in Malaysia by Tien Wah Press

1000 football clubs

TEAMS, STADIUMS, AND LEGENDS OF THE BEAUTIFUL GAME

Jean Damien Lesay

UNIVERSE

CONTENTS

PREFACE 7

EUROPE 8

THE AMERICAS 172

AFRICA 244

ASIA AND OCEANIA 280

Across the globe football has become a social phenomenon, a part of mass culture.

Preface

ootball is by far the most popular sport in the world. From Argentina to Zimbabwe, enthusiasts of every age can be found kicking balls around or excitedly following the exploits of the teams that represent them, at national, regional, or local levels.

Across the globe, football has become a social phenomenon, a part of mass culture, and clubs are often a reflection of this reality. The club is where all of this collective passion becomes crystallized. Season after season, throughout the year, one's club gives rise to hope, immense joy, and sometimes hardships that are just as fierce. A championship title, one more cup in the display case, and supporters' hearts are lifted! A defeat in the final, or worse, relegation to a lower division, and their mood quickly changes. Yet with each new season, loyal fans return to the stadium and shout out chants of encouragement to their beloved teams

1000 Football Clubs takes the reader on an international tour of football clubs, big and small, capturing the essence of what makes each one unique. This book covers clubs from every country on earth, including iconic giants such as Real Madrid, Manchester United, and Boca Juniors, as well as local heroes such as Deportivo Motagua (Honduras), Phnom Penh Crown FC (Cambodia), and Koloale FC (Solomon Islands).

The history of 1000 important clubs across the globe is fleshed out through their victories, star players, golden eras, fiercely contested derbies, interesting anecdotes, and also a look at the fans themselves, the heart and soul of these teams.

"I feel close to the rebelliousness and vigour of the youth here. Perhaps time will separate us, but nobody can deny that here, behind the Manchester windows, there is an insane love of football, of celebration, and of music."
Eric Cantona, Manchester United player from 1992 to 1997.

MANCHESTER UNITED

The Red Devils

Founded: **1878** • Stadium: **Old Trafford (Manchester)**

Originally called Newton Heath, the club was founded by the employees of a regional railroad company. The first major successes came in the 1950s. Manchester United's fearsome record on the pitch (the club has won more league titles than any other English club) is built largely on its youth training program, while its economic success owes much to exceptional financial planning. Manchester United is one of the most popular clubs in the world and rarely has trouble filling its 78,000 capacity home at Old Trafford, nicknamed the Theatre of Dreams, which draws millions of fans in a form of pilgrimage.

20 League Titles

11 FA Cups

3 Champions League / European Cups

The number of goals scored by Manchester United striker Denis Law in all competitions during the 1963-64 season.

46

George Best
After winning the Ballon d'Or in 1968, he became a legend at Old Trafford.

963

The cost, in millions of euros, of Cristiano Ronaldo's transfer from Manchester United to Real Madrid in 2009.

94

The number of games played by Ryan Giggs in the Manchester United shirt, between 1991 and 2014.

Alex Ferguson
As manager of Manchester United from 1986 to 2013, he brought 38 titles to the Red Devils.

February 6, 1968
Manchester United's players pose together one last time before getting on their plane, in Munich.

THE MUNICH AIR DISASTER

On February 6, 1958, an air crash in Munich ripped a hole in the team, at a time when Manchester United dominated English football—having won the league title in 1956 and 1957—and was preparing to conquer Europe. This exceptional generation was trained by Jimmy Murphy and then coached by Matt Busby, and many of the players were barely over twenty years old. The team were returning from Belgrade, where they had played a match against Red Star that had qualified them for the semi-finals of the European Cup for the second year running. Eight "Busby Babes" perished in the disaster. But Manchester United recovered, and ten years later the club won its first European title. In commemoration of the tragedy, the Munich Clock was installed at Old Trafford, its hands permanently stopped at 3:30—the time of the crash.

THE INCREDIBLE SHOWDOWN IN BARCELONA

In 1999, under the direction of Alex Ferguson, charismatic coach of Manchester United for twenty-seven years, a generation embodied by Ryan Giggs, David Beckham, and Paul Scholes had reached maturity. The team were playing in the finals of the Champions League, in Barcelona, and were 1–0 down against Bayern Munich at the end of regulation time. But United's determination would see Teddy Sheringham and Ole Gunnar Solskjær score a goal each during the three minutes of injury time to snatch victory for Manchester United, along with their second Champions League trophy.

May 26, 1999
During the last seconds of the final, Ole Gunnar Solskjær gives United an unexpected victory, making the club champions of Europe for the third time in their history.

ENGLAND

They wrote the history of the Red Devils.
1. Jack Rowley (1937-1954); 2. Dennis Viollet (1950-1962);
3. Bill Foulkes (1951-1970); 4. Bobby Charlton (1956-1973);
5. Denis Law (1962-1973); 6. Peter Schmeichel (1991-1999);
7. Ryan Giggs (1991-2014); 8. David Beckham (1992-2003);
9. Gary Neville (1992-2011); 10. Roy Keane (1993-2005);
11. Paul Scholes (1994-2011, then 2012-2013);
12. Cristiano Ronaldo (2003-2009);
13. Wayne Rooney (since 2004).

ENGLAND

ERIC CANTONA, KING OF OLD TRAFFORD

In 1992, when Eric Cantona arrived at Manchester United from Leeds, a team that had been crowned champions, the club managed by Alex Ferguson had not won a title for twenty-six years. Through his audacity, technical prowess, charisma, and tenacity, the French player would provide his new club with that magic element it needed to triumph. In 1993, this canny addition helped Man United become champions of England. By the time Cantona left in 1997, the club had won three more titles and two cups. As renowned for his crafty footwork as he was for his feisty temper, Eric Cantona earned himself a reputation as a rebel genius who could wow the fans. Initially known as "Frenchie," he was soon dubbed "The King," and was named "player of the century" in 2001 by Manchester United supporters.

Star players: Dennis Viollet, Duncan Edwards, Bobby Charlton, Denis Law, George Best, Bryan Robson, Mark Hughes, Ryan Giggs, Peter Schmeichel, Eric Cantona, Roy Keane, Paul Scholes, David Beckham, Cristiano Ronaldo, Wayne Rooney.

Honours: League: 1908, 1911, 1952, 1956, 1957, 1965, 1967, 1993, 1994, 1996, 1997, 1999, 2000, 2001, 2003, 2007, 2008, 2009, 2011, 2013; FA Cup: 1909, 1948, 1963, 1977, 1983, 1985, 1990, 1994, 1996, 1999, 2004; League Cup: 1992, 2006, 2009, 2010; European Cup/Champions League: 1968, 1999, 2008; UEFA Cup Winners' Cup: 1991; Intercontinental Cup: 1999; FIFA Club World Cup: 2008.

"For a player to be good enough to play for Liverpool, he must be prepared to run through a brick wall for me then come out fighting on the other side."
Bill Shankly, Liverpool manager, 1959–1974.

LIVERPOOL FC

The Reds

Founded: **1892** · Stadium: **Anfield (Liverpool)**

Liverpool Football Club would never have seen the light of day if Everton—the tenant at Anfield Road—hadn't left the stadium in 1892, forcing the owner to find another club. The Reds built on the strength of this original local rivalry against Everton and have accrued the second best set of honours in English football after Manchester United. Since the 1960s, the determination shown by their players on the pitch has been equalled only by the fervour emanating from the Anfield grandstands during matches. But alongside this sporting glory and effervescent support, the club's history has also been marked by two tragedies: the Heysel Stadium disaster in 1985, and the Hillsborough disaster in 1989.

18 League Titles

7 FA Cups

5 Champions League / European Cups

3 UEFA Cups

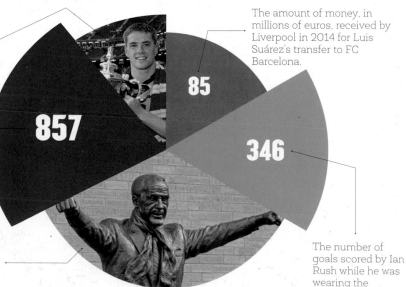

Michael Owen
On May 6, 1997, during a game against Wimbledon, he became the youngest striker in the history of the Reds: he was 17 years and 144 days old.

The amount of money, in millions of euros, received by Liverpool in 2014 for Luis Suárez's transfer to FC Barcelona.

85

The number of games played by midfielder Ian Callaghan for Liverpool.

857

346

Bill Shankly
At the entrance of the Kop at Anfield, a statue pays tribute to the legendary manager of the Reds between 1959 and 1974.

The number of goals scored by Ian Rush while he was wearing the Liverpool shirt.

LIVERPOOL FC
YOU'LL NEVER WALK ALONE

YOU'LL NEVER WALK ALONE

*When you walk through a storm / Hold your head up high / And don't be
afraid of the dark / At the end of the storm / And the sweet silver
song of a lark / Walk on through the wind / Walk on through
the rain / Though your dreams be tossed and blown / Walk on, walk
on with hope in your heart / And you'll never walk alone*

THE KOP, SYMBOL OF THE RED TRIBE

The word "kop" has now become common currency to describe a grandstand where a club's fiercest fans gather for home matches, but the usage was started by the Liverpool fans whose historic base was one of the terraces at Anfield, dubbed Spion Kop in 1906. The name comes from a hill in Natal (South Africa), scene of a battle in the Boer War, where many British soldiers from Liverpool met their deaths in January, 1900. Liverpool's original Kop had a capacity of 28,000 (standing), but this was reduced to 12,000 (seated) in 1994.

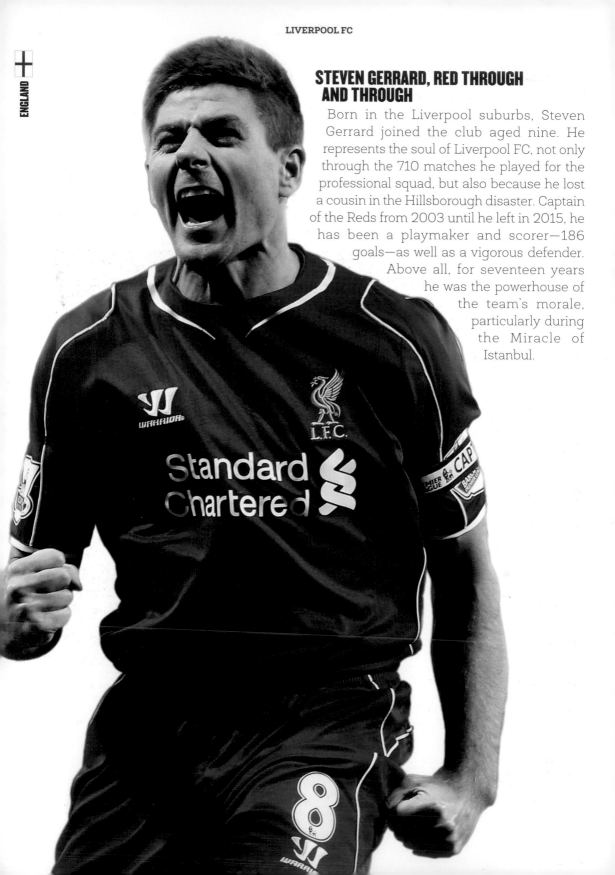

ENGLAND

STEVEN GERRARD, RED THROUGH AND THROUGH

Born in the Liverpool suburbs, Steven Gerrard joined the club aged nine. He represents the soul of Liverpool FC, not only through the 710 matches he played for the professional squad, but also because he lost a cousin in the Hillsborough disaster. Captain of the Reds from 2003 until he left in 2015, he has been a playmaker and scorer—186 goals—as well as a vigorous defender. Above all, for seventeen years he was the powerhouse of the team's morale, particularly during the Miracle of Istanbul.

ENGLAND

THE MIRACLE OF ISTANBUL

Liverpool had won the European Cup four times, but their 2005 Champions League victory was unexpected. At half-time in the final—played in Istanbul against the AC Milan of Pirlo, Shevchenko, and Seedorf—the Reds were losing 3–0. Could the players hear the chanting of the 40,000 fans who had made the long journey and were still full of hope? Whatever it was, the miracle happened, and by the end of the second half, Liverpool had pulled back to 3–3, and went on to win after a penalty shootout that recalled the one that had handed them victory in 1984, against Roma. In 2005, goalkeeper Jerzy Dudek managed to unsettle the opposing penalty-takers, just as Bruce Grobbelaar had done twenty-one years earlier.

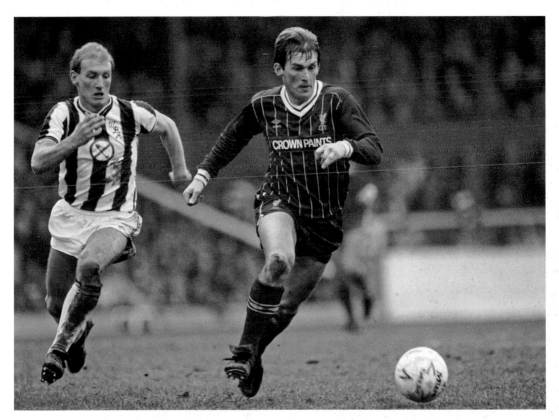

Star players: Roger Hunt, Tommy Smith, Billy Liddell, Phil Neal, Ian Callaghan, Kevin Keegan, Ian Rush, Emlyn Hughes, Ray Clemence, Graeme Souness, Kenny Dalglish, Bruce Grobbelaar, John Barnes, Robbie Fowler, Steven Gerrard, Michael Owen, Jamie Carragher, Fernando Torres, Luis Suarez.

Honours: League: 1901, 1906, 1922, 1923, 1947, 1964, 1966, 1973, 1976, 1977, 1979, 1980, 1982, 1983, 1984, 1986, 1988, 1990; FA Cup: 1965, 1974, 1986, 1989, 1992, 2001, 2006; League Cup: 1981, 1982, 1983, 1984, 1995, 2001, 2003, 2012; European Cup/Champions League: 1977, 1978, 1981, 1984, 2005; UEFA Cup: 1973, 1976, 2001.

Kenny Dalglish
Seven-time champion of England and three-time European champion, Dalglish was a hero in the 1980s. He became player-manager, then after coaching Scotland, returned two decades later to manage the club.

"At some clubs success is accidental. At Arsenal it is compulsory."
Arsène Wenger, Arsenal manager, 1996–.

ARSENAL FC
The Gunners

Founded: **1886** · Stadium: **Emirates (London)**

Founded by workers from an armaments factory, Arsenal was the first club in London to turn professional, in 1897. The club has had some wonderful periods, dominating England in the 1930s under manager Herbert "The Great Innovator" Chapman, and, in 1971, pulling off the second league/cup double in the twentieth century. Arsenal's greatest successes, however, have come since the arrival of the French coach, Arsène Wenger, in 1996. In 2006, the Gunners just missed winning the final of the Champions League, losing 1–2 to FC Barcelona. Arsenal maintains a rivalry with Tottenham that goes back to 1887, and which was amplified when the Gunners moved to North London, close to their adversaries.

13 League Titles

12 FA Cups

2 League Cups

2 European Titles

Thierry Henry
With 228 goals in 377 games, Henry is the top scorer in Arsenal's history.

The number of goals scored in the league by Gunner Ted Drake during the 1934-35 season.

42

722
The number of games played by defender David O'Leary while he was wearing the Gunners' shirt.

38

Dennis Bergkamp
As they did for Thierry Henry, the club erected a statue in front of the stadium in honour of the Dutchman, who helped Arsenal become English champions in 1998, 2002 and 2004.

The number of successive games without defeat in the Premier League during the 2003-04 season out of 38 games in total.

A PRAYER FOR ARSENAL

"You Haven't Got A Prayer, Arsenal" ran one tabloid headline the morning of the last day of the English league title race in 1989. That day, the Gunners were playing away at Liverpool—who were top of the league—and needed to win by a two-goal difference to overtake the Reds and grab the title. One minute from the end of the match, with a solid Liverpool having conceded just one goal, Arsenal launched their final attack, and the young Michael Thomas managed to dribble past the last Liverpool defender before slipping the ball past the goalkeeper, Grobbelaar. Eighteen years after their last league title, Arsenal were back on top.

May 30, 2015
Arsène Wenger's Gunners celebrate their club's twelfth victory in the final of the FA Cup.

Star players: Alex James, Cliff Bastin, Ted Drake, Bob Wilson, Frank McLintock, George Graham, Charlie George, Liam Brady, Pat Jennings, David O'Leary, Lee Dixon, Tony Adams, David Seaman, Ian Wright, Dennis Bergkamp, Emmanuel Petit, Patrick Vieira, Thierry Henry, Theo Walcott, Olivier Giroud, Mesut Özil, Alexis Sanchez.

Honours: League: 1931, 1933, 1934, 1935, 1938, 1948, 1953, 1971, 1989, 1991, 1998, 2002, 2004; FA Cup: 1930, 1936, 1950, 1971, 1979, 1993, 1998, 2002, 2003, 2005, 2014, 2015; League Cup: 1987, 1993; UEFA Cup Winners' Cup: 1994; UEFA Cup: 1970.

"I had a lot of offers but Chelsea were the only club I would have signed for." **George Best.**

CHELSEA FC

The Blues

Founded: **1905**

Stadium: **Stamford Bridge (London)**

It might appear unfair, but that's the way it is: after a century of history, a golden period in the 1960s, and despite enjoying a popularity as strong as ever, Chelsea would not be what they are today without the hundreds of millions of pounds invested by their owner, Roman Abramovich, since 2003. By hiring some of the best players in the world, he enabled the fans to touch the holy grail: a league title in 2005—fifty years after their first—and a Champions League trophy in 2012, four years after their defeat in the final to their rivals, Manchester United.

5 League Titles

7 FA Cups

5 League Cups

4 European Titles

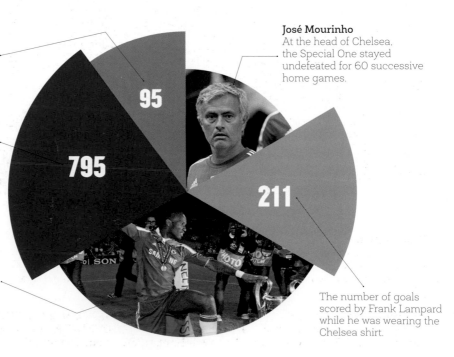

The number of points obtained by Chelsea in the Premier League during the 2004-05 season: an unforgettable record.
95

The number of games played for Chelsea by defender Ron Harris between 1961 and 1980.
795

Didier Drogba
As Chelsea's top scorer in the Champions League, he scored the equaliser (1-1) against Bayern in the 2012 final, just before the Blues' win in the penalty shoot-out.

José Mourinho
At the head of Chelsea, the Special One stayed undefeated for 60 successive home games.

211

The number of goals scored by Frank Lampard while he was wearing the Chelsea shirt.

BULLDOG SPIRIT: CHAMPION, LEADER, LEGEND

Amidst the star players brought in from all over the world, there is one man who embodies the English spirit within the Chelsea squad: John Terry. By June 2015, he had racked up no fewer than 669 matches for the club. Terry didn't hesitate to take over in goal during a match in 2006, when the first and second string goalkeepers were injured and Chelsea had no substitutions left. It seemed quite appropriate that he should take over as captain in 2005, the year that Chelsea won the league title again after fifty dry years.

May 19, 2012
John Terry (right) and Frank Lampard celebrate Chelsea's victory in the Champions League final.

April 30, 1970
Ron Harris (left) and Peter Bonetti parade through the streets of London with the FA Cup, the first in the club's history.

Star players: William Foulke, Jimmy Greaves, Terry Venables, Ian Hutchinson, Ray Wilkins, Ruud Gullit, Mark Hughes, Gianluca Vialli, Frank Leboeuf, Gianfranco Zola, Marcel Desailly, Claude Makelele, John Terry, Petr Cech, Ricardo Carvalho, Carlo Cudicini, Jimmy Floyd Hasselbaink, Didier Drogba, Ashley Cole, Frank Lampard.

Honours: League: 1955, 2005, 2006, 2010, 2015; FA Cup: 1970, 1997, 2000, 2007, 2009, 2010, 2012; League Cup: 1965, 1998, 2005, 2007, 2015; UEFA Champions League: 2012; UEFA Cup Winners' Cup: 1971, 1998; UEFA Europa League 2013.

"The United fans love George Best because he was such a great player, but the City fans love him too because he liked to have a good time and was a bit of a mod." **Noel Gallagher, musician and Manchester City fan.**

MANCHESTER CITY FC

The Sky Blues

Founded: **1880** · Stadium: **City of Manchester (Manchester)**

Founded as St. Mark's (West Gorton), the club was renamed Ardwick in 1887, and became a founding member of the second division in 1892, two years before they took the name Manchester City. In 1899, they were the first club in history to be promoted to the first division, then the first club in Manchester to win a major trophy: the 1904 FA Cup. And so their long rivalry with Manchester United began. Although there have been some highs, mainly in the 1970s, City have tended to remain in the shadow of their giant neighbours. In 2008, history took a fresh turn when City were bought by investors from Abu Dhabi, making the club one of the wealthiest in the world, with the buying power to sign major players. After decades of waiting, Manchester City became league champions in 2012 and 2014.

4 League Titles

5 National Cups

3 League Cups

1 Cup Winners' Cup

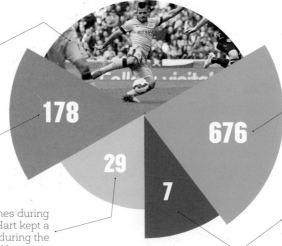

Sergio Agüero
He played a major role in the success of Manchester City during the 2012 and 2014 seasons of the Premier League. He is also City's top scorer in the history of their European campaigns.

The number of goals scored by Eric Brook for Manchester City.

The number of games during which goalkeeper Joe Hart kept a clean sheet during the 2010-11 season.

The number of games played by English midfielder Alan Oakes while he was wearing the Manchester City shirt (1959-1976).

The number of English minor league titles won by Manchester City (1899, 1903, 1910, 1928, 1947, 1966, 2002).

178

29

7

676

"BLUE MOON," THE CITY ANTHEM

The English grandstands of the 1980s were marked by the appropriation of popular songs rewritten to the glory of the respective clubs. For Manchester City, the choice fell upon "Blue Moon," an American standard that was notably covered by Elvis Presley. The fans of neighbouring Crewe Alexandra FC were the first to sing it in the stands. And it was in 1989, while playing in Liverpool, that City fans sung for the first time this melancholy number that would become their anthem. In 2010, a film about Manchester City supporters was entitled Blue Moon Rising.

May 11, 2014
Manchester City celebrate their fourth English champions title.

Star players: Billy Meredith, Eric Brook, Tommy Johnson, Roy Clarke, Alan Oakes, Johnny Hart, Joe Corrigan, Francis Lee, Colin Bell, Mike Summerbee, Neil Young, Shaun Goater, Joe Hart, Robinho, Pablo Zabaleta, Vincent Kompany, David Silva, Samir Nasri, Yaya Touré, Carlos Tevez, Sergio Agüero.

Honours: League: 1937, 1968, 2012, 2014; FA Cup: 1904, 1934, 1956, 1969, 2011; League Cup: 1970, 1976, 2014; Cup Winners' Cup: 1970.

"They always manage to serve up football of the highest scientific order."
Steve Bloomer, English international, speaking about Everton in 1928.

EVERTON FC

The Toffees

Founded: **1878** • Stadium: **Goodison Park (Liverpool)**

Everton are giants of English football, with a record 111 seasons in the first division and nine league titles. Founded by the parishioners of a Methodist church, the club's historic rivals are Liverpool FC, themselves derived from a split within "The Blues." Everton built their success and their popularity on a "scientific" style of play, rather than the traditional "long ball" style of British football. ⚽ The Golden Vision. In 1968, director Ken Loach made a film for television about Everton supporters. It was called The Golden Vision, after the nickname of Scottish player Alex Young, a star of the successful Toffees squad of the 1960s. Young helped Everton come back from two goals down to win the 1966 FA Cup final (3-2).

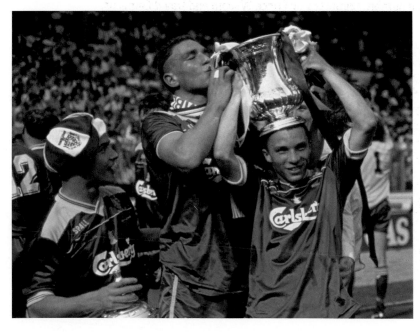

9
League Titles

5
FA Cups

1
Cup Winners' Cup

May 11, 1987
Everton win the First Division trophy for the ninth time.

Star players: Jack Sharp, Dixie Dean, Alex Young, Brian Labone, Alan Ball, Peter Reid, Graeme Sharp, Kevin Ratcliffe, Gary Stevens, Trevor Steven, Neville Southall, Mikel Arteta.

Honours: League: 1891, 1915, 1928, 1932, 1939, 1963, 1970, 1985, 1987; FA Cup: 1906, 1933, 1966, 1984, 1995; Cup Winners' Cup: 1985.

"There's a good ball in for Tony Morley. Oh, it must be and it is! It's Peter Withe." **Brian Moore, ITV, May 26, 1982.**

ASTON VILLA
The Claret and Blue Army

Founded: **1874**
Stadium: **Villa Park (Birmingham)**

Aston Villa started playing at Villa Park in 1897, and soon found themselves centre-stage, as the most successful club in England at the turn of the twentieth century, before dipping, then finding glory again in the early 1980s. In 1982, the team reached the final of the European Cup in Rotterdam where they faced Bayern Munich. Substitute goalkeeper Nigel Spink, who had only ever played one match for the side, was brought on after veteran goalkeeper Jimmy Rimmer's recurring shoulder injury flared up. Spink became a hero, repelling all of the German team's attacks. In the sixty-seventh minute, Peter Withe scored the goal that made Villa the fourth English club to be crowned European champions. Aston Villa are still the major club of England's second largest city, where they contest a derby against Birmingham City. Villa are notably supported by Prince William and David Cameron.

7
League
Titles

7
FA
Cups

1
European
Cup

April 19, 2015
Aston Villa at home against Liverpool in the FA Cup semi-finals.

Star players: Charlie Aitken, Dennis Mortimer, Gary Shaw, Gordon Cowans, Peter Withe, Gareth Southgate, David Platt, Paul McGrath, Dwight Yorke, Stiliyan Petrov, Ashley Young.

Honours: League: 1894, 1896, 1897, 1899, 1900, 1910, 1981; FA Cup: 1887, 1895, 1897, 1905, 1913, 1920, 1957; League Cup: 1961, 1975, 1977, 1994, 1996; European Cup: 1982.

"Here in Newcastle they work all week, pick their wages up on a Thursday or a Friday, and they want to spend it. It's a great place to play football, because they're so fanatical." **Alan Shearer**.

NEWCASTLE UNITED
The Magpies

Founded: **1892** · Stadium: **St James' Park (Newcastle)**

Newcastle United won most of their trophies in the early twentieth century, but were much talked about in the 1990s, when the new owner's wealth allowed manager Kevin Keegan—who had taken over when the club was in the second division—to recruit such stars as Alan Shearer, David Ginola, and Les Ferdinand. As a result, the Magpies finished second in the Premier League: in 1996 then 1997, behind Manchester United. ⚽ Fans who are prepared to circle the globe: The Magpies have a devoted following, with an average attendance at home games of over 40,000 for the past fifteen years. In 2011, a study showed that over the course of the season, the average Newcastle fan travelled the equivalent of circling the globe to follow their team when they played away.

4 League Titles

6 FA Cups

Two legendary Magpies
Chris Waddle (left) started his professional career in 1982 by joining Newcastle, where he stayed for three years. Alan Shearer (right), Magpies striker between 1996 and 2006, is the top scorer in the history of the club with 206 goals in 405 games.

Star players: Hughie Gallagher, Jacky Milburn, Bobby Mitchell, Bobby Moncur, Kevin Keegan, Malcolm McDonald, Chris Waddle, Paul Gascoigne, Alan Shearer, Andy Cole, Les Ferdinand, David Ginola, Faustino Asprilla, Peter Beardsley.

Honours: League: 1905, 1907, 1909, 1927; FA Cup: 1910, 1924, 1932, 1951, 1952, 1955; UEFA Cup: 1969.

"It's no use just winning, we've got to win well."
Bill Nicholson, Tottenham manager 1958–1974.

TOTTENHAM HOTSPUR
Spurs

Founded: **1882**
Stadium: **White Hart Lane (London)**

Although Tottenham are not the most successful of English clubs, they have long stood out, owing to their beautiful game in a country where the "long ball" or "kick and rush" style has often been many teams' sole tactic. This aesthetic quest is not surprising when you consider that the club was founded by grammar school pupils, who picked the club's name—Hotspur—after a character from Shakespeare's play Henry IV, Part I. The "glory game" was being played at White Hart Lane from the 1950s. And it worked, with Spurs becoming the first English team to win a European title, in 1963. In the 1980s and 1990s, Ardiles, Hoddle, Hateley, Klinsmann, and Ginola delighted spectators with their inspired play.

2 League Titles

8 FA Cups

3 European Titles

May 20, 1967
Dave Mackay, Spurs' captain, receives the FA Cup trophy from Harold Wilson, Prime Minister of the United Kingdom.

Star players: Alf Ramsey, Danny Blanchflower, Jimmy Greaves, Osvaldo Ardiles, Ricardo Villa, Ray Clemence, Chris Waddle, Paul Gascoigne, Glenn Hoddle, Gary Lineker, Jürgen Klinsmann, Teddy Sheringham, David Ginola, Sol Campbell, Robbie Keane.

Honours: League: 1951, 1961; FA Cup: 1901, 1921, 1961, 1962, 1967, 1981, 1982, 1991; League Cup: 1971, 1973, 1999, 2008; Cup Winners' Cup: 1963; UEFA Cup: 1972, 1984.

"I wouldn't say I was the best manager in the business. But I was in the top one." **Brian Clough.**

NOTTINGHAM FOREST

Forest

FOREST

Founded: **1865** • Stadium: **City Ground (Nottingham)**

Legendary head coach Brian Clough demanded he be given complete authority, and promised to give Forest's poor supporters unhoped-for riches when he arrived at Nottingham in 1975. Forest were then in the second division, but they moved up to the first division in 1977, before becoming league champions the following season, then European champions in 1979. In 1980, Forest successfully defended their European title, becoming the only club to have been national league champions once and European champions twice. ⚽ The man who was worth a million pounds: One of the surprises that Brian Clough had in store for the Forest fans was the hiring of Trevor Francis. Loaned to Detroit Express by Birmingham City, Francis was bought by Clough in February 1979 for a million pounds, a record in England at the time. A few months later, Francis scored the winning goal in the final of the European Cup.

May 2, 1959
Tommy Wilson scores the second goal, leading to Nottingham's victory (2-1) over Luton Town in the FA Cup final.

1 League Title

2 FA Cups

2 European Cups

Star players: Peter Shilton, Viv Anderson, Archie Gemmill, Trevor Francis, Roy Keane, Stuart Pearce, Des Walker, Teddy Sheringham.

Honours: League: 1978; FA Cup: 1898, 1959; League Cup: 1978, 1979, 1989, 1990; European Cup: 1979, 1980.

SHEFFIELD FC
The Club

Founded: **1857** • Stadium: **Coach and Horses Ground (Sheffield)**

Sheffield FC was the first club in the world to be founded outside of a school, and was a founding member of the FA (in 1863). In 1885, the club refused the move towards the professionalizing of the game. In 2004, it was made a member of the FIFA Order of Merit. The team currently plays in the Northern Premier League.

NOTTS COUNTY FC
The Magpies

Founded: **1862** • Stadium: **Meadow Lane (Nottingham)**

Notts County are the oldest active professional club in the world. In 1903, Juventus adopted the Notts colours as their own. Winners of the FA Cup in 1894, they maintain a strong rivalry with Forest, whose stadium is separated from theirs by the River Trent.

STOKE CITY FC
The Potters

Founded: **1863** • Stadium: **Britannia (Stoke-on-Trent)**

A founding member of the Football League, and the second oldest professional club in the world, Stoke City had to wait until 2011 to contest an FA Cup final, though they won the League Cup in 1972. The official club anthem, "We'll Be With You," was recorded by the players themselves.

SHEFFIELD WEDNESDAY FC
The Owls

Founded: **1867** • Stadium: **Hillsborough (Sheffield)**

Four-time champions of the league, between 1903 and 1930, and three-time FA Cup winners, Sheffield Wednesday have historic importance in England as founding members of the Football Alliance in 1889. Always popular, they managed to draw 42,000 supporters to Cardiff to contest the 2005 third-division title.

READING FC
The Royals

Founded: **1871** • Stadium: **Madejski (Reading)**

Although Reading FC had to wait until 2006 to play in the top flight, the club is memorable for their "Player of the Millennium" in 1999: Robin Friday. In the 1970s, this undisciplined forward delighted the fans with his flamboyant style, whether scoring himself or setting up goals for his teammates.

BOLTON WANDERERS FC
The Trotters

Founded: **1874** • Stadium: **Macron (Bolton)**

Founded by the Reverand Thomas Ogden, a school headmaster, this club won four FA Cups between 1923 and 1958, and has spent seventy-three seasons in the league's top division. To lighten the mood during some matches, Bolton fans have a chant: "Let's pretend we've scored a goal."

BLACKBURN ROVERS FC
The Riversiders
Founded: **1875** • Stadium: **Ewood Park (Blackburn)**

A founding member of the Football League, in 1888, the club won six FA Cups between 1891 and 1928, and won the Premier League in 1995, more than eighty years after their initial two first-division titles. Margaret Thatcher was once honorary vice-president of the club.

MIDDLESBROUGH FC
Boro
Founded: **1876** • Stadium: **Riverside (Middlesbrough)**

The club has counted some of Britain's top players among its ranks, including Paul Gascoigne, Bryan Robson, and Graeme Souness. Middlesbrough's glory years came in 2004, when they won the League Cup, and in 2006, when they were runners-up in the UEFA Cup.

PORT VALE FC
The Valiants
Founded: **1876** • Stadium: **Vale Park (Stoke-on-Trent)**

A pioneer of professional football in 1885, Port Vale have never played in a league higher than the second division. Their most famous fan is the singer Robbie Williams, who became a major shareholder in 2006.

WOLVERHAMPTON WANDERERS FC Wolves
Founded: **1877** • Stadium: **Molineux (Wolverhampton)**

A founding member of the Football League, the club had their golden age in the 1950s, winning the first division league title three times. The press nicknamed them "Champion of the World," due to their wins over several European and international clubs at the time.

IPSWICH TOWN FC
The Tractor Boys
Founded: **1878** • Stadium: **Portman Road (Ipswich)**

Winners of the league title in 1962, their first season in the first division, the club can also boast one FA Cup and one UEFA Cup. They can be proud of never having been beaten at home in a European Cup, even after hosting such teams as Real Madrid, AC Milan, and FC Barcelona.

WEST BROMWICH ALBION FC
The Baggies
Founded: **1878** • Stadium: **The Hawthorns (West Bromwich)**

West Bromwich Albion were established by workers from a factory making weighing scales. The club won a first division title in 1920, as well as five FA Cups and one League Cup. The singer Eric Clapton is a West Brom supporter. Their match programme is considered one of the best published.

SUNDERLAND AFC
The Black Cats
Founded: **1879** • Stadium: **Stadium of Light (Sunderland)**

Six-time league champions between 1892 and 1936, and twice winners of the FA Cup (1937, 1973), Sunderland are today best known for their supporters, named the noisiest in England in 2007. They are particularly loud during the Tyne-Wear Derby against Newcastle.

WATFORD FC
The Hornets
Founded: **1881** • Stadium: **Vicarage Road (Watford)**

Watford are famous for having been owned by the singer Elton John, who was also chairman for twenty-five years, starting in 1976 and taking the club from the fourth to the first division. Watford were runners-up in the 1983 first division, as well as in the 1984 FA Cup, to the great displeasure of their local rivals, Luton Town.

QUEENS PARK RANGERS FC
The Hoops
Founded: **1882** • Stadium: **Loftus Road (Londres)**

The club holds just one League Cup (1967), but counts many famous supporters including members of such groups as The Clash, The Cure, Depeche Mode, Deep Purple, and The Sex Pistols. Pete Doherty even used to run a club fanzine.

COVENTRY CITY FC
The Sky Blues
Founded: **1883** • Stadium: **Ricoh Arena (Coventry)**

Founded by employees of a local bicycle firm, the club played in the first division without interruption from 1967 to 2001, and won the FA Cup in 1987. When the club's youth academy was threatened with closure, it was saved by a trust set up by the fans.

DERBY COUNTY FC
The Rams
Founded: **1884** • Stadium: **Pride Park (Derby)**

A founding member of the Football League, in 1888, the club holds two first-division titles (1972, 1975) and one FA Cup (1946). They were the first team in England to employ a mascot full-time to maintain links with fans and the local community.

LEICESTER CITY FC
The Foxes
Founded: **1884** • Stadium: **King Power (Leicester)**

Leicester City are the English kings of yo-yoing, having experienced twenty-two relegations to the second division. They have won three League Cups (1964, 1997, 2000). Through their ranks have passed such football legends as Gordon Banks, Peter Shilton, and Gary Lineker.

TRANMERE ROVERS FC
Rovers
Founded: **1884** • Stadium: **Prenton Park (Birkenhead)**

This historic Merseyside club hit the headlines in 1988, when they participated in the Football League Centenary Tournament at Wembley, then reached the final of the League Cup in 2000. Since 2004, their supporters have invested in the club by buying shares in it.

BURY FC
The Shakers
Founded: **1885** • Stadium: **Gigg Lane (Bury)**

These pioneers of the professional game have won two FA Cups (1900, 1903), and hold the record for the largest winning margin in a final: 6–0 against Derby County in 1903. As of 2015, Bury were still based at Gigg Lane, where they played their first match in 1885.

MILLWALL FC
The Lions
Founded: **1885** • Stadium: **The Den (Londres)**

Although their results don't make them a top level club—runners-up in the 2004 FA Cup, and they have only played in a European competition once—Millwall are known for their fiercely loyal, even aggressive, supporters. Their infamous terrace chant is "No one likes us, we don't care."

SHREWSBURY TOWN FC
The Shrews
Founded: **1886** • Stadium: **New Meadow (Shrewsbury)**

This club, which has never played in the Premier League, holds the English record for victories in the Welsh Cup, with six trophies picked up between 1891 and 1985. They have also performed well in the FA Cup, reaching the quarter finals twice, in 1979 and 1982.

BLACKPOOL FC
The Tangerines
Founded: **1887** • Stadium: **Bloomfield Road (Blackpool)**

Winners of the FA Cup in 1953, the club is associated with one of the greatest names in football: Stanley Matthews. A Blackpool player from 1947 to 1961, "The Wizard of the Dribble" was named the very first European Footballer of the Year in 1956, while wearing Blackpool FC colours.

BRISTOL CITY FC
The Robins
Founded: **1894** • Stadium: **Ashton Gate (Bristol)**

Bristol City, the favourite club of Monty Python actor John Cleese, were runners-up in the 1909 FA Cup, and count the 1934 Welsh Cup among their honours. They play one of the most fiercely-contested derbies in England, against their local rivals, Bristol Rovers.

WEST HAM UNITED FC
The Hammers
Founded: **1895** • Stadium: **Upton Park (Londres)**

Founded originally by workers from a shipyard and ironworks on the Thames, West Ham have spent fifty-six seasons in the top flight, as well as winning three FA Cups and one European Cup Winners' Cup (1965). Their supporters are famous for their rendition of "I'm Forever Blowing Bubbles."

SCUNTHORPE UNITED FC
The Iron
Founded: **1899** • Stadium: **Glanford Park (Scunthorpe)**

Although they have never played in the first division, Scunthorpe are currently the only professional side in Lincolnshire. It was in their ranks that two stars of English football—Ray Clemence and Kevin Keegan (twice named European Footballer of the Year)—made their professional debuts.

NORWICH CITY FC
The Canaries
Founded: **1902** • Stadium: **Carrow Road (Norwich)**

Twice winners of the League Cup (1962, 1985), the club relishes the "Old Farm Derby" against Ipswich Town, although Norwich are currently in the Premier League, a division above their neighbours. "On The Ball, City" has been sung in the stands since 1902—it is considered to be the oldest football song in the world still being chanted.

HULL CITY AFC
The Tigers
Founded: **1904** • Stadium: **KC (Kingston-upon-Hull)**

Founded in traditional rugby territory, the club didn't enter the Premier League until 2008, and it wasn't until 2014 that they played their first cup final. In 2013, strong local opposition prevented a name change to "Hull Tigers"—which the new owner wanted to make happen.

CHARLTON ATHLETIC
The Addicks
Founded: **1905** • Stadium: **The Valley (London)**

Charlton won the 1947 FA Cup. Up until 2008, they gave a seat in the boardroom to a supporter elected by their peers. Their oldest rivalry is with Millwall, while the most recent is with Crystal Palace.

CRYSTAL PALACE
The Eagles
Founded: **1905** • Stadium: **Selhurst Park (London)**

Founded to occupy the host stadium of the FA Cup final from 1895 to 1914, the club reached the first division in 1969. Runners-up in the 1990 FA Cup, Crystal Palace were bought by several wealthy supporters in 2010, saving the club from financial disaster.

EASINGTON COLLIERY AFC
The Colliery
Founded: **1913** • Stadium: **Easington Welfare Park (Easington Colliery)**

This amateur club formed by miners played an important role of social cohesion during the miners' strike of 1984–1985, keeping the strikers occupied and distributing meals to the poorest. The club also allowed both strikers and non-strikers to share some peaceful moments together.

DICK, KERR'S LADIES
Munitioneers
Founded: **1917** • Stadium: **Deepdale (Preston)**

This pioneering club in women's football was established by workers at a munitions factory in Preston during the First World War. In 1920, they played the first women's international match in history, against a French side, in front of 25,000 spectators.

LEEDS UNITED FC
The Peacocks
Founded: **1919** • Stadium: **Elland Road (Leeds)**

Three-time league champions, Leeds reached their peak in 1975, when they were runners-up in the European Cup competition. They have a loyal and enthusiastic fan base, while also being one of the most divisive clubs in English football—which might be another badge of pride.

LONDON XI
The Londoners
Founded: **1955** • Stadium: **Various (London)**

This squad of players from different London clubs was formed especially to participate in the 1955–1958 Inter-Cities Fairs Cup, going as far as the final, where they were beaten by FC Barcelona. The team played in various stadiums, including Wembley, Highbury, and Stamford Bridge.

DONCASTER ROVERS BELLES LADIES FC Donny Belles
Founded: **1969** • Stadium: **Keepmoat stadium (Doncaster)**

Founded by young women who sold lottery tickets in the stands of Doncaster Rovers, the club has twice been league champion of England, and has won the FA Women's Cup six times. Doncaster Rovers Belles have a longstanding rivalry with Arsenal Ladies.

ARSENAL LADIES FC
The Gunners
Founded: **1987** • Stadium: **Meadow Park (London)**

Arsenal Ladies are affiliated with Arsenal FC, and are the most successful English women's football club, with twelve league titles and thirteen FA Women's Cups. They also won the 2007 UEFA Women's Cup. The club has been professional since 2002, and once a year they play at the Emirates Stadium.

AFC WIMBLEDON
The Dons
Founded: **2002** • Stadium: **Cherry Red Records Stadium (London)**

Founded by supporters of FC Wimbledon to protest against the relocation of their club to Milton Keynes—fifty-six miles away—AFC Wimbledon moved up from the ninth to the fourth division in 2011, allowing them to turn professional. They have won numerous minor trophies.

FC UNITED OF MANCHESTER
Red Rebels
Founded: **2005** • Stadium: **Broadhurst Park (Manchester)**

Founded by supporters of Manchester United to protest against the takeover of their club by the American businessman Malcolm Glazer, FCUM is a semi-professional club run democratically by their thousands of fans. Having started out in the tenth division, they now play in the seventh.

WREXHAM FC
The Dragons
Founded: **1864** • Stadium: **Racecourse Ground (Wrexham)**

The third oldest club in the world, Wrexham have won twenty-three Welsh Cups, and played in the quarter-finals of the 1976 Cup Winners' Cup. They were relegated in 2008, after eighty-seven seasons in the English league. Since 2011, they belong to their supporter-shareholders.

CEFN DRUIDS AFC
The Ancients
Founded: **1872** • Stadium: **The Rock (Wrexham)**

The second oldest Welsh club, after their rivals, Wrexham, Cefn Druids were the first to take part in the English Cup, in 1876. Eight times winners of the Welsh Cup before 1904, they reached the final again in 2012, and re-entered the first division in 2014.

CARDIFF CITY FC
The Bluebids
Founded: **1899** • Stadium: **Cardiff City (Cardiff)**

The only non-English club to have won the cup (in 1927), Cardiff City have played more than fifteen seasons in the English top flight over the past century. Runners-up in the 2008 FA Cup, as well as in the 2012 League Cup, this former club of John Toshack is the most successful in the history of Welsh football.

SWANSEA CITY
The Swans
Founded: **1912** • Stadium: **Liberty (Swansea)**

The club played their first professional match in 1912—against their eternal rivals, Cardiff. Promoted to the Premier League in 2011, they were the first Welsh club at this level since the establishment of the new English league. Their supporters own 20 percent of the club.

"The wives of Celtic fans used to send me letters thanking me for sending their husbands home early." **Jim Baxter, Rangers midfielder, 1960–1965, 1969–1970.**

GLASGOW RANGERS FC

The Gers

Founded: **1872** • Stadium: **Ibrox (Glasgow)**

The Rangers legend began in 1872, when four friends decided to found their own football club, just for the pleasure of playing. In 1891, the club won the first Scottish league championship, and another fifty-three titles would follow—a world record—including nine in a row, from 1989 to 1997, under coach Graeme Souness. During the 1960s and 1970s, European clubs discovered Ibrox Park, Rangers' home since 1899. Runners-up in the European Cup Winners' Cup of 1961 and 1967, they finally lifted the trophy in 1972. In 2008, the club reached the final of the UEFA Cup, the last time to date that a Scottish club has done so. A series of major difficulties forced the club to drop down to the fourth division in 2012, giving them the opportunity to beat another world record—that of the number of spectators for a match of this category: 49,118. By 2014, Rangers were already back in the second division.

54 League Titles

33 National Cups

1 UEFA Cup Winners' Cup

Alex Ferguson
During his career as a football player, Man U's legendary manager played for Rangers between 1967 and 1969.

The number of games played by John Greig while he was wearing the Rangers shirt.

Paul Gascoigne
From 1995 to 1998, he played 104 games with Rangers, scoring 39 goals in total.

The number of goals scored by Ally McCoist while he was wearing the Rangers shirt between 1983 and 1998.

The record attendance for a league game, played on January 2, 1939 at Ibrox Park, against Celtic.

755

355

118 567

SCOTLAND

WHEN ETERNAL RIVALS HELP EACH OTHER

Rangers initially drew their fan base from the workers of the city's shipyards, and historically they were mainly from Glasgow's Protestant population, so making them the traditional rivals of the Catholic Celtic, against whom Rangers have contested some 400 "Old Firm" derbies. Despite this strong rivalry, the two clubs have been able to bury the hatchet when circumstances required it. For example, after the Ibrox disaster, which cost the lives of sixty-six Rangers fans, on January 2, 1971, Rangers and Celtic formed a single squad to play a benefit match against a team of top Scottish players to raise funds for the victims' families.

Star players: Sandy Archibald, David Meiklejohn, Bob McPhail, Jimmy Smith, Willie Waddell, Ralph Brand, Jim Baxter, Willie Henderson, John Greig, Sandy Jardine, Derek Johnstone, Davie Cooper, Ally McCoist, Richard Gough, Mark Hateley, Andy Goram, Brian Laudrup, Paul Gascoigne, Barry Ferguson.

Honours: League: 1891, 1899, 1900, 1901, 1902, 1911, 1912, 1913, 1918, 1920, 1921, 1923, 1924, 1925, 1927, 1928, 1929, 1930, 1931, 1933, 1934, 1935, 1937, 1939, 1947, 1949, 1950, 1953, 1956, 1957, 1959, 1961, 1963, 1964, 1975, 1976, 1978, 1987, 1989, 1990, 1991, 1992, 1993, 1994, 1995, 1996, 1997, 1999, 2000, 2003, 2005, 2009, 2010, 2011; National Cup: 1894, 1897, 1898, 1903, 1928, 1930, 1932, 1934, 1935, 1936, 1948, 1949, 1950, 1953, 1960, 1962, 1963, 1964, 1966, 1973, 1976, 1978, 1979, 1981, 1992, 1993, 1996, 1999, 2000, 2002, 2003, 2008, 2009; League Cup: 1946, 1948, 1960, 1961, 1963, 1964, 1970, 1975, 1977, 1978, 1981, 1983, 1984, 1986, 1987, 1988, 1990, 1992, 1993, 1996, 1998, 2002, 2003, 2005, 2009, 2010, 2011; UEFA Cup Winners' Cup: 1972.

"I fell a bit in love with Celtic, because the atmosphere was amazing and the crowd was magnificent, the way they behaved with the Porto fans." **Jose Mourinho, June 2003**

THE CELTIC FC

The Bhoys

Founded: **1888** • Stadium: **Celtic Park (Glasgow)**

Established by a Catholic priest as a means of fund-raising to help Glasgow's Irish community, the club soon became a rallying point, as well as a trophy-winning machine. Celtic reached the final of the Scottish Cup in their first official season, and they have racked up no fewer than ninety-seven trophies in three national competitions. On the European scene, the club reached two semi-finals of the Cup Winners' Cup (1964, 1966), before their team—composed solely of local players—became the first to put an end to the dominance of the great Spanish and Italian clubs by winning the 1967 European Cup, beating Inter Milan. In 1970, Celtic failed to defend their title, but were still runners-up. The club have played one more European final, the 2003 UEFA Cup, where they lost to Porto. Since 2012, the financial problems suffered by their historic rival, Rangers, have deprived them of the pleasure of contesting the "Old Firm," the most famous derby in the world.

46 League Titles

36 National Cups

1 European Cup

May 27, 1967
Billy McNeill lifts the European Cup.

The number of games played by Billy McNeill while he was wearing the Celtic shirt.

822

The number of supporters who attended the match between Celtic and Aberdeen on April 24, 1937: it set the attendance record for a European football game.

147 365

The number of goals scored by Jimmy McGrory for Celtic.

522

77

The number of games in which Celtic remained unbeaten at home, between 2001 and 2004.

THE BEST FANS IN EUROPE?

Paolo Maldini, Michael Owen, Xavi Hernandez, Ronaldo, and many more great names have all praised the atmosphere of Celtic Park. For some people, Celtic supporters are quite simply the best in the world. Indeed, the first version of the current stadium, Celtic Park, was built by hundreds of volunteers, in 1892. Over the last few seasons, the average attendance for league championship matches has regularly exceeded 50,000, and this huge crowd never fails to seize the chance to belt out "You'll never walk alone" for European matches. Celtic can count some nine million supporters across the globe.

Star players: Jimmy Quinn, Patsy Gallacher, Jimmy McGrory, Bobby Evans, Charlie Tully, Jock Stein, Jimmy Johnstone, Billy McNeill, Bobby Murdoch, Bobby Lennox, Ronnie Simpson, Tommy Gemmell, Bertie Auld, Kenny Dalglish, Danny McGrain, Paul McStay, Tommy Burns, Henrik Larsson, Emilio Izaguirre.

Honours: League: 1893, 1894, 1896, 1898, 1905, 1906, 1907, 1908, 1909, 1910, 1914, 1915, 1916, 1917, 1919, 1922, 1926, 1936, 1938, 1954, 1966, 1967, 1968, 1969, 1970, 1971, 1972, 1973, 1974, 1977, 1979, 1981, 1982, 1986, 1988, 1998, 2001, 2002, 2004, 2006, 2007, 2008, 2012, 2013, 2014, 2015; National Cup: 1892, 1899, 1900, 1904, 1907, 1908, 1911, 1912, 1914, 1923, 1925, 1927, 1931, 1933, 1937, 1951, 1954, 1965, 1967, 1969, 1971, 1972, 1974, 1975, 1977, 1980, 1985, 1988, 1989, 1995, 2001, 2004, 2005, 2007, 2011, 2013; League Cup: 1957, 1958, 1966, 1967, 1968, 1969, 1970, 1975, 1983, 1998, 2000, 2001, 2006, 2009, 2015; European Cup: 1967.

KILMARNOCK FC
Killie

Founded: **1869** • Stadium: **Rugby Park (Kilmarnock)**

The oldest professional club in the country, Kilmarnock played in the very first Scottish Cup match, in 1873. Winners of the 1965 league championship, they also hold three Scottish Cups, one League Cup (2012), and one UEFA Cup semi-final (1967).

HAMILTON ACADEMICAL FC
The Accies

Founded: **1874** • Stadium: **New Douglas Park (Hamilton)**

Founded by the headmaster and pupils of a school, Hamilton Academical are the only professional British club with roots in a school team. Having played frequently in the first division before 1939, they returned to the top-flight in 2008, giving them the opportunity to confront their great rival, Motherwell, once again.

HEART OF MIDLOTHIAN FC
The Jam Tarts

Founded: **1874** • Stadium: **Tynecastle Stadium (Edinburgh)**

Heart of Midlothian is the oldest club in Edinburgh. "Hearts" have won four league titles and eight national cups. They have maintained a good-natured local rivalry with Hibernian since 1875, and their stadium, where they have played since 1886, draws the third largest crowds in Scotland, after Rangers and Celtic.

HIBERNIAN FC
Hibs

Founded: **1875** • Stadium: **Easter Road (Edinburgh)**

Founded by Irish immigrants, Hibernian have won four league titles, two national cups, and three league cups—their most recent trophy, in 2007. Threatened with bankruptcy in 1990, the club owe their survival to their supporters, who prevented their merging with Hearts, their ancestral rival.

PARTICK THISTLE FC
The Jags

Founded: **1876** • Stadium: **Firhill (Glasgow)**

Partick Thistle made their debut in the first division in 1897. One hundred years later, they were saved from bankruptcy by their supporters. They hold one Scottish Cup and one League Cup. Since 2013, the only two top-flight clubs in Glasgow have been Celtic and Thistle.

ABERDEEN FC
The Dons

Founded: **1903** • Stadium: **Pittodrie (Aberdeen)**

Champions in 1955 and never relegated, the club entered a golden age in 1978, when young coach Alex Ferguson took over the reins, leading Aberdeen to three more league titles, four cups and the 1983 European Cup Winners' Cup, when they beat Real Madrid.

DUNDEE UNITED FC
The Terrors
Founded: **1909** • Stadium: **Tannadice Park (Dundee)**

The club caused a sensation in 1980s Scotland, winning the title in 1983 and contesting the 1987 UEFA Cup final, after beating FC Barcelona. Dundee United have roots in the Catholic community, and their main rival is Dundee FC, whose ground is barely a goal kick away.

INVERNESS CALEDONIAN THISTLE FC   The Pride of the Highlands
Founded: **1994** • Stadium: **Caledonian (Inverness)**

Born from the merger of Caledonian and Inverness Thistle—both established in 1885—the club started out in the fourth division before entering the top flight in 2004. They placed third in the 2015 league championship and won the Scottish Cup, qualifying for their first European Cup Winners' Cup in 2015–2016.

BOHEMIAN FC
The Gypsies
Founded: **1890** • Stadium: **Dalymount Park (Dublin)**

A founder member of the League of Ireland in 1922, Bohemian have never known relegation, and they hold eleven league titles and seven cups. In 2002, they became the first Irish team to beat a British club—the Scottish team, Aberdeen—in the UEFA cup.

SHELBOURNE FC
Shels
Founded: **1895** • Stadium: **Tolka Park (Dublin)**

The club's name was chosen by drawing lots among its founders. They have won thirteen league titles and seven cups, as well as three Irish Cups in the years before independence. Popular in the north of Dublin, Shelbourne's main rivals are their neighbours, Bohemian FC.

UNIVERSITY COLLEGE DUBLIN ASSOCIATION   The Students
Founded: **1895** • Stadium: **UCD Bowl (Dublin)**

Founded within the university's medical school, this club's players are all students and they sometimes travel to matches in individual cars. This didn't stop them from winning the Irish cup in 1984.

SHAMROCK ROVERS
Hoops
Founded: **1901** • Stadium: **Tallaght (Dublin)**

With seventeen league titles and twenty cups, Shamrock Rovers are the most successful club in the country. In 1967, they played in the American league under the name Boston Rovers. The 2000s were dark years for the club, and they were only able to survive thanks to financial support from their fans.

DUNDALK FC
The Lilywhites
Founded: **1903** • Stadium: **Oriel Park (Dundalk)**

Founded by railway workers in a town close to the border with Northern Ireland, they are one of the most successful Irish clubs outside Dublin, with ten league titles and nine cups. Since 1999, they have taken part with Linfield Belfast in a project of rapprochement with Ulster through football.

DERRY CITY FC
The Candystripes
Founded: **1928** • Stadium: **Brandywell (Derry)**

This Northern Ireland club has a mainly Catholic following. Derry City became champions in 1965, before opting to enter the league of the Republic of Ireland in 1985, for political reasons. Having reached the first division in 1987, they did a historic triple two years later: league, cup, and league cup.

CLIFTONVILLE FAC
The Reds
Founded: **1879** • Stadium: **Solitude (Dublin)**

The oldest club in Irish football, Cliftonville were the first in the country to install floodlights for games. Five-time champions and eight-time winners of the cup, they are popular in nationalist Catholic circles in Belfast.

GLENTORAN FC
The Glens
Founded: **1882** • Stadium: **The Oval (Belfast)**

The most popular club in the country, along with Linfield, against whom they contest the "Belfast's Big Two" derby, Glentoran are mainly supported by Unionists. Known for having rejected the young George Best for being "too small and light," the club has won twenty-three league championships and twenty-two Irish Cups.

LINFIELD FC
The Blues
Founded: **1886** • Stadium: **Windsor Park (Belfast)**

The club holds fifty-one league titles, the first won in 1891, making them the world's second most successful club in its own league, behind Glasgow Rangers. Popular with the Protestant community, the average attendance at their games is the highest in the Northern Ireland league.

CRUSADERS FC
The Hatchetmen
Founded: **1898** • Stadium: **Seaview (Belfast)**

The club finally joined the league in 1949, following a rather tumultuous history. Five-time champions—most recently in 2015—Crusaders maintain close relations with their local community in North Belfast. Their major local rivals are Cliftonville.

HAVNAR BÓLTFELAG
The Red and Blacks
Founded: **1904** • Stadium: **Gundadalur (Tórshavn)**

The Faroe Islands' most successful club, with twenty-two league championships and twenty-six cups, they managed to get through the opening round of the 1993 UEFA Cup Winners' Cup, their first European competition. In 2014, Havnar Bóltfelag got as far as the second qualifying round of the UEFA Champions League.

B36 TÓRSHAVN
White Tigers
Founded: **1936** • Stadium: **Gundadalur (Tórshavn)**

B36 Tórshavn have always battled against their local rival, Havnar Bóltfelag, including for the right to use Gundadalur Stadium. They hold ten league titles and five cups, and have played in the preliminary rounds of a number of European competitions.

KR REYKJAVIK
KR Ingar
Founded: **1899** • Stadium: **KR-Völlur (Reykjavik)**

Iceland's oldest football club, KR were the only team in Reykjavik for a decade. They won the first national league championship, a performance they have repeated twenty-five times—most recently in 2013. Their black and white striped kit is an homage to Newcastle United.

FRAM REYKJAVIK
The Blues
Founded: **1908** • Stadium: **Laugardalsvöllur (Reykjavik)**

With eighteen league titles and eight cups, Fram Reykjavik are one of the most successful clubs in Iceland. Their 15,000-seat stadium is one of the largest in the country. They maintain a strong rivalry with their Reykjavik neighbour Valur.

KNATTSPYRNUFÉLAGI VALUR
Valsarar
Founded: **1911** • Stadium: **Hlíðarendi (Reykjavík)**

Valur—which means "falcon" in Icelandic—were named by their players, who saw a falcon flying over their training ground. A big rival of Knattspyrnufélag Reykjavíkur, the club have won twenty league titles and ten Icelandic Cups.

ÍBRÓTTABANDALAG AKRANESS
Yellow and Happy
Founded: **1946** • Stadium: **Akranesvöllur (Akranes)**

Based in a town of 6,000 inhabitants, the club was the first outside the capital Reykjavík to win the Icelandic league championship, in 1951. Since then, they have won seventeen more titles and nine cups, and have played in the first round of European competitions on several occasions.

"Remember my name and my face. My name is Zlatan Ibrahimović and I'm going to become the best footballer in the world." **Zlatan Ibrahimović (eighteen years old) to his team-mates at Malmö FF after signing his first professional contract in 1999.**

MALMÖ FF
The Sky Blues

Founded: **1910** · Stadium: **Swedbank (Malmö)**

Malmö FF hold twenty-one league titles—a Swedish record. Their aura grew to continental proportions in 1979, when they reached the final of the European Cup, only to be beaten 1-0 by Nottingham Forest. Malmö hit the headlines again in 1999, when Zlatan Ibrahimović—who was born in the town and had been a fan of the club since he was a child—commenced his professional career here. The club would return to the summit, earning three league titles since 2010. Very popular, this figurehead of Swedish football maintains one local rivalry with IFK Malmö, another (historical) one with Helsingborgs, and a third with Gothenburg.

21 League Titles

14 National Cups

Zlatan Ibrahimović
A youth player at the club, the Swede also made his professional debut at Malmö FF.

Star players: Bo Larsson, Krister Kristensson, Roy Andersson, Roland Andersson, Jan Möller, Ingemar Erlandsson, Magnus Andersson, Robert Prytz, Torbjörn Persson, Jonnie Fedel, Jonas Thern, Martin Dahlin, Stefan Schwarz, Patrik Andersson, Zlatan Ibrahimović, Jari Litmanen.

Honours: League: 1944, 1949, 1950, 1951, 1953, 1965, 1967, 1970, 1971, 1974, 1975, 1977, 1985, 1986, 1987, 1988, 1989, 2004, 2010, 2013, 2014; National Cup: 1944, 1946, 1947, 1951, 1953, 1967, 1973, 1974, 1975, 1978, 1980, 1984, 1986, 1989.

AIK FOTBOLL
Gnaget
Founded: **1891** • Stadium: **Friends Arena (Stockholm)**

AIK, who are based in the capital, hold the record for longevity in the first division, having spent eighty-six seasons in the top flight. Five-time league champions, they have played at Friends Arena—the largest stadium in the country (50,000 capacity)—since 2009. They draw the biggest crowds for the matches they play against their neighbours, Syrianska.

DJURGÅRDENS IF FOTBOLL
The Iron Stoves
Founded: **1891** • Stadium: **Tele2 Arena (Stockholm)**

Seven-time league champions, and the most successful club in Stockholm, from 1936 to 2013, they played in the magnificent stadium that housed the 1912 Olympic Games. Djurgårdens contest the "twins derby" with AIK, another club from the capital, who were founded three weeks before them.

IFK NORRKÖPING
Peking
Founded: **1897** • Stadium: **Nya Parken (Norrköping)**

Twelve-time league champions, the club dominated Swedish football in the 1950s–1960s. Their supporters have encouraged them with shouts of "Peking," ever since a Swedish explorer told them that the names, Peking and Norrköping, both mean "northern town."

IF ELFSBORG
The Elegants
Founded: **1904** • Stadium: **Borås (Borås)**

Founded by a group of teenagers, Elfsborg have spent seventy-one seasons in the top flight, and have won five league titles. Ingvar Carlsson, who would go on to become prime minister, was one of the club's young fans. Elfsborg's stadium fills up whenever they play their rivals, Gothenburg.

IFK GÖTEBORG
The Angels
Founded: **1904** • Stadium: **Gamla Ullevi (Gothenburg)**

Eighteen-time champions, IFK are known for their exceptional European record: winners of the UEFA Cup in 1982 and 1987, they have also contested one semi-final of the Champions League, in 1986, and a quarter-final, in 1995, after having eliminated Manchester United.

HELSINGBORGS IF
The Reds
Founded: **1907** • Stadium: **Olympia (Helsingborgs)**

With seven league titles and five cups, Helsingborgs are the fifth most successful club in Sweden. Henrik Larsson launched his international career while playing for the club, then went on to join Feyenoord, Celtic, and Barcelona, before returning to Helsingborgs as manager in 2015.

HAMMARBY IF
Bajen
Founded: **1915** · Stadium: **Tele2 (Stockholm)**

Swedish league champions in 2001, the club are supported by the capital's working classes. Very popular, they draw on average 10,000 more spectators than their rivals, Djurgårdens, with whom they share a stadium. Their most famous supporter is Björn Borg.

SYRIANSKA FC
Suryoye
Founded: **1977** · Stadium: **Södertälje Fotbollsarena (Stockholm)**

Based near Stockholm, Syrianska represent the Syriac people, who don't have a national team. After having started out in the seventh division, they reached the top flight in 2010. The club have supporters all over the world, and their rivals are the "Assyrians" of Assyriska.

ODDS BK
Oddrane
Founded: **1894** · Stadium: **Skagerak (Skien)**

The oldest active club in the country get their name from a character in a novel. They hold the record for cup victories, with twelve trophies. In 2011, Jone Samuelsen scored a goal for them from a header sixty-four yards out—a world record.

VIKING FK
The Dark Blues
Founded: **1899** · Stadium: **Viking (Stavanger)**

Eight-time winners of the league, the club dominated the 1970s in Norway, before handing over the reins to Rosenborg. In 1992, they nearly pulled off a coup in the Champions League against Barcelona (0–1, 0–0). Ten years later, they knocked Chelsea out of the UEFA Cup.

SK BRANN
The Reds
Founded: **1908** · Stadium: **Brann (Bergen)**

Three-time league champions, six-time winners of the Norwegian cup, and quarter-finalists in the 1997 Cup Winners' Cup, this club from Norway's second largest city regularly record the best attendances in the league. Chelsea star Tore André Flo made his debut here.

MOLDE FK
The Hawthorns
Founded: **1911** · Stadium: **Aker (Molde)**

Molde's star is rising, following a string of second places behind Rosenborg. The club has now won three league titles (2011, 2012, 2014) since the role of head coach was taken over by Ole Gunnar Solskjær—a former player for the side, who also played for Manchester United.

VÅLERENGA FOTBALL
The Bohemians

Founded: **1913** • Stadium: **Ullevaal (Oslo)**

This working-class club from the capital won the first of their five titles in 1965 with a flamboyant team nicknamed "The Bohemians." Today, the 10,000 fans who are members of "The Clan" bring their rousing support to the stadium during matches against rivals Lillestrøm.

LILLESTRØM SK
The Canaries

Founded: **1917** • Stadium: **Åråsen (Lillestrøm)**

Lillestrøm have won the league championship and cup competition five times each, making them a prominent force in Norwegian football. They can count on a loyal, and very well organized, fan base, with an average attendance of nearly 10,000 spectators at their 12,000 capacity stadium.

ROSENBORG BK
The Troll Kids

Founded: **1917** • Stadium: **Lerkendal (Trondheim)**

Holder of twenty-two league titles, Rosenborg have qualified eleven times for the group stage of the Champions League, and have managed to beat Real Madrid, AC Milan, and Dortmund. The most popular club in the country, they lead the rankings for the highest average crowd for league games at home.

TROMSØ IL
The Kids

Founded: **1920** • Stadium: **Alfheim (Tromsø)**

Based in the largest town in Norwegian Lapland, the club has served as a springboard for several Sami players, such as Morten Pedersen, Sigurd Rushfeldt, and Tom Høgli. Tromsø have won the cup twice, and have played in the European Cup a dozen times.

HIFK FOTBOLL
The Star Chested

Founded: **1897** • Stadium: **Sonera (Helsinki)**

HIFK Fotboll are supported by Finland's Swedish speakers and are rivals of HJK Helsinki. The club won seven league titles between 1930 and 1961. Having fallen as low as the fifth division, they returned to the first division in 2015 and turned to crowd funding to raise the money to finance their season.

HJK HELSINKI
The Club

Founded: **1907** • Stadium: **Sonera (Helsinki)**

Since this club became very popular among Finnish-speaking students, eventually the decision was made that only Finnish would be spoken at the club. HJK Helsinki have dominated Finnish football, winning twenty-seven national titles, and playing in the group stage of the 1998 Champions League.

TURUN PALLOSEURA
TPS
Founded: **1922** • Stadium: **Veritas (Turku)**

Eight-time league champions and three-time winners of the Finnish Cup, the club created a sensation in 1987 when they beat Inter Milan at home (1–0) in the second round of the UEFA Cup. This popular club often record the best attendances in the first division.

FC HAKA
Haka
Founded: **1934** • Stadium: **Tehtaan kenttä (Valkeakoski)**

Haka, who have their origins in the local paper industry, are one of the most successful clubs in Finland, with nine league titles and twelve cups. They reached the quarter-finals of the 1984 European Cup Winners' Cup, and reached the third qualifying round of the 2001 Champions League.

FC JAZZ
The Jazzmen
Founded: **1934** • Stadium: **Pori (Pori)**

Back when this club was still called Porin Pallo-Toverit, they played in the second division. In 1991, they changed their name in order to benefit from the renown of the Pori Jazz Festival, which takes place in the town each summer. This decision led the club to two championship titles and qualification into the UEFA Cup three times in the 1990s.

FC LAHTI
The Black Drones
Founded: **1996** • Stadium: **Lahden (Lahti)**

The club was formed by the merger of FC Kuusysi, five-time league champions, and Reipas Lahti, three-time league champions and the first club of Jari Litmanen— the greatest player in Finnish football history. Under their new name, Lahti won two Finnish League Cups (2007 and 2013).

JK TAMMEKA TARTU
The Blue and Whites
Founded: **1989** • Stadium: **Tamme (Tartu)**

This club is based in Tartu, Estonia's second largest city, and has been present in the first division since 2005, gaining promotion with a team of young players who had all been trained at the club. Although they have never placed better than fifth in the league, Tammeka are renowned for their fervent supporters.

FC FLORA
Cactus
Founded: **1990** • Stadium: **A. Le Coq Arena (Tallinn)**

Previously a second-division club in the USSR, Flora have played in the Estonian first division since it was established in 1992. The club have won nine titles, the same number as their great rivals, Levadia. They are managed by the eccentric Aivar Pohlak, who is also the chairman of the Estonian Football Association.

NÕMME KALJU FC
Pink Panthers
Founded: **1997** • Stadium: **Hiiu (Tallinn)**

By re-establishing a club that was originally founded in 1923, its directors upset the domination of Estonian football by Levadia and Flora. They bought foreign players in order to gain promotion from the amateur ranks to the professional league—a title they won in 2012.

FC LEVADIA TALLINN
The Green and Whites
Founded: **1998** • Stadium: **Kadriorg (Tallinn)**

Previously named FK Olümp Maardu, the club came into being thanks to a local factory whose name it took. In fifteen years, they became the most successful in the country, with nine league titles and eight cups. Levadia Tallinn regularly play in the preliminary rounds of the UEFA Cup.

FK SUDUVA MARIJAMPOLE
Sudovians
Founded: **1942** • Stadium: **Sūduva (Marijampolė)**

This club, one of the oldest in Lithuania, spent many years navigating the amateur divisions before reaching the first division in 2002. They have finished on the podium six times during the last ten seasons of the league championship, and have won two Lithuanian Cups.

FC ZALGIRIS
The Green and Whites
Founded: **1947** • Stadium: **LFF (Vilnius)**

FC Žalgiris were the highest profile Lithuanian football team during the Soviet era, spending eleven seasons in the first division—their best result was third place in 1987. Since independence, they have won five titles, despite relegation to the second division and their subsequent rescue by a group of players and fans.

FBK KAUNAS
The Yellow and Greens
Founded: **1960** • Stadium: **S. Darius et S. Girenas (Kaunas)**

Twice league champions of Lithuania before 1990—under the name Banga—the club is the country's most successful since independence, with eight league titles. In 2008, they pulled off a coup by beating Glasgow Rangers in the second qualifying round of the UEFA Champions League.

FK EKRANAS
The Blue-Reds
Founded: **1964** • Stadium: **Aukštaitija (Panevėžys)**

Founded in a factory producing screens, Ekranas have been league champions of Lithuania eight times—seven since independence. In 2004, they played their rivals FBK Kaunas in front of 8,000 spectators, even though the capacity of their stadium is only 4,000.

ESTONIA

LITHUANIA

AGF AARHUS
The Whites

Founded: **1880** • Stadium: **Ceres Park (Aarhus)**

Holder of a record number of victories in the Danish Cup (nine trophies), AGF Arhus have also won five league championships. They hold the record for the longest stay in the Danish first division (sixty-five seasons), and are one of the clubs that have retired the number 12 in homage to their supporters.

AALBORG BK
The Red and Whites

Founded: **1885** • Stadium: **Nordjyske Arena (Aalborg)**

Four-time national champions—most recently in 2014—and three-time winners of the Danish Cup, Aalborg BK are the only club in Denmark to have reached the group stage of the Champions League twice (1995–1996, 2008–2009). They also played in the first round of the UEFA Cup Winners' Cup in 1987.

BK FREM COPENHAGEN
True Copenhagen

Founded: **1886** • Stadium: **Valby Idrætspark (Copenhagen)**

Founded by young militants who opposed the government, this club from the south of the capital have remained popular with the working classes. They have won six league championships and two cups. Their official supporters' group, "BK Frem Support," is the oldest in the country.

ODENSE BK
The Striped

Founded: **1887** • Stadium: **TRE-FOR Park (Odense)**

Winner of three league championships and five cups, the club caused a sensation when they qualified for the quarter-finals of the 1994–1995 UEFA Cup by beating Real Madrid at home—an episode known as the "The Miracle in Madrid."

AKADEMISK BOLDKLUB
The Academics

Founded: **1889** • Stadium: **Gladsaxe (Copenhagen)**

Originally founded by academics, the club was initially only open to students—Nobel Prize winning physicist Niels Bohr was their goalkeeper for a few games. Between 1919 and 1967, they won nine league titles. In 1999 they were back on top, winning the Danish Cup before eventually being relegated in 2004.

VEJLE BOLDKLUB
Jutland Ruby

Founded: **1891** • Stadium: **Vejle (Vejle)**

In 1977, the European Footballer of the Year award was given to Vejle player Allan Simonsen, who started and finished his career at the club. Vejle hold five league titles and six Danish Cups. After merging with Kolding FC in 2011, they became independent again in 2012 and returned to the first division.

BOLDKLUBBEN AF 1893
B.93

Founded: **1893** • Stadium: **Østerbro (Copenhagen)**

This club from the Østerbro neighbourhood holds nine league titles—won between 1916 and 1946—and one Danish Cup—won in 1982. Currently in the second division, the club long had a local rival in the form of Østerbros BK, who were founded in 1894, until the latter dropped into the lower divisions and merged with another club in 1998.

STAEVNET
Copenhague XI

Founded: **1904** • Stadium: **Idrætsparken (Copenhagen)**

Formed by players from other Copenhagen clubs—hence their nickname—Stævnet played friendly matches all over the world. Between 1955 and 1964, they took part in the Inter-Cities Fairs Cup, the ancestor of today's Europa League. The club was dissolved in 1994.

BRØNDBY IF
The Boys from the Western Outskirts

Founded: **1964** • Stadium: **Brøndby (Brøndby)**

Brøndby have played in the Danish first division since 1982 (a record). In the years 1985–2005, the club were dominant, winning ten league championships. In 1998–1999, they played in the group stage of the Champions League, after serving as a springboard for Peter Schmeichel and the Laudrup brothers, Brian and Michael.

CHRISTIANIA SC
CSC

Founded: **1982** • Stadium: **Kløvermarkens (Copenhagen)**

Founded by young residents of the "free town" of Christiana, a self-governed neighbourhood in the Danish capital, this amateur club have yo-yoed between the ninth and fifth divisions. They nevertheless enjoy a certain amount of support, particularly among the city's artistic community.

FC NORDSJÆLLAND
The Wild Tigers

Founded: **1991** • Stadium: **Farum Park (Farum)**

Established following the merger of two clubs, FC Nordsjælland started out in the fourth division. They turned professional in 1997, and entered the first division in 2002. In 2012, the club won the domestic league and played in the group stage of the Champions League.

FC COPENHAGEN
The Lions

Founded: **1992** • Stadium: **Telia Parken (Copenhagen)**

FC Copenhagen were formed from the merger of Kjøbenhavns Boldklub (fifteen league titles) and Boldklubben 1903 (seven titles). Between 1993 and 2013, the club won ten championships. They contest the "New Firm" derby against Brøndby. In 2010, the club reached the last sixteen of the Champions League.

"We have a bow and arrow, and if we aim well, we can hit the target. The problem is that Bayern has a bazooka." **Jurgen Klopp, manager of Borussia Dortmund (2008–2015).**

BAYERN MUNICH
Star of the South

Founded: **1900** • Stadium: **Allianz Arena (Munich)**

Although they were not selected for inclusion in the Bundesliga when it was founded in 1963, Bayern Munich soon proved that they were the best team in Germany. Champions for the first time in 1969, they have won the trophy twenty-five times in fifty-two seasons. They won the 1967 UEFA Cup Winners' Cup—their first participation in a European competition—and won three European Cups in a row from 1974 to 1976, with a team who formed the backbone of Germany's 1974 World Cup winning squad. Crowned European champions five times, they have also lost five Champions League/European Cup finals. They are ranked third for third-place finishes, behind Real Madrid and AC Milan.

25 League Titles

17 National Cups

5 Champions League / European Cups

3 FIFA Club World Cups

Manuel Neuer
The Bavarian goalkeeper was captain of the German team during the 2014 World Cup in Brazil and became one of the twenty-three Bayern Munich players crowned world champions

632

2013

The year that Bayern won it all: domestic league and cup, Champions League, FIFA Club World Championship.

525

The number of goals scored by Gerd Müller, in all competitions, while he was wearing the Bayern shirt.

The number of games played for Bayern by goalkeeper Oliver Kahn, beating his famous predecessor Sepp Maier (623).

Karl-Heinz Rummenigge
He received the Ballon d'Or twice (1980 and 1981), just like Franz Beckenbauer, and became a legend at Bayern.

A KAISER "MADE IN MUNICH"

There can be few careers as glittering as that of Franz Beckenbauer, dubbed Der Kaiser, the greatest player in the history of Bayern. Born in Munich, he dreamed of playing for Munich 1860, but he was hit by one of their players during a youth tournament, and at thirteen years old he opted for "The Reds," playing his first professional match at the age of eighteen. He started out at leftwing, before switching to midfield, later becoming a sweeper. During the 1960s and 1970s, he was one of the greatest defenders in the world, but he never lost his attacking abilities. Famed for his dribbling raids deep inside the opposition's half, he scored seventy-two goals in 567 matches for Bayern. Three times European Champion, he won two Footballer of the Year awards in the red strip.

THE ALLIANZ ARENA, SYMBOL OF BAYERN'S POWER

This huge, tyre-shaped stadium, which has stood on the northern edge of Munich since 2005, takes on a striking red colour on match day. The Allianz Arena is the symbol of the club's vigorous financial health. The ground was previously jointly owned with Munich 1860, the city's other club, but the latter was bought out by Bayern in 2008, making Bayern Munich the sole proprietor. In 2014, the club even announced that it had reimbursed its loan for the construction of the stadium sixteen years early. The stadium has also been a popular success: the 69,000 seats were selling out for every league match, so 2,000 extra had to be added in 2012.

FC HOLLYWOOD IN THE STANDS

Bayern Munich has been nicknamed FC Hollywood, owing to the star players who have worn its red strip, but the list of celebrity supporters is just as impressive. Among the best known are current and retired sportsmen, including Boris Becker, Wladimir Klitschko; and Nico Rosberg; Robbie Williams, the singer; and even Joseph Ratzinger, better known as Pope Benoît XVI.

THE ELDERS AT THE CONTROLS

Bayern have that quality possessed by the truly great clubs: they combine modernity and tradition in order to evolve without losing their character. They operate rather like a family, where the greatest players naturally find their place in management when their career comes to an end. Franz Beckenbauer was president of the club from 1994 to 2009, to be replaced by Uli Hoeness—president until 2014. Karl-Heinz Rummenigge, who was vice-president from 1991 to 2002, is currently president of the management committee.

June 4, 2013
Karl Heinz Rummenigge, Jupp Heynckes and Uli Hoeness (from left to right) pose triumphantly in front of their four trophies.

Star players: Sepp Maier, Klaus Augenthaler, Franz Beckenbauer, Gerd Müller, Paul Breitner, Karl-Heinz Rummenigge, Lothar Matthaus, Stefan Effenberg, Mehmet Scholl, Oliver Kahn, Giovane Elber, Michael Ballack, Bastian Schweinsteiger, Philipp Lahm, Thomas Müller, Franck Ribéry, Arjen Robben.

Honours: League: 1932, 1969, 1972, 1973, 1974, 1980, 1981, 1985, 1986, 1987, 1989, 1990, 1994, 1997, 1999, 2000, 2001, 2003, 2005, 2006, 2008, 2010, 2013, 2014, 2015; National Cup: 1957, 1966, 1967, 1969, 1971, 1982, 1984, 1986, 1998, 2000, 2003, 2005, 2006, 2008, 2010, 2013, 2014; European Cup/Champions League: 1974, 1975, 1976, 2001, 2013; UEFA Cup Winners' Cup: 1967; UEFA Cup 1996; FIFA Club World Cup: 1976, 2001, 2013.

"We will never install seats. It's the tradition, the culture of our club: The Yellow Wall." **Hans-Joachim Watzke, Borussia Dortmund's chief executive.**

BORUSSIA DORTMUND

The Black and Yellows

Founded: **1909**
Stadium: **Westfalenstadion (Dortmund)**

Named after the local beer drunk by their founders—workers and miners—the Black and Yellows have strong local roots. The club played well in the 1930s, but didn't attain their first major successes until the 1950s-1960s, and their true glory days came in the 1990s. The first German club to win a European competition—the 1966 UEFA Cup Winners' Cup—they were also the first to win the revamped Champions League, in 1997. The team comprised Footballer of the Year Matthias Sammer, Stefan Reuter, Jürgen Kohler, Steffen Freund, and Andreas Möller, all of whom were European Champions following Germany's 1996 victory. Borussia Dortmund were also runners-up in the UEFA Cup (1993, 2002) and in the 2013 Champions League, where they lost to Bayern Munich. Throughout the years, the club's working-class roots have been evident in their attacking style of play, based on commitment and mental strength.

8 League Titles

3 National Cups

1 Champions League Title

1 UEFA Cup Winners' Cup

Matthias Sammer
Winner of the European Cup in 1997 with Borussia, Matthias Sammer became the club's first player to win the Ballon d'Or that same year.

The number of games played by midfielder Michael Zorc while he was wearing the Dortmund shirt. It was the only club he played for during his professional career (1981-1998).

463

31

1997

The number of goals scored in one season (1965-66) by Borussia striker Lothar Emmerich.

The year that Borussia won the Club World Championship, after their victory against Cruzeiro (2-0) during the Intercontinental Cup.

Mario Götze
The German hero of the 2014 World Cup final is a product of Borussia Dortmund's youth academy.

"THE FAMOUS YELLOW WALL OF BORUSSIA." —ANGELA MERKEL

Dortmund's WestfallenStadion—or Signal Iduna Park to give its current sponsored name—boasts the highest average attendance in the world, with a little over 80,000 spectators at each league match over these last few years (the maximum capacity is 80,700). Among them are 25,000 "ultra" fans, belonging to over a hundred different groups, who fill the "Yellow Wall" of the south terrace—the largest terrace in Europe, which has the peculiarity of allowing the supporters to remain standing, an arrangement that is prohibited for international games, since FIFA regulations dictate that seats must be fitted. The one match not to be missed in a season is the Revierderby, which has been contested against Schalke 04 since 1925. It is sometimes possible to spot the German Chancellor, Angela Merkel, the most famous supporter of the Black and Yellows, in attendance.

Star players: Hans Tilkowski, Lothar Emmerich, Alfred "Adi" Preißler, Heinrich Kwiatkowski, August Lenz, Matthias Sammer, Stefan Reuter, Karl-Heinz Riedle, Michael Zorc, Stephan Chapuisat, Andreas Möller, Marcel Raducanu, Aki Schmidt, Jürgen Kohler, Manni Burgsmüller, Robert Lewandowski, Marco Reus.

Honours: League: 1956, 1957, 1963, 1995, 1996, 2002, 2011, 2012; National Cup: 1965, 1989, 2012; Champions League: 1997; UEFA Cup Winners' Cup: 1966; Intercontinental Cup: 1997.

"I can't think of any other club in Europe where the club is so closely associated with the community. Schalke is now one of the biggest employers in Gelsenkirchen; the area literally depends on the club." **A Schalke 04 fan, BBC Sports News.**

SCHALKE 04

The Miners

Founded: **1904**
Stadium: **Veltins Arena (Gelsenkirchen)**

Founded by a group of high school students, Schalke have excelled at football since the 1930s. They are known for their mesmerising ball control, earning them the nickname "Spinning-top Schalke." Historically, their players were often former miners. After a period without success, the club got back on track in the 1990s. In 2001, they missed out on the league title by just one goal, when Bayern scored in injury time on the last day of the season. In European competitions, Schalke 04 have performed less well than the other major German teams, but they did win the 1996 UEFA Cup against Inter Milan, and reached the semi-finals of the 2011 Champions League after beating Valencia and Inter. Located in the centre of North Rhine-Westphalia, one of the most densely inhabited parts of Europe, Schalke 04 are the most popular German club after Bayern Munich.

7 League Titles

5 National Cups

1 UEFA Cup

July 23, 2011
Schalke 04 win the DFL-Supercup after their victory against Borussia Dortmund (0-0 FT, 5-4 on penalties).

Star players: Fritz Szepan, Ernst Kuzorra, Norbert Nigbur, Bernhard Dietz, Reinhard Libuda, Klaus Fichtel, Rolf Rüssmann, Klaus Fischer, Rüdiger Abramczik, Olaf Thon, Ingo Anderbrügge, Jens Lehmann, Marc Wilmots, Kevin Kurányi, Manuel Neuer, Émile Mpenza, Christian Poulsen, Raùl, Klaas-Jan Huntelaar.

Honours: League: 1934, 1935, 1937, 1939, 1940, 1942, 1958; National Cup: 1937, 1972, 2001, 2002, 2011; UEFA Cup: 1997.

"Hamburg, my pearl / you wonderful city / you are my home / you are my life." **"Hamburg meine Perle," song of the supporters of Hamburger SV.**

HAMBURGER SV

The Dinosaur

Founded: **1887** · Stadium: **Volksparkstadion (Hamburg)**

The only German club to have never known relegation—earning them the nickname "dinosaur"—the club's golden age was between the years 1976 and 1987, a success symbolized by the Austrian coach, Ernst Happel. Following defeat to Nottingham Forest in the 1980 European Cup, Hamburg became European champions in 1983, beating Michel Platini's Juventus thanks to a goal from Felix Magath. ⚽ HSV supporters forever! Uwe Seeler once declared: "I am a native of this town, and HSV's crest will remain forever engraved in my heart." The day he departs this world, the Hamburg legend of the 1950s-1960s could be buried one hundred and fifty feet from the stadium in the first cemetery in Europe dedicated to football players, which opened in 2008.

6 League Titles

3 National Cups

1 European Cup

1 European Cup Winners' Cup

Star players: Uwe Seeler, Horst Hrubesch, Franz Beckenbauer, Kevin Keegan, Manfred Kaltz, Felix Magath, Dietmar Beiersdorfer, Ulrich Stein, Daniel Van Buyten, Rafael Van der Vaart.

Honours: League: 1923, 1928, 1960, 1979, 1982, 1983; National Cup: 1963, 1976, 1987; European Cup: 1983; European Cup Winners' Cup: 1977.

May 9, 1980
Goalkeeper Rudolf Kargus, HSV's captain, leads his team to their first European Cup final, following the club's victory against Real Madrid in the semi-final (0-2, 5-1).

GERMANY

"Mönchengladbach is Vesuvius . . . and all the cataclysms of creation embodied in football."
Jacques Thibert, *L'Année du football*, 1976.

BORUSSIA MÖNCHENGLADBACH
The Foals

Founded: **1900** • Stadium: **Borussia Park (Mönchengladbach)**

Having entered the Bundesliga in 1965, Mönchengladbach soon became one of German football's major assets. Their three consecutive league titles (1975–1977) made the club very popular in a Germany stunned by the domination of Bayern Munich—three-time champions of Europe. ⚽ The Weisweiler method. In the mid-1960s, the club stood out in Germany because of their spirited playing style, earning their players the nickname "Foals." The coach, Hennes Weisweiler, applied a training programme—similar to that of Ajax Amsterdam—that instilled speed and adaptability in his players. Also important was the choice hiring of foreign players, such as the Danish striker Allan Simonsen, named 1977 European Footballer of the Year while wearing the club's strip.

5 League Titles

3 National Cups

2 UEFA Cups

May 21, 1975
Hans-Jürgen Wittkamp, Dietmar Danner, Jupp Heynckes, Henning Jensen, Frank Schaeffer and Allan Simonsen (from left to right) enjoy their club's first European title.

Star players: Günter Netzer, Jupp Heynckes, Berti Vogts, Wolfgang Kleff, Uli Stielike, Rainer Bonhof, Allan Simonsen, Lothar Matthäus, Stefan Effenberg, Martin Dahlin, Oliver Neuville.

Honours: League: 1970, 1971, 1975, 1976, 1977; National Cup: 1960, 1973, 1995; UEFA Cup 1975, 1979.

TSV 1860 MÜNCHEN
The Lions

Founded: **1860** • Stadium: **Allianz Arena (Munich)**

The club may be overshadowed by giants Bayern—and a few years ago had to sell their share in the Allianz Arena to their rival—but they were German league champions in 1966, and runners-up in the 1965 European Cup Winners' Cup. München have strong working-class roots, and are known as "Munich's great love."

HERTHA BERLIN
The Old Lady

Founded: **1892** • Stadium: **Olympic (Berlin)**

Before the Second World War, Hertha Berlin were one of the best clubs in the country, winning the league championship in 1930 and 1931. They played in the amateur league after the war, before taking advantage of the many players fleeing from East Germany to rebuild, gaining promotion to the Bundesliga in 1968.

FC LOKOMOTIVE LEIPZIG
Loksche

Founded: **1893** • Stadium: **Bruno-Plache (Leipzig)**

Crowned the first league champions of Germany in 1903, the club won the title again in 1906 and 1913. In 1954, they entered the East German league, and undertook eighteen European campaigns, finally winning the 1987 Cup Winners' Cup. They now play in the fourth division.

VFB STUTTGART
The Swabians

Founded: **1893** • Stadium: **Mercedes-Benz Arena (Stuttgart)**

Initially comprised of middle-class schoolchildren, VFB Stuttgart have been champions on five occasions, and won the cup three times. Runners-up in the 1989 UEFA Cup and the 1998 UEFA Cup Winners' Cup, the club's local rivals are Stuttgarter Kickers and Karlsruher SC.

EINTRACHT BRAUNSCHWEIG
The Lions

Founded: **1895** • Stadium: **Eintracht (Braunschweig)**

A founding member of the German FA, in 1900, and of the Bundesliga, in 1963, Eintracht Braunschweig have historically been one of the most popular clubs in Northern Germany. In 1967 they became league champions, and in 1973 they were the first club in Germany to wear a sponsor's name on their strip.

FORTUNA DÜSSELDORF
Flingeraner

Founded: **1895** • Stadium: **Esprit Arena (Düsseldorf)**

Fortuna Düsseldorf were the 1933 German league champions. In 1940, they shared the billing with Schalke 04 during the first television broadcast of a football match. They were runners-up in the 1979 European Cup Winners' Cup. In 2009, they drew 50,000 spectators to a third-division match.

HANOVER 96
The Reds
Founded: **1896** • Stadium: **HDI (Hanover)**

Founded by a German schoolteacher, Hanover 96 won their first German league championship in 1938, in front of 95,000 spectators, beating Schalke 04—the best team at the time. They won the league again in 1954, and the cup in 1992. Their main rivals are Eintracht Braunschweig.

CHEMNITZER FC
Sky Blues
Founded: **1899** • Stadium: **An der Gellertstraße (Chemnitz)**

Founded by students, Chemnitzer were one of the founders of the German Football Association. Under the East German regime, they took the new name of the city, becoming FC Karl-Marx-Stadt, and won the league title in 1967. Following reunification, they changed their name back to Chemintzer and launched Michael Ballack's career.

EINTRACHT FRANKFURT
The Eagles
Founded: **1899** • Stadium: **Commerzbank (Frankfurt)**

A stronghold of German football, Eintracht were league champions in 1959, and reached the final of the 1960 European Cup, where they were beaten by Real Madrid. Winner of the 1980 UEFA Cup, they have since shown a lack of consistency that has earned them the nickname "moody diva."

TSG 1899 HOFFENHEIM
Hoffe
Founded: **1899** • Stadium: **Rhein-Neckar (Sinsheim)**

Hoffenheim are based in a village of 3,000 inhabitants. In the years 2000 to 2008, they ascended from the fifth division to the Bundesliga, thanks to Dietmar Hopp, a businessman and former player at the club. In 2009, Hopp commissioned the building of a 30,000-capacity stadium in neighbouring Sinsheim.

WERDER BREMEN
The River Islanders
Founded: **1899** • Stadium: **Weser (Bremen)**

Founded by high-school students who had won sports equipment during a school competition, Werder Bremen were one of the founders of the German Football Association in 1900. Winner of four league championships, six cups and one Cup Winners' Cup (1992), Werder Bremen's major rivals are Hamburg.

FC KAISERSLAUTERN
The Red Devils
Founded: **1900** • Stadium: **Fritz-Walter (Kaiserslautern)**

Twice champions in the 1950s, and twice again in the 1990s, Kaiserslautern are somewhat mercurial but can boast some dramatic victories. In 1973, the club scored six goals against Bayern in thirty-three minutes, and in 1982, they beat Real Madrid 5-0.

1. FC NÜRNBERG
The Legend

Founded: **1900** • Stadium: **Grundig (Nuremberg)**

1. FC Nürnberg were dominant in the early twentieth century, winning eight titles between 1920 and 1961, and earning themselves the nickname, "The Club." They have won the league championship once since the creation of the Bundesliga, as well as picking up four cups. Their rivalry with Fürth is the oldest in the country.

FC CARL ZEISS JENA
FCC

Founded: **1903** • Stadium: **Ernst-Abbe-Sportfeld (Jena)**

Founded by workers from the Carl Zeiss optics factory, the club's heyday came during the 1960s and 1970s, when they won the East German league three times, and lifted four East German cups, and one UEFA Cup Winners' Cup (1981). They were runners-up in the 1992 second-division of reunited Germany, before falling to the fourth division.

BAYER 04 LEVERKUSEN
Factory Team

Founded: **1904** • Stadium: **BayArena (Leverkusen)**

Established by employees of the chemical giant, Bayer, which became their owners, Bayer Leverkusen are the first club to have contested the final of the Champions League (in 2002) without ever having been national league champions. They also won the 1988 UEFA Cup.

SC FREIBURG
The Brazilians of Breisgau

Founded: **1904** • Stadium: **Schwarzwald (Freiburg)**

Sport-Club Freiburg have a slick playing style, which has earned them the nickname "Brazilians," even though promotion to the Bundesliga only came in 1993. In the 1980s, while in the second division, Joachim Löw was the club's top scorer. Günter Grass, winner of the Nobel Prize for Literature, supported them until his death.

1. FSV MAINZ 05
Carnival Club

Founded: **1905** • Stadium: **Coface (Mainz)**

This historic club from Rhineland-Palatinate played in the Bundesliga for the first time in 2004. Since then, they have regularly filled their new 34,000-capacity stadium, where a carnival atmosphere reigns every time the team score a goal.

UNION BERLIN
Iron Union

Founded: **1906** • Stadium: **An der Alten Försterei (Berlin)**

The club previously known as FC Olympia Oberschöneweide won the 1968 East German cup and have always had a strong working-class following. In 2008, their fans carried out stadium-enlargement works themselves. They now play in the second division.

FC AUGSBURG
Fuggerstädter
Founded: **1907** · Stadium: **WWK (Augsburg)**

C Augsburg have strong working-class roots, and over 12,000 members, the current club being the result of a merger between TSV Schwaben and BC Augsburg. Despite their popularity, it wasn't until 2011 that they played their first season in the first division. Their traditional local rivals are Munich 1860.

ROT WEISS ESSEN
RWE
Founded: **1907** · Stadium: **Essen (Essen)**

Winner of the cup in 1953, the club became league champions of Germany in 1955, earning them the right to contest the first UEFA European Cup. They still draw 8,000 spectators per match, despite currently playing in the fourth division.

FC ST. PAULI
Buccaneers of the League
Founded: **1910** · Stadium: **Millerntor (Hamburg)**

Hamburg's second most successful club, FC St. Pauli are known for their "alternative" supporters waving pirate flags in their stadium near the city's famous red-light district, the Reeperbahn. Despite only three brief appearances in the Bundesliga, the 30,000-capacity stadium is always full.

VFL WOLFSBURG
The Wolfes
Founded: **1945** · Stadium: **Volkswagen Arena (Wolfburg)**

Established for the workers of the Volkswagen factory, of which they are a subsidiary, the club entered the first division in 1997 and became league champions in 2009 under the management of Felix Magath. In 2014, Wolfsburg signed the striker André Schürrle—a member of the 2014 World Cup winning squad.

1. FC KÖLN
The Billy Goats
Founded: **1948** · Stadium: **RheinEnergie (Cologne)**

The first winner of the Bundesliga, in 1963, FC Köln have racked up three league titles and four cups, and were runners-up in the 1986 UEFA Cup, when they were beaten by Real Madrid. Their mascot, a goat picked by the fans, can be viewed via webcam at Cologne Zoo.

BERLINER FC DYNAMO
The Wine Reds
Founded: **1953** · Stadium: **Friedrich-Ludwig-Jahn Sportpark (Berlin)**

Originally affiliated with the East German police, Berliner FC Dynamo were given Dynamo Dresden's players in 1954, but with little success. Eventually they won ten titles in a row, from 1979 to 1988. Now playing in the fourth division, they can draw 10,000 spectators for important matches.

DYNAMO DRESDEN
Dynamo

Founded: **1953** • Stadium: **Glücksgas (Dresden)**

Another club that was originally affiliated with the East German police, Dynamo won eight league championships between 1953 and 1990, despite their players being moved to Berlin in 1954. Although they now play in the second division, they still draw average crowds of 27,000 spectators.

1. FC MAGDEBURG
The Club

Founded: **1965** • Stadium: **MDCC (Magdeburg)**

The first football club established by the East German regime, they won the 1974 UEFA Cup Winners' Cup– the only European football trophy ever won by an East German team. Three-time league champions and seven-time winners of the cup, 1. FC Magdeburg have just managed to survive since reunification. In 2001, they were saved by their fans from bankruptcy.

FC HANSA ROSTOCK
Hanseaten

Founded: **1965** • Stadium: **Ostsee (Rostock)**

The club won their only title in 1991, the final season of the East German league. This success catapulted them directly into the Bundesliga, but they were relegated in 1992, before returning in 1995 and spending ten seasons competing at the top of the league, a record for a former East German club.

ENERGIE COTTBUS
Energie

Founded: **1966** • Stadium: **Freundschaft (Cottbus)**

Energie Cottbus are a modest East German club and one of the few from the former DDR-Oberliga to have carved out a niche in German football since reunification in 1990. Runners-up in the 1997 cup, they entered the Bundesliga in 2000, fielding the first team to be composed entirely of foreign players.

FC ROT-WEISS ERFURT
The Reds

Founded: **1966** • Stadium: **Steigerwald (Erfurt)**

Erfurt were formed from the merger of FC Turbine—twice champion of East Germany—and BSG Optima. They ended the final season of the DDR-Oberliga (1991) in third place. That same year, they became the last ever representative of East German football in a European competition (UEFA Cup, second round).

RASENBALLSPORT LEIPZIG
The Bulls

Founded: **2009** • Stadium: **Red Bull Arena (Leipzig)**

This is the fourth football club owned by Red Bull, who bought the licence from a fifth-division club. In just four years, they managed to reach the second division. In 2013–2014, while in the third division, they boasted an average attendance of 16,000 spectators at the former Zentralstadion.

"Come on Rapid, fight and win!"
(Traditional club chant).

RAPID WIEN

The Green-Whites

Founded: **1899** · Stadium: **Ernst Happel (Vienna)**

Originally a workers' football club, Rapid have always been at the top of Austrian football, thanks to their fighting spirit. This mentality is symbolized by the crowd, who traditionally applaud in the seventy-fifth minute of each match to boost team morale. This practice, which has continued uninterrupted since 1913, has helped Rapid reach the finals of the European Cup Winners' Cup on two occasions. ⚽ Champion of Germany during World War Two: Following the annexation of Austria by Germany in 1938, Rapid joined the elites of German football. In 1938, the club won the German Cup, and in 1941 became Champions of Germany. To this day, Rapid remain the only champion club in a foreign country.

32
League Titles

14
National Cups

August 19, 2015
Rapid welcome Shakhtar Donetsk in the qualifying round of the Champions League.

Star players: Josef Bican, Gerhard Hanappi, Ernst Happel, Franz Hasil, Hans Krankl, Antonín Panenka, Trifon Ivanov, Carsten Jancker, Michael Konsel.

Honours: League: 1912, 1913, 1916, 1917, 1919, 1920, 1921, 1923, 1929, 1930, 1935, 1938, 1940, 1941, 1946, 1948, 1951, 1952, 1954, 1956, 1957, 1960, 1964, 1967, 1968, 1982, 1983, 1987, 1988, 1996, 2005, 2008; National Cup: 1919, 1920, 1927, 1946, 1961, 1968, 1969, 1972, 1976, 1983, 1984, 1985, 1987, 1995.

GRAZER AK
The Red Jackets
Founded: **1902** • Stadium: **UPC Arena (Graz)**

Having won the Austrian Cup four times, Grazer AK had long been overshadowed by their local rival, Sturm Graz, before winning the league in 2004. Declared bankrupt in 2012, a new club was set up by its supporters shortly thereafter, and they play in the Austrian amateur division.

ADMIRA WACKER
The Southerners
Founded: **1905** • Stadium: **BSFZ Arena (Mödling)**

Founded in Vienna and a historic club in Austrian football, Admira Wacker had won eight national titles by 1966, before commencing a series of mergers that ended with them being based in the town of Mödling. Having returned to the first division in 2011, the club have since played in the Europa League.

STURM GRAZ
The Blacks
Founded: **1909** • Stadium: **UPC Arena (Graz)**

Founded as a workers' team, Sturm Graz were the first non-Viennese team to join the Austrian league. A triple winner of the championship (1998, 1999, 2011), Graz are also the second most popular in the country, behind Rapid Wien, with whom they maintain a rivalry.

AUSTRIA WIEN
The Violets
Founded: **1910** • Stadium: **Franz Horr (Vienna)**

Austria Wien dominated Central European football during the 1930s, thanks to the superb Matthias Sindelar. The club have won the national championship twenty-four times, and were runners-up in the 1978 European Cup Winners' Cup. Their great rivals are Rapid, with whom they have contested more than 300 derbies.

FC WACKER INNSBRUCK
The Black and Greens
Founded: **2002** • Stadium: **Tivoli Neu (Innsbruck)**

This club has a twin heritage: Wacker Innsbruck, winner of five league titles and five cups in the 1970s; and FC Tirol, which took over the licence from the former in 1993, and were three times champions. FC Wacker Innsbruck are now Tyrol's leading football club.

FC RED BULL SALZBURG
The Red Bulls
Founded: **2005** • Stadium: **Red Bull Arena (Salzburg)**

Formerly known as SV Austria Salzburg, the club were bought by the Red Bull company in 2005. With a major injection of funds, and Giovanni Trapattoni as head coach, the club won six national titles between 2006 and 2014.

"I have achieved more with Ajax in six years than Barcelona has in one hundred years." **Louis Van Gaal, in 1997 just before moving from Ajax to become manager of FC Barcelona.**

AFC AJAX
Sons of the Gods

Founded: **1900** • Stadium: **Amsterdam Arena (Amsterdam)**

Ajax have dominated in the Netherlands since the 1930s, but they have also long stamped their mark on European competitions. As effective as they are spectacular, Ajax won the European Cup three seasons in a row, with a generation that composed the backbone of the Netherlands team that were runners-up in the 1974 and 1978 World Cups. Renowned for their youth academy and their keen nose for recruiting players, Ajax have been marking time since 1995, and the Bosman ruling that opened the floodgates for the richest clubs in Europe. Although Ajax are the most popular club in the country, they are also the most disliked by a great number of fans, especially by the supporters of Feyenoord, their eternal rivals, against whom they play in the *Klassieker*.

33 League Titles

18 National Cups

4 Champions League / European Cups

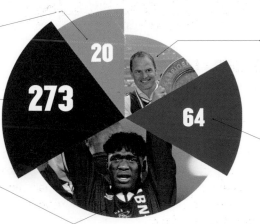

The number of goals scored in the Champions League by Jari Litmanen while he was wearing the Ajax shirt.

The total number of goals scored by Piet van Reenen, an Ajax player during the 1930s.

Clarence Seedorf
European champion in 1995 with Ajax, he was also the youngest striker in the history of the club.

Frank de Boer
An Ajax legend during his career as a player, he's also one of their most successful managers and the first to win four consecutive Eredivisie titles.

The number of goals scored in a single season (1960-61) by Henk Groot.

AJAX, THE SCHOOL FOR FOOTBALL

Ajax have had a unique club culture since 1917 and the arrival of Jack Reynolds as manager. Over a period of twenty-five years, the English coach laid the foundations of a system developed later by Rinus Michels, then continued by Louis van Gaal. This system—or rather

a style of play—called "total football" consists of discipline, physical fitness, technical craft, and collective intelligence. This is handed down from one generation to the next, thanks to a training programme that is identical for each of the club's teams, from the youngest age, and particularly for the members of De Toekomst ("The Future"), the academy that trains the most promising players. In 2015, Ajax were still the biggest supplier of players to the top-flight European leagues.

May 24 1995
Patrick Kluivert, a pure product of the Ajax school, lifts the Champions League trophy.

"WE ARE THE CHAMPIONS," FIRST!

After Ajax achieved a promising draw (2–2) in the away leg of the final of the 1992 UEFA Cup against Torino FC, 5,000 Dutch supporters were still packed into the visitors' stand of Turin's Delle Alpi stadium one hour after the final whistle. Suddenly, Louis van Gaal's players walked out of the dressing rooms and crossed the pitch to salute them. The supporters started singing Queen's "We are the Champions," accompanied by a brass band that was in the stand with them. The singing was repeated during the home leg in Amsterdam, as Ajax took another European title. From that moment on, the song originally sung by Freddie Mercury—who had died just a few months previously—has entered the repertoire of football fans the world over.

NETHERLANDS

JOHAN CRUYFF, LUCKY NUMBER FOURTEEN

Although he made a splash in the colours of FC Barcelona—and even with Ajax's sworn enemy, Feyenoord, the name of Johan Cruyff will forever be associated with Ajax. Not only was the striker the main architect of the club's success during its most successful period, when they won the European Cup three years in a row (1971, 1972, 1973), but he embodied the spirit of the club even after he left it. Cruyff arrived at Ajax when he was just ten years old, and by eighteen he was its kingpin. Elegant, inventive, and always effective, the player who popularized the number fourteen proved that the total football promoted by the coach Rinus Michels was no fantasy. When he joined Barcelona as a player, from 1973 to 1978, then as coach, from 1988 to 1996, he brought the Ajax philosophy with him.

April 27, 2014
Ajax celebrate their thirty-third title as Dutch champions.

Star players: Gerrit Fischer, Johan Cruyff, Johnny Rep, Frank Rijkaard, Ronald de Boer, Frank de Boer, Jari Litmanen, Dennis Bergkamp, Marco van Basten, Arie Haan, Johan Neeskens, Ruud Krol, Danny Blind, Edgar Davids, Patrick Kluivert, Zlatan Ibrahimović, Wesley Sneijder, Luis Suàrez.

Honours: League: 1918, 1919, 1931, 1932, 1934, 1937, 1939, 1947, 1957, 1960, 1966, 1967, 1968, 1970, 1972, 1973, 1977, 1979, 1980, 1982, 1983, 1985, 1990, 1994, 1995, 1996, 1998, 2002, 2004, 2011, 2012, 2013, 2014; National Cup: 1917, 1943, 1961, 1967, 1970, 1971, 1972, 1979, 1983, 1986, 1987, 1993, 1998, 1999, 2002, 2006, 2007, 2010; European Cup/Champions League: 1971, 1972, 1973, 1995; European Cup Winners' Cup: 1987; UEFA Cup: 1992; Intercontinental Cup: 1972, 1995.

NETHERLANDS

"Yes Eindhoven, will always be red and white!
Passion and Pride! Co hand in hand here!
So we put the lighttown on the map"
"PSV is in my heart," Lighttown Madness (PSV fans group)

PSV EINDHOVEN
The Farmers

Founded: **1913**
Stadium: **Philips (Eindhoven)**

Philips' sports association were established within the famous electrical goods company, and initially recruited players for their professional team from among its employees. The most successful club in the Netherlands after Ajax, they had a period of domination in the late 1980s, when they joined Ajax and Feyenoord as champions in the European Cup, with another such period in the 2000s. Their style of play may be less flamboyant than that of their two rivals, but they can put up a fight, such as during the 10-0 victory over Feyenoord in 2010. They are also the club that introduced the Brazilians, Romário and Ronaldo, to Europe.

22 League Titles

9 National Cups

1 European Cup

April 7, 1991
Romário fools the Ajax goalkeeper and PSV become champions.

Star players: Willy and René Van de Kerkhof, Jan van Beveren, Jan Poortvliet, Eric Gerets, Søren Lerby, Ruud Gullit, Ronald Koeman, Romário, Ronaldo, Phillip Cocu, Jaap Stam, Mark van Bommel, Ruud van Nistelrooy, Mateja Kežman, Arjen Robben, Memphis Depay.

Honours: League: 1929, 1935, 1951, 1963, 1975, 1976, 1978, 1986, 1987, 1988, 1989, 1991, 1992, 1997, 2000, 2001, 2003, 2005, 2006, 2007, 2008, 2015; National Cup: 1950, 1974, 1976, 1988, 1989, 1990, 1996, 2005, 2012; European Cup 1988; UEFA Cup: 1978.

"Last week we were able to see that football isn't just about accumulating quality. The right attitude and formation are just as important, as Feyenoord proved against us. Holland can be very proud of this club." **Clarence Seedorf, after losing a match with Inter Milan in Rotterdam, in 2002.**

FEYENOORD ROTTERDAM

The Pride of the South

Founded: **1908** • Stadium: **De Kuip (Rotterdam)**

A worker's club that fielded an amateur team for many years, Feyenoord caused a stir in 1938 by beating the English professional team, Arsenal. In 1970, when their coach was the Austrian, Ernst Happel, their highly elaborate play gave Dutch football its first European Cup. The eternal rivals of Ajax, the club succeeded in 1983 in signing the national hero, Johan Cruyff, in the twilight of his career, along with a future star, Ruud Gullit. The result was that the club won their first title in ten years. Very popular, thousands of their fans—nicknamed "The Legion"— have travelled across Europe to support them since the 1960s.

May 3, 1984
Johann Cruyff and Ruud Gullit lead Feyenoord to the league and cup double.

14 League Titles

11 National Cups

1 European Cup

Star players: Rinus Bennaars, Ove Kindvall, Henk Schouten, Hans Venneker, Wim Jansen, Joop van Daele, Wim van Hanegem, Johan Cruyff, Ruud Gullit, Peter Houtman, Giovanni van Bronckhorst, Clarence Seedorf, Pierre van Hooijdonk, Robin van Persie.

Honours: League: 1924, 1928, 1936, 1938, 1940, 1961, 1962, 1965, 1969, 1971, 1974, 1984, 1993, 1999; National Cup: 1930, 1935, 1965, 1969, 1980, 1984, 1991, 1992, 1994, 1995, 2008; European Cup: 1970; UEFA Cup: 1974, 2002; Intercontinental Cup: 1970.

SPARTA ROTTERDAM
The Castle Lords
Founded: **1888** • Stadium: **Sparta (Rotterdam)**

The oldest professional club in the country, they took their colours from the English club, Sunderland. By the 1960s, they had won the league title six times, and had never been relegated up until 2002. Their stadium, nicknamed "The Castle," has two red-brick towers as part of its facade.

SBV VITESSE
Vitas
Founded: **1892** • Stadium: **GelreDome (Arnhem)**

This historic club racked up a succession of runners-up places in the early twentieth century. In 2010, they were the first club in the country to be bought by a foreign investor. Their outlays earned them the nickname of "FC Hollywood on the Rhine," at a time when they were returning to the Europa League.

WILLEM II
The Tricolours
Founded: **1896** • Stadium: **Konig Willem II (Tilburg)**

Renamed two years after their founding, in homage to Willem II of Orange, the club have won the league championship three times, including the first professional season in 1955. They have also taken two cups, and have spent thirty-seven seasons in the first division.

MVV MAASTRICHT
Wearers of Stars
Founded: **1902** • Stadium: **De Geussell (Maastricht)**

Promoted to the first division in 1957, MVV have played twenty-six consecutive seasons in the top flight. In 1980, they inflicted a heavy defeat (6–3) on Ajax at the De Meer stadium in Amsterdam. That squad included the future Netherlands coach, Bert van Marwijk.

ADO DEN HAAG
The Residentionclub
Founded: **1905** • Stadium: **Kyocera (The Hague)**

Twice league champions during the amateur era, ADO, who are based in the Dutch capital, were coached by Ernst Happel when they won the 1968 Cup against Ajax, their first professional trophy. Every summer, they organize an international tournament for their supporters.

NAC BREDA
The Pearl of the South
Founded: **1912** • Stadium: **Rat Verlegh (Breda)**

Nicknamed "football masters" for having beaten Real Madrid 4–0 in 1920, the club won the (amateur) league championship in 1921, and the cup in 1973. They were the first Dutch club to establish a supporters' council to protect their culture.

SC HEERENVEEN
The Super Frisians
Founded: **1920** • Stadium: **Abe Lenstra (Heerenveen)**

Despite a historic 6–5 victory over Ajax in 1950, the club only entered the first division in 1990. Runners-up to PSV in 2000, and a regular qualifier for the European Cup over the past fifteen years, they were a springboard for Ruud van Nistelrooy and Klaas-Jan Huntelaar.

RODA JC KERKRADE
The Miners
Founded: **1962** • Stadium: **Parkstad Limburg (Kerkrade)**

The result of a merger between two clubs—one of which was a champion with a team composed of former miners—Roda JC have won the cup twice. A great rival of MVV Maastricht, they have called one of the stands in their new stadium the "Miner Stand," in honour of their supporters.

FC TWENTE
The Pride of the East
Founded: **1965** • Stadium: **De Crolsch Veste (Enschede)**

Runners-up in the 1975 UEFA Cup, three-time winners of the Dutch Cup, and league champions for the first time in 2010, the club manages to fill their 30,000-capacity stadium for each match. Like at Liverpool, the song "You'll Never Walk Alone" is sung at each match.

ALKMAAR ZAANSTREEK NV
The Cheese Farmers
Founded: **1967** • Stadium: **Afas (Alkmaar)**

Initially called AZ 67, the club had their hour of glory in 1981, when they won the league title, and reached the final of the UEFA Cup. In the 2000s, they became league champions again, and got as far as the semi-finals of the Europa League.

FC UTRECHT
Utreg
Founded: **1970** • Stadium: **Galgenwaard (Utrecht)**

Dutch league champions in 1958, through VV Dos—a club founded in 1901 from which they took over—they are the only team outside of the big three (Ajax, PSV, Feyenoord) to have never been relegated. Three-time winners of the KNVB Cup, they have played in nineteen European Cup competitions.

FC GRONINGEN
The Pride of the North
Founded: **1971** • Stadium: **Euroborg (Groningen)**

Groningen had their first successes in the 1980s, led by the Koeman brothers, Erwin and Ronald. In 2015, they won their first Dutch Cup. Their 22,000-capacity stadium—"the green cathedral"—opened in 2006 and is sold-out for every match.

"We remain the benchmark in Belgium. Every time a Belgian club distinguishes themselves, they are compared to Anderlecht." **Roger Vanden Stock, President of Anderlecht.**

RSC ANDERLECHT

The Mauves

Founded: **1908** · Stadium: **Constant Vanden Stock (Brussels)**

Present in the Belgian first division since 1935, Royal Sporting Club Anderlecht have always been among the country's elite clubs, amassing a fine collection of honours in Belgian soccer. They have also impressed on a European level, winning three titles from seven finals played. The club's success, and their 'middle-class' image, have not only earned them the biggest following in Belgian soccer, but have also made them the club other fans most love to beat, particularly those of Liège, against whom Royal Sporting Club Anderlecht play the Belgian clasico.

33 League Titles

9 National Cups

2 UEFA Cup Winners' Cups

1 UEFA Cup

Star players: Paul Van Himst, Robbie Rensenbrink, Juan Lozano, Erwin Vandebergh, Franky Vercauteren, Enzo Scifo, Vincent Kompany.

Honours: League: 1947, 1949, 1950, 1951, 1954, 1955, 1956, 1959, 1962, 1964, 1965, 1966, 1967, 1968, 1972, 1974, 1981, 1985, 1986; 1987, 1991, 1993, 1994, 1995, 2000, 2001, 2004, 2006, 2007, 2010, 2012, 2013, 2014; National Cup: 1965, 1972, 1973, 1975, 1976, 1988, 1989, 1994, 2008; UEFA Cup Winners' Cup: 1976, 1978; UEFA Cup: 1983.

April 23, 1978
Captain Franky Vercauteren lifts the Cup Winners' Cup trophy.

BELGIUM

"Oh FC Bruges / Super Bruges / We're wonderful / They say our days are numbered we're not famous anymore / But Bruges rules the country like we've always done before."

CLUB BRUGGE

Blue-Black

Founded: **1891** • Stadium: **Jan Breydel (Bruges)**

Club Brugge are the only Belgian club to have remained a worthy challenger to Anderlecht for the past forty years. Every year, the two sides play a hotly anticipated match nicknamed *Le Topper*. Under Austrian coach Ernst Happel, Brugge reached two European finals: the 1976 UEFA Cup, and the 1978 European Cup. They are the most popular club in Flanders. In homage to their fans (the twelfth man), Club Brugge doesn't assign the number twelve to players. One of their supporters' groups, the Blue Army, was the first (in 2003) to sing The White Stripes' "Seven Nation Army," which has since become a popular anthem in football stadiums the world over.

13 League Titles

11 National Cups

March 22, 2015
Club Brugge win the eleventh Belgian Cup in their history.

Star players: Franky van der Elst, Gert Verheyen, Raoul Lambert, Jan Ceulemans, Georges Leekens, Jean-Pierre Papin, Mario Stanic.

Honours: League: 1920, 1973, 1976, 1977, 1978, 1980, 1988, 1990, 1992, 1996, 1998, 2003, 2005; National Cup: 1968, 1970, 1977, 1986, 1991, 1995, 1996, 2002, 2004, 2007, 2015.

ROYAL ANTWERP FOOTBALL CLUB — The Great Old
Founded: **1880** · Stadium: **Bosuilstadion (Antwerp)**

These pioneers of Belgian soccer have spent ninety-six seasons among the elite, with many a dramatic match, such as the first round of the 1989 UEFA Cup, when they scored the three goals necessary for qualification during injury time. Their greatest achievement was reaching the final of the 1992 UEFA Cup Winners' Cup.

UNION SAINT-GILLOISE — The Apaches
Founded: **1897** · Stadium: **Joseph-Marien (Brussels)**

Eleven-time league champions of Belgium, Union Saint-Gilloise are a monument of Belgian football, and hold the record for undefeated matches in the first division (sixty). Now playing in the third division, Union remain the most popular club in Brussels after Anderlecht.

STANDARD LIÈGE — The Reds
Founded: **1898** · Stadium: **Maurice Dufrasne (Liège)**

These giants of Walloon soccer have the third best record in Belgium (ten championships, six cups). A regular in European cups, they reached the final in 1982, playing FC Barcelona. They boast the most enthusiastic supporters in Belgium, including a good number of Flemish fans.

K BEERSCHOT VAC — The Kiel Rats
Founded: **1899** · Stadium: **Le Kiel (Antwerp)**

Upon its founding, the club poached the best players from Royal Antwerp, beginning a rivalry that would last a century. Owing to financial problems, the club was dissolved in 1999, after one hundred years of existence, eighty-one seasons in the first division, seven Belgian league championships, and two Belgian cups.

CERCLE BRUGGE — Green and Black
Founded: **1899** · Stadium: **Jan Breydel (Bruges)**

Cercle were founded by Catholic students, and were the first Flemish club to win the Belgian championship. This old rival of Club Brugge has an army of loyal fans, who saved the club from bankruptcy in the 1980s.

KAA GENT — The Buffalos
Founded: **1900** · Stadium: **Ghelamco Arena (Ghent)**

In 2015, KAA Gent won their first title after seventy-five seasons in the first division. They have also won three cups (1964, 1984, 2010). Their recent title gives their fans even more reason to launch into their famous cry of "Buffalo" at the start of each match.

SPORTING CHARLEROI
The Zebras

Founded: **1904** • Stadium: **Pays de Charleroi (Charleroi)**

Sporting Charleroi have never won any major titles, despite playing in two finals of the Belgian Cup and one final of the first division. Yet they remain very popular. Their supporters' clubs, founded in the 1920s, provide strong encouragement in the derbies played against Standard Liège.

KV MECHELEN
The Yellow Reds

Founded: **1904** • Stadium: **Achter de Kazerne (Mechelen)**

The club's fortunes have fluctuated wildly over the years—they have been relegated twenty-two times; won the top flight on four occasions; and are the last Belgian club to lift a European trophy, in 1988. The club went into liquidation in 2002, but were saved by their fans—united behind the slogan: "We'll do it ourselves!"

LIERSE SK
De Pallieters

Founded: **1906** • Stadium: **Herman Vanderpoortenstadion (Lier)**

In 1960, this habitué of top flight Belgian soccer (four league titles, two cups) played their first European Cup against FC Barcelona when they were still an amateur club. Since absorbing its local rival, Lyra, in 1972, Lierse have played derbies against Mechelen.

WATERSCHEI THOR
Thorians

Founded: **1919** • Stadium: **André Dumont (Genk)**

Founded by Flemish miners, the "Thor" part of the name is an acronym of Tot Herstel Onzer Rechten, meaning "To recover our rights" (from the bosses, who were mostly French-speaking). The club won the Belgian Cup in 1980 and 1982, and reached the semi-finals of the European Cup Winners' Cup in 1983. In 1988, they merged with Racing Genk.

KSC LOKEREN
The Tricolours

Founded: **1923** • Stadium: **Daknamstadion (Lokeren)**

Despite thirty-seven seasons in the first division, the club's top honours are limited to two Belgian Cups (2012, 2014), which hasn't prevented them from playing in the UEFA Cup seven times over the years. The club maintains a great rivalry with Beveren.

RACING GENK
Dirty Men

Founded: **1923** • Stadium: **Cristal Arena (Genk)**

Racing Genk was born out of the merger in 1988 of two working-class clubs, Winterslag and Waterschei, and went on to wow their fans (comprising many former miners) by winning two league titles. In 2002, they brought excitement to their home region when they reached the group stage of the Champions League.

KSK BEVEREN
Little Anderlecht
Founded: **1934** • Stadium: **Freethiel (Beveren)**

The club's golden age was in the 1970s and 1980s, when they won two league titles, earning the nickname "Little Anderlecht." KSK Neveren have also claimed a few scalps at European level, including Valencia and Inter Milan. In 2010, the club merged with Red Star Waasland.

OH LEUVEN
The University Students
Founded: **2002** • Stadium: **Den Dreef (Louvain)**

Born from the merger of three lower-division clubs (Stade Leuven, Daring Club Leuven, and FC Zwarte Duivels), OH Leuven managed to reach the first division in less than ten years. The club also succeeded in unifying all of the old fans behind their new colours.

CD FOLA ESCH
The Red-Whites
Founded: **1906** • Stadium: **Émile Mayrisch (Esch)**

Founded by a British professor, CD Fola Esch are the oldest Luxembourg club. They won the league championship five times between 1918 and 1930. A big rival of Jeunesse d'Esch, they were relegated to the third division in 2004, before returning to the limelight, winning two titles in 2013 and 2015.

AS JEUNESSE D'ESCH
The Little Steelworkers
Founded: **1907** • Stadium: **Stade de la Frontière (Esch)**

With their twenty-eight league titles, AS Jeunesse d'Esch, who were established in a region with a large steelmaking industry, have largely dominated Luxembourg football since the 1950s. In 1973, they stood up to Liverpool FC (1–1) in the European Cup before losing the second leg at Anfield (0–2).

FC AVENIR BEGGEN
Pixies
Founded: **1915** • Stadium: **Rue Henri Dunant (Luxembourg)**

Founded by children who were prevented from attending school by the Germans during the First World War, FC Avenir Beggen have been league champions of Luxembourg six times. Their golden age came between 1984 and 1994, during which time they won three league/cup doubles.

F91 DUDELANGE
The Red-Yellows
Founded: **1991** • Stadium: **Jos Nosbaum (Dudelange)**

Formed from the merger of three local clubs, including Stade Dudelange—ten-time league champions—the club has dominated the league for the past fifteen years, winning eleven titles. In 2005, F91 Dudelange became the first Luxembourg club to reach the second round of the UEFA Champions League.

"Following a Grasshopper defeat, I can't write for a week."
Friedrich Dürrenmatt, Swiss author.

GRASSHOPPER CLUB ZURICH

The Grasshoppers

Founded: **1886** · Stadium: **Letzigrund (Zurich)**

Founded by an English student, who gave the club the colours of his favourite team, Blackburn Rovers, the club won the first season of the Swiss league championship, and would follow with another twenty-six titles over more than a century—a record. In the 1930s, GC were part of the European top flight, thanks to the "Swiss lock," a defensive tactic that was a precursor of the *catenaccio* dreamt up by the head coach, Karl Rappan, and previously tested at Servette. As semi-finalists of the 1978 UEFA Cup, the club caused a stir the following season by knocking Real Madrid out of the European Cup. They initially drew their support from Zurich's upper classes; and for more than a century have maintained a rivalry with FC Zurich—whose stadium they have borrowed since 2007, when their own historic stadium of Hardturm was demolished.

27
League Titles

19
National Cups

May 1937
The Grasshoppers win the league and cup double.

Star players: Max Abegglen, Martin Andermatt, Stéphane Chapuisat, Giovane Elber, Kurt Jara, Marcel Koller, Stephan Lichtsteiner, Raimondo Ponte, Ciriaco Sforza, Alain Sutter, Ramon Vega, Johann Vogel, Roger Vonlanthen, Hakan Yakin, Murat Yakin, Reto Ziegler.

Honours: League: 1898, 1900, 1901, 1905, 1921, 1927, 1928, 1931, 1937, 1939, 1942, 1943, 1945, 1952, 1956, 1971, 1978, 1982, 1983, 1984, 1990, 1991, 1995, 1996, 1998, 2001, 2003; National Cup: 1926, 1927, 1932, 1934, 1937, 1938, 1940, 1941, 1942, 1943, 1946, 1952, 1956, 1983, 1988, 1989, 1990, 1994, 2013.

FC SANKT-GALLEN
Espen

Founded: **1879** • Stadium: **AFG Arena (Saint-Gall)**

Sankt-Gallen are the oldest club in Switzerland. They have won the league twice, first in 1904, and again, nearly a century later, in 2000. Relegated to the second division in 2008, the club managed to return to the top flight in 2009. They draw on average a crowd of 12,000 spectators—a Swiss record.

SERVETTE FC
The Garnets

Founded: **1890** • Stadium: **Genève (Geneva)**

It was at Servette that Karl Rappan invented the "lock" in the 1930s. The club hold seventeen league titles, and are the third most successful club in Switzerland. Twice quarter-finalists in the Cup Winners' Cup, the Brazilian striker Sonny Anderson made his European debut here.

FC BASEL 1893
Bebbi

Founded: **1893** • Stadium: **St Jakob Park (Basel)**

Eighteen-time league champions (ten times since 2002), the club, who gave their colours to FC Barcelona, have also hit the headlines outside of Switzerland: in 2012, they eliminated Manchester United from the Champions League, and in 2013, they reached the quarter-finals of the Europa League.

FC LAUSANNE-SPORT
LS

Founded: **1896** • Stadium: **Olympique de La Pontaise (Lausanne)**

Lausanne-Sport, founded by a group of teenagers, are one of the most successful clubs in Swiss football, having won seven league titles and nine cups. Semi-finalists in the 1958 UEFA Cup, it was here that the Italian giant, Giancarlo Antognoni, finished his career.

FC ZÜRICH
The Lions

Founded: **1896** • Stadium: **Letzigrund (Zurich)**

Co-founded by Hans Gamper—who also founded FC Barcelona—FCZ have been league champions twelve times, and have twice contested the semi-finals of the Champions League. In 2009, they beat AC Milan on their home ground. In Zurich, they enjoy greater popularity than their rivals, Grasshopper.

BSC YOUNG BOYS
YB

Founded: **1896** • Stadium: **Suisse (Berne)**

Based in the federal capital, Young Boys are the fifth most successful club in the country, with eleven league titles to their credit. In 1959, at the height of their glory, they were the first Swiss club to reach the semi-finals of the European Cup.

FC THUN
The Reds
Founded: **1898** • Stadium: **Stockhorn (Thun)**

Based in a small town in the canton of Berne, the club made a splash during the 2005 and 2006 seasons, when they eliminated Dynamo Kiev and Malmö from the Champions League, having qualified for the group stage with the smallest budget of any team.

FC LUGANO
Bianconeri
Founded: **1908** • Stadium: **Comunale Cornaredo (Lugano)**

Three-time champions, the former club of Brazilain goalkeeper, Dida, knocked Inter Milan out of the UEFA Cup in 1995. Relegated to the fourth division in 2003, after going bankrupt, the club retrieved their historic name in their centenary year. They play the Tessin derby against Bellinzona.

FC SION
The Red and Whites
Founded: **1909** • Stadium: **Tourbillon (Sion)**

Sion were at their peak in the 1990s, winning two league titles, in 1992 and 1997, when Fernando de Assis— Ronaldinho's older brother— was playing for the club. Atlético Madrid and Olympique de Marseille have both been beaten by Sion in international competitions.

NEUCHÂTEL XAMAX FCS
Xamax
Founded: **1912** • Stadium: **la Maladière (Neuchâtel)**

Xamax were named after Max Abbelgen, a founding member, whose first name is written backwards and then forwards. Their heyday was in the 1980s, when they were twice league champions and twice quarter-finalists in the UEFA Cup.

FC VADUZ
Residenzler
Founded: **1932** • Stadium: **Rheinpark (Vaduz)**

In a country that has too few teams to form a league, the club instead play in Switzerland. Promoted to the first division in 2008, Vaduz have also played in the Europa League for over twenty years thanks to their domination of the Liechtenstein Cup, which they have won forty-three times, a world record.

USV ESCHEN/MAUREN
The Blue and Yellows
Founded: **1963** • Stadium: **Sportpark Eschen-Mauren (Eschen)**

The club play in the Swiss division, but have won five Liechtenstein Cups, most recently in 2012, putting an end to FC Vaduz's uninter-rupted string of victories that commenced in 1998. This success earned them the right to play in the Europa League for the first time.

"PSG represents the capital, where all the political and sporting authorities are located. It's good to be seen at Parc des Princes. Not at all at Stade Vélodrome. People don't come here to be seen, but to see OM win. Nobody wears suits and ties here." **José Anigo, former OM player, coach, and sports director.**

OLYMPIQUE DE MARSEILLE

OM

DROIT AU BUT

Founded: **1899** · Stadium: **Stade Vélodrome (Marseille)**

A founding member of the professional league championship, in 1932, OM soon experienced their first successes, and became extremely popular. With nine league titles, ten cups (a record), and one Champions League trophy, they are the most successful club in French football. Among their other honours, they can also be proud of having been runners-up in the 1991 European Cup, and twice runners-up in the UEFA Cup (1999, 2004). Their glory years have been associated with charismatic presidents such as Bernard Tapie, member of parliament and cabinet minister, who steered the club through a series of audacious signings and a few scandals. OM have maintained a fierce rivalry with PSG since the early 1990s. They play in the largest stadium in the first division.

9 League Titles

10 National Cups

1 Champions League Title

Jean-Pierre Papin
The 1991 Ballon d'Or winner scored 184 goals while he was playing for Marseille.

The number of goals scored by Swedish striker Gunnar Andersson, the top scorer in the history of the club.

The number of goals scored in one season (1970-71) by Croatian forward Josip Skoblar.

192

49

453

The number of games played by Roger Scotti while he was wearing the Marseille shirt (1942-1958).

Didier Deschamps
Marseille's captain during the club's victory in the 1993 Champions League. Later, as manager, he helped the club regain national success.

MARSEILLE, THE MOST FERVENT FANS IN FRANCE

In a city whose heart beats to the rhythm of its football club, OM supporters are something special. After having financed the building of the stadium in the 1930s, they were the first fans in France to invest in the "ultra" movement, with the creation of the Commando Ultra in 1984. From 1987, groups of supporters were recruited by the club to sell season tickets in the stands. The supporters used the resulting profits to fund the giant flags and banners that have made Marseille fans the most spectacular in France. With a hundred supporters' fans across the country, all linked to the main groups in Marseille, OM is France's favourite team, with nine million supporters, as well as drawing the largest crowds to both home and away matches.

May 26, 1993
Basile Boli scores with a header, the only goal of the Champions League final, against AC Milan.

Star players: Mario Zatelli, Josip Skoblar, Roger Magnusson, Marius Trésor, Eric Di Meco, Jean-Pierre Papin, Abedi Pelé, Carlos Mozer, Chris Waddle, Basile Boli, Didier Deschamps, Fabien Barthez, Laurent Blanc, Fabrizio Ravanelli, Didier Drogba, Steve Mandanda, Mathieu Valbuena.

Honours: League: 1937, 1948, 1971, 1972, 1989, 1990, 1991, 1992, 2010; National Cup: 1924, 1926, 1927, 1935, 1938, 1943, 1969, 1972, 1976, 1989; League Cup: 2010, 2011, 2012; Champions League: 1993.

"I had an offer to sign for Manchester United in 2005. I even met with Sir Alex Ferguson in Nice. We had lunch together and he told me he had faith in me. But in the end I chose to extend my contract with PSG."
Bernard Mendy.

PARIS SAINT-GERMAIN FC

The Parisians

Founded: **1970** • Stadium: **Parc des Princes (Paris)**

Paris Saint-Germain grew out of the desire of several politicians to resolve the lack of a major Paris football club. PSG entered the first division in 1974. They began to dominate French football in the 1990s, nurturing a strong rivalry with Marseille, then the strongest club in the country. PSG have pulled off many a victory in European competition, against the likes of Real Madrid, Barcelona, Liverpool, and Chelsea. They won their first Cup Winners' Cup in 1996, and were runners-up in 1997 against Barcelona. When PSG were bought by a group of Qatari investors in 2011, they became one of the richest clubs in the world, enabling them to attract players such as Zlatan Ibrahimović, the club's highest ever scorer.

5 League Titles

9 National Cups

1 UEFA Cup Winners' Cup

Bruno N'Gotty
He scored the only goal of the Cup Winners' Cup final against Rapid Vienna, bringing victory to PSG in 1996.

The number of games played by Jean-Marc Pilorget while he was wearing the PSG shirt.

Zlatan Ibrahimovic
He arrived in Paris in the summer of 2012, and by 2015, the Swede had broken the record for the number of goals scored by a player at PSG, which was until then held by Pedro Miguel Pauleta.

The amount of money, in millions of euros, spent by PSG in 2013 to sign Edinson Cavani.

The number of games that Luis Fernandez oversaw as coach of PSG.

435

64

244

THE CRAZIEST MATCH

In 1993, PSG played Real Madrid at home in the quarter-finals of the UEFA Cup. Having been beaten 3-1 away, the Parisians led 2-0 with just ten minutes left to play, thanks to a superb goal from Ginola. Valdo slotted a third, but after three minutes of injury time, Zamorano scored for Real. PSG made a final attack and won a free kick. The fourth goal flew into the net from a Kombouaré header, causing the stadium to erupt.

March 18, 1993
Antoine Kombouaré and his teammates eliminate the favourites Real Madrid.

A DESIGNER SHIRT

The fashion designer Daniel Hechter was chairman of the management committee from 1973 to 1978, and it was he who designed the shirt the club wore as they won promotion to the first division and encountered their first successes. The team used the colours of the city of Paris—red and blue—with two thin, white, vertical lines to separate them.

Star players: Mustapha Dahleb, Carlos Bianchi, Luis Fernandez, Dominique Bathenay, Dominique Rocheteau, Safet Sušić, Joël Bats, Paul Le Guen, Alain Roche, Ricardo, David Ginola, Daniel Bravo, George Weah, Bernard Lama, Youri Djorkaeff, Rai, Nicolas Anelka, Pedro Pauleta, Zlatan Ibrahimović.

Honours: League: 1986, 1994, 2013, 2014, 2015; National Cup: 1982, 1983, 1993, 1995, 1998, 2004, 2006, 2010, 2015; League Cup: 1995, 1998, 2008, 2014, 2015; UEFA Cup Winners' Cup: 1996.

"When it comes to football, Lyon will always be a suburb of Saint-Étienne." **Roger Rocher, president of AS Saint-Étienne (1961–1981).**

AS SAINT-ÉTIENNE

The Greens

Founded: **1919** • Stadium: **Geoffroy-Guichard (Saint-Étienne)**

Formed by workers of a grocery store chain, the club's style is one of self-sacrifice and teamwork. In the early 1970s, Saint-Etienne developed a new generation of French players, and enjoyed success in European competitions. The Greens remain hugely popular, and maintain a strong rivalry with Lyon, the regional capital. ⚽ If only the posts hadn't been square: During the final of the 1976 European Cup, in Glasgow, Saint-Étienne were dominating Bayern Munich, before Roth scored the goal that secured victory for the Germans. Scientists have proved that the two shots made by Saint-Étienne that hit the square goalposts would have gone in if the posts had been round. Despite the defeat, the men from Saint-Étienne paraded down the Champs-Elysées, in Paris.

10
League Titles

6
National Cups

May 12, 1976
Jean-Michel Larqué's AS Saint-Étienne (left) face Franz Beckenaueur's Bayern Munich during the European Cup final.

Star players: Kees Rijvers, Eugène N'Jo Léa, Robert Herbin, Ivan Ćurković, Oswaldo Piazza, Dominique Bathenay, Jean-Michel Larqué, Dominique Rocheteau, Michel Platini, Johnny Rep, Laurent Blanc, Willy Sagnol, Grégory Coupet.

Honours: League: 1957, 1964, 1967, 1968, 1969, 1970, 1974, 1975, 1976, 1981; National Cup: 1962, 1968, 1970, 1974, 1975, 1977; League Cup: 2013.

"We could opt to be like a concrete block, but that's not to my taste. The aim is for each player to feel fulfilled as part of the collective." **José Arribas, coach, 1960-1976.**

FC NANTES
The Canaries

Founded: **1943** · Stadium: **la Beaujoire (Nantes)**

Nantes have been one of the bigger clubs of the first division since the 1960s, building a game comprising multiple passes and joint attacks, and winning the league eight times. In 1972, the creation of France's first youth academy allowed the club to train generations of international-class players, several of whom became world champions. Nantes were semi-finalists in the 1996 Champions League. ⚽ Bob Marley and FC Nantes: During a world tour in July 1980, Bob Marley stopped off in Nantes and asked if he and the Wailers could play a friendly match against the Canaries—the league champions of France at the time. The high priest of reggae wore an FC Nantes shirt for the occasion.

8 League Titles

3 National Cups

May 27, 1995
The Canaries celebrate their seventh league title.

Star players: Bernard Blanchet, Philippe Gondet, Henri Michel, Vahid Halilhodžić, Maxime Bossis, José Touré, Mickael Landreau, Marcel Desailly, Didier Deschamps, Christian Karembeu, Patrice Loko.

Honours: League: 1965, 1966, 1973, 1977, 1980, 1983, 1995, 2001; National Cup: 1979, 1999, 2000.

"We play in the Champions League, while the guys from Saint-Étienne play on PlayStation." **Jean-Michel Aulas, president of Olympique Lyonnais, 2010.**

OLYMPIQUE LYONNAIS
The Kids

Founded: **1950** • Stadium: **Gerland (Lyon)**

Olympique Lyonnais, from France's second biggest city, have long been overshadowed by their neighbours Saint-Étienne. Semi-finalists in the 1964 Cup Winners' Cup, the club's only major success was in the French Cup until the arrival of President Jean-Michel Aulas in 1987. With patience, he built up a club capable of dominating in the long term, and it worked: from 2002 to 2008, Lyon won a record seven consecutive titles in the league, aided by the wizard of free kicks, Juninho. In 2010, they eliminated Real Madrid in the Champions League before losing in the semi-final. Meanwhile, the club was also building its own 60,000-capacity stadium, a first in France.

7 League Titles

5 National Cups

May 17, 2008
Benzema, Fred and Govou (from left to right) celebrate OL's seventh successive league title.

Star players: Fleury Di Nallo, Jean Djorkaeff, Serge Chiesa, Nestor Combin, Bernard Lacombe, Rémi Garde, Jean Tigana, Daniel Xuereb, Simo Nikolić, Florian Maurice, Ludovic Giuly, Sonny Anderson, Claudio Caçapa, Cris, Grégory Cupt, Florent Malouda, Juninho Pernambucano, Karim Benzema.

Honours: League: 2002, 2003, 2004, 2005, 2006, 2007, 2008; National Cup: 1964, 1967, 1973, 2008, 2012; League Cup: 2001.

"We are the Galactics." **Ludovic Giuly after Monaco's victory (3–1) over Real Madrid that qualified the club for the 2004 Champions League.**

AS MONACO
The Red and Whites

Founded: **1924**
Stadium: **Louis-II (Monaco)**

The only foreign club in the French league, AS Monaco have often benefited from the generosity of Prince Rainier, and his son, Albert, to acquire major foreign players. This policy has been continued by the club's new owner, the Russian businessman Dmitry Rybolovlev. The combination of international stars and youngsters from the youth academy have led the club close to success: runners-up in the 1992 Cup Winners' Cup, twice semi-finalists in the Champions League (1994, 1998), and runners-up in the 2004 Champions League, losing to Porto, after having beaten Real Madrid and Chelsea. This is a record that Monaco's great rivals, Marseille and Nice, are not currently able to equal.

7 League Titles

5 National Cups

April 6, 2004
Ludovic Giuly's AS Monaco defeat Zinédine Zidane's Real Madrid during the Champions League quarter-finals.

Star players: Michel Hidalgo, Marcel Artelesa, Jean Petit, Delio Onnis, Jean-Luc Ettori, Manuel Amoros, Bruno Bellone, Glenn Hoddle, George Weah, Emmanuel Petit, Youri Djorkaeff, Jürgen Klinsmann, Thierry Henry, David Trezeguet, Marco Simone, Fabien Barthez, Ludovic Giuly, Radamel Falcao.

Honours: League: 1961, 1963, 1978, 1982, 1988, 1997, 2000; National Cup: 1960, 1963, 1980, 1985, 1991; League Cup: 2003.

LE HAVRE AC
The Doyen
Founded: **1872** • Stadium: **Océane (Le Havre)**

Founded by British employees of the Port of Le Havre, they were the first football club in France, and became professional in 1933. They won the 1959 cup, despite playing in the second division. Famed for their youth academy, the club launched the career of world-class midfielder, Paul Pogba.

FC GIRONDINS DE BORDEAUX
The Navy and Whites
Founded: **1881** • Stadium: **Nouveau Stade de Bordeaux (Bordeaux)**

Professional since 1937, the club dominated French football in the early 1980s, reaching the semi-finals of the 1985 European Cup. In 1996, they were runners-up in the UEFA Cup, with Zidane in their squad. In all, they have won six league titles and four cups.

RACING CLUB DE PARIS
The Penguins
Founded: **1882** • Stadium: **Lucien-Choine (Paris)**

This historic club, founded by high-school students, played in the first professional championship in 1932. They have won the league once and the cup five times. The club disappeared in 1962 before being reborn as Matra Racing from 1982 to 1992. They are now an amateur club.

RED STAR FC
The Red Star
Founded: **1897** • Stadium: **Bauer (Saint-Ouen)**

Established by Jules Rimet, the future founder of FIFA, the club won five cups between the wars. As popular as ever in the Paris suburbs, they play their gala matches at the Stade de France. In 2015, Red Star moved back up into the second division, and the professional league.

AS CANNES
The Red Dragons
Founded: **1902** • Stadium: **Pierre de Coubertin (Cannes)**

Cannes were one of the pioneers of the professional game, and won a French Cup in 1932. In the 1990s, the quality of their youth academy—which produced the likes of Zinedine Zidane, Patrick Vieira, and Johan Micoud—saw them compete twice in the European Cup.

OGC NICE
The Eaglets
Founded: **1904** • Stadium: **Allianz Riviera (Nice)**

A founding member of the professional league (1932), the club had a brisk rivalry with Reims in the 1950s, and beat Real Madrid in the quarter-finals of the 1960 European Cup. They are four-time league champions and three-time winners of the French Cup.

AJ AUXERRE
AJA

Founded: **1905** • Stadium: **Abbé-Deschamps (Auxerre)**

This club, from the small town of Auxerre, played in the first division from 1981 to 2012. Winner of four cups, and league champions in 1996, Auxerre reached the quarter-finals of the 1997 Champions League. Famed for their youth academy, they had only one manager between 1961 and 2005: Guy Roux.

RC LENS
Blood and Gold

Founded: **1906** • Stadium: **Bollaert-Delelis (Lens)**

Linked historically to the mines of Northern France, the club initially hired Polish workers to play for them. Known for the fervour of their supporters, Lens were French league champions in 1998, and semi-finalists in the 2000 UEFA Cup.

RC STRASBOURG
Le Racing

Founded: **1906** • Stadium: **la Meinau (Strasbourg)**

Established at a time when Alsace was part of Germany, the club played in German competitions up until 1919. They hold one league title, and have won the French Cup three times. Among the major European clubs they have beaten are AC Milan, FC Barcelona, and Liverpool.

EN AVANT DE GUINGAMP
The Red and Blacks

Founded: **1912** • Stadium: **Roudourou (Guingamp)**

Based in a small town whose stadium could house the town's population twice over, the club entered the first division in 1995. Twice winner of the French Cup (2009, 2014), they were fielding the duo of Didier Drogba and Florent Malouda in 2002, well before Chelsea signed them.

FC METZ
The Maroons

Founded: **1919** • Stadium: **Saint-Symphorien (Metz)**

Metz, who have spent fifty-eight seasons in the first division, have won two French Cups, and are noteworthy for two other reasons: in 1972, they refused to sign the young Michel Platini— considered to be too weak physically—and in 1984, they beat FC Barcelona 4-1 at Camp Nou in the European Cup Winners' Cup.

MONTPELLIER HÉRAULT SC
La Paillade

Founded: **1919** • Stadium: **la Mosson (Montpellier)**

Established in a working class area, Montpellier have signed such notable players as Eric Cantona and Laurent Blanc. Used to yo-yoing between the first and second divisions, they won their first league title in 2012, after lifting two cups (1929, 1990). Their regional rivals are Nîmes Olympique.

FC SOCHAUX-MONTBÉLIARD
The Lion Cubs
Founded: **1928** • Stadium: **Auguste Bonal (Sochaux)**

Sochaux were founded with the support of the car manufacturer, Peugeot, and were the first to advocate professionalizing French football. They also pioneered the training of young players. They have won two league titles and two cups, and hold the French record for number of seasons played in the first division: sixty-six.

STADE DE REIMS
The Red and Whites
Founded: **1931** • Stadium: **Auguste-Delaune (Reims)**

Thanks to their "champagne" football based around an attacking game, the club won six league titles between 1949 and 1962. They were runners-up in the first European Cup (1956), as well as in 1959—both times against Real Madrid. After a subsequent unremarkable period, they returned to the first division in 2012.

LILLE OSC
The Mastiffs
Founded: **1944** • Stadium: **Pierre-Mauroy (Lille)**

Created from the merger of two clubs who dominated the first years of the professional game, Lille were nicknamed "The War Machine" when they won two league titles and five cups in their first eleven seasons. In 2011, they achieved their second cup/league double.

OLYMPIQUE LYONNAIS (LADIES)
OL Ladies
Founded: **1970** • Stadium: **Gerland (Lyon)**

Originally called FC Lyon, the club reached the first division in 1978, before becoming part of Olympique Lyonnais in 2004. Thirteen-time French league champions, they contested four consecutive Champions League finals from 2010 to 2013, winning two of them (2011, 2012).

UNIÓ ESPORTIVA SANT JULIÀ
Le Saint
Founded: **1982** • Stadium: **DEVK arena (Sant Julià de Lòria)**

Two-time league champions, UE Sant Julià are best known for becoming the first Andorran club to reach the second round of the Champions League (in 2009), following a win on penalties over Tre Fiori (San Marino). El Clàssic, the Andorran derby, is played between UE Sant Julià and Santa Coloma.

FC SANTA COLOMA
The Dove
Founded: **1986** • Stadium: **DEVK arena (Sant Julià de Lòria)**

FC Santa Coloma have won the Andorran league title nine times and the cup on eight occasions. In 2007, they became the first Andorran club to win a match in any European competition, when they played Maccabi Tel-Aviv in the UEFA Cup. In 2014, they reached the second qualifying round of the Champions League.

"In the Fiorentina-Juve match in April 1991, Juve won a penalty. Baggio refused to take it, and it was missed. He was then substituted, and on his way to the bench picked up and put on a Fiorentina scarf." **John Foot, *Calcio: A History of Italian Football*.**

ACF FIORENTINA

Viola

Founded: **1926** • Stadium: **Artemio Franchi (Florence)**

Runners-up in the second year of the European Cup against Real Madrid (1957), Fiorentina went on to become the first Italian club to win a European trophy, in 1961. Yet in their Artemio Franchi stadium, a masterpiece of 1930s architecture, Fiorentina have not been able to achieve successes worthy of their quality. Similarly, their No. 10, Giancarlo Antognoni, eclipsed by Platini and Maradona in the 1980s, should have deserved a greater slice of glory. Runners-up in the 1990 UEFA Cup with Roberto Baggio, the club went bankrupt in 2002, started out again in the fourth division, and then gained promotion back into Serie A in just two years.

2 League Titles

6 National Cups

1 European Cup Winners' Cup

May 1956
Fiorentina become champions of Italy for the first time.

Star players: Julinho, Giancarlo De Sisti, Amarildo, Ugo Ferrante, Giancarlo Antognoni, Giovanni Galli, Daniele Massaro, Daniel Passarella, Roberto Baggio, Gabriel Batistuta, Francesco Toldo, Rui Costa, Angelo di Livio, Luca Toni, Adrian Mutu, Alberto Gilardino.

Honours: League: 1956, 1969; National Cup: 1940, 1961, 1966, 1975, 1996, 2001; European Cup Winners' Cup 1961.

"I grew up playing for Roma and I want to die playing for Roma, because I have always been a Roma fan!"
Francesco Totti, AS Roma player (1993–).

AS ROMA
The Wolves

Founded: **1927** • Stadium: **Olimpico (Rome)**

Created from a merger between all the clubs in Rome, with the exception of Lazio, AS Roma had to wait until the 1980s to take their place among the great Italian clubs. Champions in 1983, they reached the final of the European Cup a year later, losing at home to Liverpool. The arrival of Francesco Totti as captain, scorer of 299 goals for the club, enabled AS Roma to lift the Champions League trophy in 2001. The first Italian club to be bought by foreigners (in 2011), they are one of the most popular in the country, far ahead of their great local rival, Lazio, and just behind Naples, a club with whom Roma fans share a great friendship.

3 League Titles

9 National Cups

1 UEFA Cup

June 17, 2001
Totti helps Roma win its third Serie A title.

Star players: Bruno Conti, Toninho Cerezo, Falcão, Carlo Ancelotti, Rudi Voeller, Aldair, Abel Balbo, Marco Delvecchio, Gabriel Batistuta, Cafu, Giuseppe Giannini, Antonio Cassano, Vincenzo Montella, Francesco Totti, Daniele De Rossi, Christian Panucci.

Honours: League: 1942, 1983, 2001; National Cup: 1964, 1969, 1980, 1981, 1984, 1986, 1991, 2007, 2008; UEFA Cup: 1961.

"The Laziali are natural fighters. It's because of this I choose this squad and these colours. In order to be Laziale you need to be strong — morally, physically and spiritually." **Paolo Di Canio, Lazio player (1985–1986, 1987–1990, 2004–2006)**

SS LAZIO
The Eagles

Founded: **1900** • Stadium: **Olimpico (Rome)**

Rome's oldest football club—a plaque on the Piazza della Libertà commemorates their centenary—Lazio have always excited their fans, both on the pitch and in the stands. Their greatest successes came in the late twentieth century. The Manchester United manager, Alex Ferguson, even went as far as to say they were the best team in the world, after losing the 1999 UEFA Supercup to them. Twice a year, the Olimpico stands fill with screaming fans, as the supposedly more middle-class Lazio play the supposedly more working-class Roma in the *Derby della Capitale*.

2 League Titles

6 National Cups

1 European Cup Winners' Cup

Star players: Silvio Piola, Giorgio Chinaglia, Bruno Giordano, Paolo Di Canio, Michael Laudrup, Alessandro Nesta, Pierluigi Casiraghi, Giuseppe Signori, Pavel Nedved, Roberto Mancini, Dejan Stankovic, Fernando Couto, Sinisa Mihajlovic, Diego Simeone, Angelo Peruzzi, Dino Baggio, Hernan Crespo.

Honours: League: 1974, 2000; National Cup: 1958, 1998, 2000, 2004, 2009, 2013; UEFA Cup Winners' Cup: 1999.

May 19, 1999
Lazio win their first European title.

"I can assure Inter fans that the Serie B is not in our DNA." **Giuseppe Prisco, vice-president of Inter, 1963–2001.**

INTER MILAN

The Cherished One

Founded: **1908** • Stadium: **Giuseppe-Meazza (Turin)**

A number of supporters of AC Milan did not agree with the rule prohibiting foreign players, so they decided to establish their own team, which they called Internazionale. After winning their first title in 1920, Inter have won at least one *scudetto* per decade, with the exception of the 1990s. The only Italian club never to have been relegated to Serie B, they have racked up eighteen league titles—the same number as AC Milan. Their European record is also impressive: Inter have won three of the four UEFA Cup finals they have played. In the European Cup/Champions League, they have taken three victories from five finals. In 2010, when the club won the Champions League under the reins of José Mourinho, the squad comprised eleven foreign players at kick-off. Internazionale: a name well merited.

18 League Titles

7 National Cups

3 Champions League / European Cups

2010
The year that Inter won it all: Serie A, Coppa Italia and Supercoppa Italiana, Champions League, Club World Cup.

858
The number of games played by Javier Zanetti while he was wearing the Inter shirt.

Ronaldo
In 1997, the Brazilian won the Ballon d'Or. The following year he and Inter Milan lifted the UEFA Cup.

284
The number of goals scored by Giuseppe Meazza while he was wearing the Inter shirt. The stadium took the name of this famous centre forward, who played for the club from 1927 to 1940.

Lothar Matthäus
World champion with Germany, he won the Ballon d'Or in 1990 while he was playing with the Nerazzurri.

THE INVENTION OF MODERN FOOTBALL

Modern football was born at Inter Milan in 1960, with the arrival of Helenio Herrera. The Argentine coach put an end to the style of play hitherto practised by the club, which consisted of fielding up to five forwards. By sealing up the defence, thanks to one player serving as a "door-bolt" (*catenaccio*), Inter gave itself a weighty tactical advantage. Firstly, the club's strengthened defence blunted adversaries' attacks. Secondly, the use of corridors to launch swift counterattacks was very effective. In eight years, Herrera's Inter won three *scudetti* and two European Cups.

September 17, 1965
Helenio Herrera led Inter to its second successive Intercontinental Cup

May 22, 2010
Winner (2-0) over Bayern thanks to Diego Milito's two goals, Inter wins the coveted Champions League trophy.

Star players: Giuseppe Meazza, Antonio Angelillo, Mario Corso, Giacinto Facchetti, Luis Suarez, Sandro Mazzola, Tarciso Burgnich, Gabriele Oriali, Alessandro Altobelli, Guiseppe Bergomi, Walter Zenga, Lothar Matthaus, Javier Zanetti, Ronaldo, Wesley Sneijder, Alvaro Recoba, Dejan Stanković, Diego Milito.

Honours: League: 1910, 1920, 1930, 1938, 1940, 1953, 1954, 1963, 1965, 1966, 1971, 1980, 1989, 2006, 2007, 2008, 2009, 2010; National Cup: 1939, 1978, 1982, 2005, 2006, 2010, 2011; European Cup/Champions League: 1964, 1965, 2010; UEFA Cup: 1991, 1994, 1998; FIFA Club World Cup: 1964, 1965, 2010.

"There's music playing, the song 'Live is Life,' and to the rhythm of the song Maradona started juggling the ball. So we stopped our warm-up. What's this guy doing? He's juggling off his shoulders. And we couldn't warm up anymore because we had to watch this guy." **Jürgen Klinsmann talking about Diego Maradona before the Napoli–Stuttgart UEFA Cup final in 1989.**

SSC NAPOLI

The Little Donkeys

Founded: **1926** · Stadium: **San Paolo (Naples)**

A name and a word sum up this club, founded by an Englishman, a worker at the port of Naples: Maradona and passion. Maradona is, of course, the name of the Argentine player who became a saint for the inhabitants of the city. He arrived in 1984, giving Naples its pride back, and helping them to their two *scudetti* and their only European trophy, the UEFA Cup. Passion is the word that best describes the 50,000 spectators who came to support the team one day when they were playing in the third division—to which they were relegated in 2004. Having hauled themselves out of serious financial difficulties, thanks to the intelligence of their new president, the film producer Aurelio De Laurentiis, the club got itself back on the podium of Serie A in 2011.

2 League Titles

5 National Cups

1 UEFA Cup

May 3, 2014 Napoli wins the Italian Cup by defeating Fiorentina (3-1) in the final.

The number of games played by Giuseppe Bruscolotti while he was wearing the Napoli shirt (1972-1988).

511

115

The number of goals scored by Diego Maradona while he was playing for Napoli.

265

The number of games managed by Bruno Pesaola, who coached Napoli in the 1960s and 1970s.

Edinson Cavani Napoli striker between 2010 and 2013, he became the third highest scorer in the history of the club, with 104 goals.

April 22, 1990
Diego Maradona greets the Napoli supporters, as the club heads towards its second Serie A title.

SAINT MARADONA

"He made us hold our heads up against Northern Italy." That is just one of the many things Neapolitans say about Diego Maradona. They venerate he who was the architect of their great successes on the pitch. In Café Moreno, located in the centre of Naples, his admirers can pay homage before a few relics of the "saint." A lock of hair and a tear are on public view, amid a décor that looks more like a chapel than a bar. To add to the religious atmosphere, a photograph of Pope Francis, a compatriot of Maradona and a big football fan, was even added recently.

Star players: Attila Sallustro, Amedeo Amadei, Omar Sivori, Jose Altafini, Beppe Savoldi, Ruud Krol, Diego Maradona, Ciro Ferrara, Andrea Carnevale, Fernando De Napoli, Antonio Careca, Ricardo Alemão, Bruno Giordano, Gianfranco Zola, Fabio Cannavaro, Ezequiel Lavezzi, Gonzalo Higuain.

Honours: League: 1987, 1990; National Cup: 1962, 1976, 1987, 2012, 2014; UEFA Cup: 1989.

"At Juventus, winning isn't important. It's the only thing that counts." **Giampiero Boniperti, president of Juventus, 1971–1990.**

JUVENTUS FC
The Old Lady

Founded: **1897** • Stadium: **Juventus (Turin)**

The club initially wore a pink strip, but in 1903 they were given a set of black and white striped shirts that came from the English team, Notts County. It was in this strip that the Juventini won the first of their thirty-one *scudetti*—a national record. Beyond Italy's borders, Juventus were the first Italian team to win three European cups (1985), after their victory over Liverpool, which was marked by the Heysel stadium disaster that cost the lives of thirty-nine of its supporters. Juventus have contested thirteen European finals, and have fielded some of the best Italian players, forming the backbone of the World Cup winning squads of 1934, 1982, and 2006. The club maintain two strong rivalries. One is local, against FC Torino—founded by a former president of Juventus. The other is national, against Inter Milan in the *Derby d'Italia*. Despite being involved in various scandals, Juventus have always managed to work their way back to the top.

31 League Titles

10 National Cups

2 Champions League / European Cups

Fabio Cannavaro
In 2006, he became the seventh Ballon d'Or winner in Juventus' history .

The number of games played by Alessandro Del Piero while he was wearing the Juve shirt (1993-2012).

705

54

596

The cost, in millions of euros, of Gianluigi Buffon's transfer from Parma to Juventus in 2001, a record-breaking amount for a goalkeeper.

The number of Juventus games managed by Giovanni Trapattoni.

Alessandro Del Piero
He is the Old Lady's top striker with 291 goals.

PLATINI, THE KING OF TURIN

With eight Footballer of the Year awards won by its players, Juventus are ranked second, behind FC Barcelona. One of those players has won the award three times: Michel Platini, in 1983, 1984, and 1985. Having arrived at the club in 1982, the French attacking midfielder blew apart the Italian championship with his class. Unequalled in his ability to supply his strikers, Paolo Rossi and Zbigniew Boniek, with chances, Platini was unbeatable when taking a free kick, and developed skills as a finisher that earned him the title of top scorer of Serie A three years in a row. Initially sceptical about this player, who had arrived from the unknown world of the French championship, the *tifosi* would make "Michele" their king.

August 6, 1978
President Giovanni Agnelli (right) attends the players' training session. They were crowned Italian champions a few months previously.

LA FIDANZATA D'ITALIA (ITALY'S FIANCÉE)

Founded by high-school students, in 1923 the club was bought by the Agnelli family—owners of the FIAT automobile factory, which has its head office in Turin. The story goes that the idea to buy the club came to Edoardo Agnelli—president of Juventus from 1923 to 1935—when a Juventus player who was also a FIAT worker was having some difficulties balancing sport and work. The first club to pay a wage—and provide a car—Juve attracted the best players, beginning, in the 1930s, an era of domination. By building a strong link between the club and the factory workers, who often came from poor parts of Italy, the Agnellis made Juventus the most supported club in Italy—almost one in three Italians are fans of the team. Juventus have 170 million supporters across the world.

HURRÀ JUVENTUS, THE CENTURY-OLD MAGAZINE OF THE OLD LADY

In 1915, Juventus had already been league champions, and were one of the biggest clubs in Italy. In order to maintain contact between management, players, and supporters during the First World War, the club decided to publish a monthly magazine, *Hurrà Juventus*. In the first issue, dated June 10, 1915, the fans read: "The *Juventini* are brothers." Publication ceased in 1925, before recommencing in 1963, and continuing to this day. With 60,000 copies sold every month, it has the widest circulation in its category. Even the launch of the Juventus Channel on television in 2006 hasn't affected its popularity.

May 23, 2015
The Bianconeri celebrate the club's thirty-first Scudetto.

Star players: Giampiero Boniperti, John Charles, Omar Sivori, Franco Causio, Roberto Bettega, Dino Zoff, Claudio Gentile, Gaetano Scirea, Marco Tardelli, Paolo Rossi, Zbigniew Boniek, Michel Platini, Roberto Baggio, Alessandro Del Piero, Gianluca Vialli, Didier Deschamps, Zinedine Zidane, David Trézeguet, Gianluigi Buffon.

Honours: League: 1905, 1926, 1931, 1932, 1933, 1934, 1935, 1950, 1952, 1958, 1960, 1961, 1967, 1972, 1973, 1975, 1977, 1978, 1981, 1982, 1984, 1986, 1995, 1997, 1998, 2002, 2003, 2012, 2013, 2014, 2015; National Cup: 1938, 1942, 1959, 1960, 1965, 1979, 1983, 1990, 1995, 2015; European Cup/Champions League: 1985, 1996; European Cup Winners' Cup: 1984; UEFA Cup: 1977, 1990, 1993; Intercontinental Cup: 1985, 1996.

"We should be the devil and scare everyone."
Herbert Kilpin, founder of AC Milan.

AC MILAN
I Rossoneri

Founded: **1899** • Stadium: **San Siro (Milan)**

Founded by Englishmen in 1908, they initially refused to hire foreign players, so some dissidents went off to form Internazionale, and AC Milan saw a period of drought that lasted until 1951. Having fought back to equal the success of their eternal rivals—eighteen national titles each—the Rossoneri went even further, with success in international competitions. They have won the European Cup/Champions League seven times, and been runners-up on five occasions, making them the second most successful club in the history of that competition, behind Real Madrid. As far as popularity is concerned, they may lie behind Juventus and Inter within Italy, but are the leaders at a European level. Their style is also rather un-Italian. Contrary to many of the great Italian clubs, who are often calculating and sometimes short on spectacle, AC Milan have always known how to wow the crowds with their attacking game inspired by coaches such as Arrigo Sacchi and Fabio Capello.

18 League Titles

5 National Cups

7 Champions League / European Cups

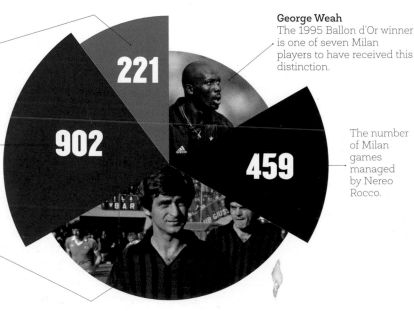

The number of goals scored by Swedish striker Gunnar Nordahl while he was playing for Milan (1948-1956).

221

George Weah
The 1995 Ballon d'Or winner is one of seven Milan players to have received this distinction.

The number of games Paolo Maldini played with the Rossoneri.

902

459

The number of Milan games managed by Nereo Rocco.

Gianni Rivera
The 1969 Ballon d'Or winner was the youngest striker in the history of the club, scoring his first goal at the age of 17.

PAOLO MALDINI, A LIFE IN RED AND BLACK

His father, Cesare, played nearly 350 matches for AC Milan in the 1950s and 1960s, and even captained them. This might have been a hard act to follow for Paolo, but it was nothing of the sort. After passing through the club's youth academy, the son spent twenty-four years (1985–2009) in the red and black strip, setting the record for number of matches played, with 902 appearances. Elegant, effective, and always known for his fair play, Maldini was a modern defender, never hesitating to make deep counterattacks. The most fitting compliment paid to him came courtesy of Zlatan Ibrahimović: one of the most talented and outspoken strikers in history declared that Paolo Maldini was the best defender he had ever confronted. It goes without saying that his number three was retired by the club.

ITALY

A TOUCH OF DUTCH CLASS

AC Milan have fielded squads of exceptional quality throughout their rich history, but there was one team which not only swiped numerous titles, but did so while enchanting all fans of the beautiful game. In 1986, Silvio Berlusconi took over the club and bought the best European players of the era, including three Dutchmen from the 1988 European champions side: Frank Rijkaard, Ruud Gullit, and Marco van Basten. This trio—comprising a centre-back, an attacking midfielder, and an elegant finisher—were at their peak in 1989. After eliminating Real Madrid in the semi-finals of the European Cup 5–0, the Rossoneri beat Steaua Bucarest 4–0 in the final. That evening in Barcelona, the Dutch trio gave a lesson in attacking football. Gullit and van Basten each scored two goals, with Rijkaard, uncompromising in midfield, supplying them with the opportunities.

May 24, 1989
Milan face Steaua Bucureşti in the European Cup final. The Italians can count on the Dutch trio of Gullit, Rijkaard, and van Basten, as well as Carlo Ancelotti (second from the left).

ITALY

IN THE LIONS' DEN

Originally a working-class club, AC Milan contests the *Derby della Madonnina* against Inter—with whom they share a stadium. Since 1968, the Rossoneri have been supported by the members of the *Fossa dei Leoni* (The Lions' Den), Italy's oldest "ultra" group.

Leoni armati,
Siam marciando,
Siam la Fossa dei leoni,
Dei leon leon leon,
Leon leon,
Siam la Fossa dei leoni,
Sangue violenza,
Fossa dei leoni,
Milan Milan Milan

(Lions armed,
We're marching,
We're the lions' den,
Lions, lions, lions,
We're the lions' den,
Blood, violence,
Lions' den,
Milan, Milan, Milan)

Star players: Cesare Maldini, Juan Schiaffino, Jose Altafini, Knut Nordahl, Nils Liedholm, Giovanni Trapattoni, Gianni Rivera, Ruud Gullit, Marco van Basten, Frank Rijkaard, Franco Baresi, Roberto Donadoni, Paolo Maldini, George Weah, Demetrio Albertini, Andriy Shevchenko, Kaka, Andrea Pirlo, Gennaro Gattuso.

Honours: League: 1901, 1906, 1907, 1951, 1955, 1957, 1959, 1962, 1968, 1979, 1988, 1992, 1993, 1994, 1996, 1999, 2004, 2011; National Cup: 1967, 1972, 1973, 1977, 2003; European Cup/Champions League: 1963, 1969, 1989, 1990, 1994, 2003, 2007; European Cup Winners' Cup: 1968, 1973; Intercontinental Cup: 1969, 1989, 1990; FIFA Club World Cup: 2007.

GENOA CRICKET AND FOOTBALL CLUB The Griffin

Founded: **1893** • Stadium: **Luigi Ferraris (Genoa)**

Founded by British business-men, the club dominated Italian football in the first quarter of the twentieth century, winning nine league titles. They play one of the most hotly contested derbies in the world against Sampdoria, and enjoy support from some particularly creative *tifosi*.

UDINESE
The Little Zebras

Founded: **1896** • Stadium: **Friuli (Udine)**

Udinese is the second oldest club in Italian football, after Genoa. They won the first unofficial league champion-ship, and were runners-up in the first Italian Cup (1922). A regional rival of Triestina, they have fielded two world champions: Franco Causio and Vincenzo Iaquinta.

US CITTÀ DI PALERMO
The Pink Blacks

Founded: **1900** • Stadium: **Renzo Barbera (Palerme)**

Founded by an English ornithologist, Città di Palermo have been runners-up in the Italian Cup three times. They are one of the ten most popular clubs in the country, mainly thanks to Sicilians living in Northern Italy. The club play the Sicilian derby against Catania.

VICENZA CALCIO
Berici

Founded: **1902** • Stadium: **Romeo Menti (Vicenza)**

Although Vicenza have just one major trophy in its display case—the 1997 Italian Cup—they have fielded some of the biggest names in Italian football: Paolo Rossi became a star here between 1976 and 1980, and European Footballer of the Year Roberto Baggio made his professional debut at the club in 1982.

FC PRO VERCELLI 1892
Lions

Founded: **1892** • Stadium: **Silvio Piola (Vercelli)**

Based in a small town in the Piedmont between Milan and Turin, the club dominated the early years of Italian football, winning seven league titles from 1908 to 1922. Having sunk into oblivion, Pro Vercelli fought back into Serie B in 2012, after an absence of sixty-four years.

HELLAS VERONA
Yellow Blues

Founded: **1903** • Stadium: **Marc'Antonio Bentegodi (Verona)**

Founded by high-school students, and named after the Greek word for "Greece"—at the suggestion of a classics teacher—Hellas Verona were Italian league champions in 1984. They were promoted back into Serie A in 2013 after an absence of eleven years, and must now contend with a local rival, Chievo.

TORINO FC
The Bull
Founded: **1906** • Stadium: **Olimpico (Turin)**

The club dominated Italian football in the post-war period, winning four titles between 1946 and 1949, before they were ripped apart by an air crash in 1949. Great rivals of Juventus, Torino enjoy greater popularity than their Piedmont neighbour.

ATALANTA BERGAMASCA
The Goddess
Founded: **1907** • Stadium: **Ateli Azzurri d'Italia (Bergamo)**

Founded by students, the club has racked up fifty-seven seasons in Serie A without ever winning the title—a record. Winners of the 1963 Italian Cup, Atalanta were a semi-finalist in the 1988 Cup Winners' Cup, when they were playing in Serie B. Their great rivals are Brescia.

FC BARI 1908
The Cockerels
Founded: **1908** • Stadium: **San Nicola (Bari)**

Out of all the Southern Italian clubs, Bari have made the third most appearances in the top flight, having played over 1,000 matches in thirty seasons of Serie A. A rival of Lecce, the club can count on a loyal fan base to create a stirring atmosphere in their 58,000–capacity stadium.

BOLOGNA FC 1909
The Red Blues
Founded: **1909** • Stadium: **Renato Dall'Ara (Bologna)**

Seven-time winners of the league title between 1925 and 1964, and twice winners of the cup, they contest the Emilia-Romagna derby against Modena—which did not prevent their "ultra" fans from mobilizing to provide aid to Modena during the floods of 2014.

BRESCIA CALCIO
Little Swallows
Founded: **1911** • Stadium: **Mario Rigamonti (Brescia)**

Brescia have spent twenty-two seasons in Serie A, but have never won a major title. Although their supporters maintain a strong regional rivalry with Atalanta, they share a thirty-year-old friendship with Milan AC, a unique situation in Italy.

PARMA FC
The Duchy Men
Founded: **1913** • Stadium: **Ennio Tardini (Parma)**

The club played in Serie B for many years, before being bought by the dairy giant Parmalat in the 1980s. Promoted to Serie A, they won the 1993 UEFA Cup Winners' Cup, followed by the UEFA Cup in 1995 and 1999. Their downfall was just as swift: the club went bankrupt in 2015.

COSENZA
Wolves
Founded: **1914** • Stadium: **San Vito (Cosenza)**

This Calabrian club, who have never played higher than Serie B, are known for their number-one fan: the Franciscan monk, Padre Fedele Bisceglia. President of the club in 2004, Fedele Bisceglia was struck off by the church because of his links to "ultra" fan organisations.

AS LIVORNO CALCIO
The Mullets
Founded: **1915** • Stadium: **Armando Picchi (Livorno)**

Livorno have played in Serie A since 1929, the year the new top Italian league was created. They were declared bankrupt in 1991, and became an amateur club again. Promoted back into Serie A in 2004, they made their first appearance in the UEFA Cup in 2006. Their supporters are among the most fervent in Italy.

TRIESTINA
The Halberdiers
Founded: **1918** • Stadium: **Nereo Rocco (Trieste)**

From 1947 to 1954, when Trieste was a "Free Territory," the club was the only one in history to play in Serie A without being based on Italian soil. They placed second in the 1948 championship, despite finishing last the previous year—when they had to be saved from relegation for "patriotic" reasons.

CAGLIARI CALCIO
The Sardinians
Founded: **1920** • Stadium: **Sant'Elia (Cagliari)**

Led by the great Gigi Riva, the club from the capital of Sardinia were Italian champions in 1970, three years after playing a season in the USA under the name Chicago Mustangs. In 1994, they were semi-finalists in the UEFA Cup, their best European performance to date.

US CATANZARO
Southern Eagles
Founded: **1929** • Stadium: **Nicola Ceravolo (Cantazaro)**

The club, who played in Serie A from 1978 to 1983 with Claudio Ranieri in their ranks, have a great rivalry with Cosenza. Just like their neighbour, they are supported by a religious figure: Madre Vitaliana del Carmine—a famous nun who leads the fans in the stands.

CHIEVO VERONA
Flying Donkeys
Founded: **1929** • Stadium: **Marc'Antonio Bentegodi (Verona)**

Although they played in the preliminary stage of the 2006 Champions League, this could be considered an over achievement. They were only promoted to the fourth division in 1986. Chievo have played in Serie A since 2001, and contest the Derby della Scala against Hellas.

ITALY

CALCIO CATANIA
The Elephants
Founded: **1946** • Stadium: **Angelo Massimino (Catania)**

Catania, who wear red for Etna and blue for the sky, have played seventeen seasons in Serie A. In 1961, their 2–0 victory at home against the great Inter gave rise to an Italian expression meaning "surprise result": "Clamoroso al Cibali!" ("Cibali resounds"—the stadium was previously called "Cibali").

UC SAMPDORIA
The Blue-ringed
Founded: **1946** • Stadium: **Luigi Ferraris (Genoa)**

In the late 1980s and early 1990s, the club played among the big clubs in both Italy and Europe, winning the 1990 UEFA Cup Winners' Cup, and coming second in the last European Cup competition (1992). They play the *Derby della Lanterna* against Genoa.

SAN MARINO

SP TRE FIORI
Ultras
Founded: **1949** • Stadium: **Florentino (Fiorentino)**

With seven league titles and six cups, Tre Fiori are the most successful of San Marino's amateur teams. In 2009, they drew twice against the Andorrans of Sant Julià in the qualifying round of the Champions League, but were eliminated in a penalty shootout.

SAN MARINO CALCIO
Titans
Founded: **1959** • Stadium: **Olimpico (Serravalle)**

The only club in the principality of San Marino authorized to take part in the Italian championship, they played in the fourth division for many years before gaining promotion to the third division in 2005, drawing a crowd of 4,500 spectators for a home game against Genoa.

MALTA

FLORIANA FC
Tal-Irish
Founded: **1894** • Stadium: **Independence Ground (Floriana)**

Floriana were one of the first clubs to be founded in Malta. They are one of the most popular, and also one of the most successful, with twenty-five league titles and twenty-six cups. They maintain a great rivalry with their neighbours, Valletta FC.

SLIEMA WANDERERS FC
The Wanderers
Founded: **1909** • Stadium: **Ta' Qali (Sliema)**

Their twenty-six league titles and twenty cup victories make the club the most successful on the island. They have also qualified for the second round of a European competition on four occasions—a record for Maltese clubs. Their main supporters' group is called the Blue Gladiators.

"No one in the Europa League can beat us. Only if we go into the Champions League there might be some problems with Real Madrid and Barcelona. The rest . . . we're destroying them."
Gigi Becali, Steaua's president, 2013.

STEAUA BUCUREŞTI
The Army Men

Founded: **1947** • Stadium: **Ghencea (Bucharest)**

Founded by the army, Steaua became football's "golden team" during the 1950s. But it was in the 1980s that they astounded Europe, by playing a series of 104 matches without defeat that lasted from 1986 until 1989—a record. Also in 1986, they reached the final of the European Cup, playing FC Barcelona in Seville. The rock-solid defence put up by the Romanians meant that the score sheet was 0-0 at full time, and so the title had to be decided by a penalty shootout. Their goalkeeper, Helmut Duckadam, took the stage and saved four Catalan penalty kicks. Steaua were champions of Europe. In 1989, they reached the final again, but this time lost to AC Milan.

26 League Titles

22 National Cups

1 European Cup

May 7, 1986
Steaua win the European Cup, nicknamed "old big ears".

Star players: Gheorghe Constantin, Miodrag Belodedici, Helmut Duckadam, Anghel Iordanescu, Gheorghe Hagi, Marius Lacatus, Gavril Balint, Dan Petrescu, Ilie Dumitrescu, Laszlo Boloni, Constantin Galca, Adrian Ilie.

Honours: League: 1951, 1952, 1953, 1956, 1960, 1961, 1968, 1976, 1978, 1985, 1986, 1987, 1988, 1989, 1993, 1994, 1995, 1996, 1997, 1998, 2001, 2005, 2006, 2013, 2014,2015; National Cup: 1950, 1951, 1952, 1955, 1962, 1966, 1967, 1969, 1970, 1971, 1976, 1979, 1985, 1987, 1989, 1992, 1996, 1997, 1999, 2011, 2015; European Cup: 1986.

CFR 1907 CLUJ
The Railwaymen
Founded: **1907** • Stadium: **Dr. Constantin Rădulescu (Cluj)**

Founded by railway workers, the club moved up from the third to the first division between 2000 and 2004, then won the title in 2008, 2010 and 2012, relying on foreign players. In their first Champions League match in 2008, they beat AS Roma, in Rome.

FC RAPID BUCURESTI
The Burgundy Eagles
Founded: **1923** • Stadium: **Giuleşti-Valentin Stănescu (Bucharest)**

Founded by a group of railway workers, Rapid have won three league titles, and have been runners-up fourteen times. Popular among the working class—even if one of their supporters' groups is composed of artists—it has some of the most expressive "ultras" in the country.

FC PETROLUL PLOIESTI
The Yellow Wolves
Founded: **1924** • Stadium: **Ilie Oană (Ploieşti)**

Founded in Bucharest as Juventus, the club has always maintained a major rivalry with its former neighbour, Rapid Bucureşti, despite having moved to Ploieşti in 1952. The club has won four league titles and three cups. Adrian Mutu finished his career here.

FC DINAMO BUCURESTI
The Red Dogs
Founded: **1948** • Stadium: **Dinamo (Bucharest)**

Founded by the Ministry of the Interior, Dinamo have won eighteen championship titles and played in two European semi-finals: the 1984 European Cup and 1990 Cup Winners' Cup. They hold the record for the highest score in the European Cup: 11–0 against Crusaders FC.

FC UNIVERSITATEA CRAIOVA
The Students
Founded: **1948** • Stadium: **Municipal (Craiova)**

Four-time league champions between 1974 and 1991, Universitatea Craiova were for a long time the only club capable of rivalling the Bucharest clubs, and also the first in the country to play in a European semi-final (1983). They were banned from the federation in 2014 for legal reasons.

FC OTELUL GALATI
The Steelworkers
Founded: **1964** • Stadium: **Oţelul (Galaţi)**

Oţelul are linked to the steelmaking industry in the east of the country, and were champions in 2011. The following season, they played Manchester United in the Champions League—the average annual salary of the club's players was equivalent to the English club's players' average weekly salary.

"It was in 1988, a little before Christmas. He knocked at the door of my office, came in, and introduced himself: 'I am Miodrag Belodedić, I am Serbian, and I want to play for Red Star.'"

Dragan Dzajic, technical director of Red Star.

RED STAR
Red and White

Founded: **1945**

Stadium: **Crvena Zvezda (Belgrade)**

Founded by representatives of the Yugoslavian communist party, Red Star are today a strong symbol of Serbia, where they are supported by more than half the population. This popularity can be explained above all by their results: twenty-six league titles, and victory in the 1991 Champions League, where they beat Marseille—twelve years after they first played a UEFA Cup final. Internationally, the club have also come to symbolize the Yugoslavian style of play—elegant and technical—as embodied by Dragan Stojković or Dejan Savićević. Their supporters, the "Delije" (Braves) are known throughout Europe for the feisty atmosphere they bring to the "Marakana"—the nickname of Red Star's stadium.

26 League Titles

24 National Cups

1 European Cup

May 29, 1991
Red Star rise to the top of Europe.

Star players: Rajko Mitić, Branko Stanković, Dragoslav Šekularac, Dragan Džajić, Vladimir Petrović, Dušan Savić, Slavo Muslin, Dragan Stojković, Dejan Savićević, Robert Prosinečki, Vladimir Jugović, Darko Pančev, Siniša Mihajlović, Miodrag Belodedić, Dejan Stanković, Darko Kovačević, Nemanja Vidić.

Honours: League: 1951, 1953, 1956, 1957, 1959, 1960, 1964, 1968, 1969, 1970, 1973, 1977, 1980, 1981, 1984, 1988, 1990, 1991, 1992, 1995, 2000, 2001, 2004, 2006, 2007, 2014; National Cup: 1948, 1949, 1950, 1958, 1959, 1964, 1968, 1970, 1971, 1982, 1985, 1990, 1993, 1995, 1996, 1997, 1999, 2000, 2002, 2004, 2006, 2007, 2010, 2012; European Cup: 1991; Intercontinental Cup: 1991.

OFK BELGRADE
The Romantics
Founded: **1911** • Stadium: **Omladinski (Belgrade)**

The oldest club currently playing in the Serbian first division, they won five league titles and five cups in the former Yugoslavia. They have also reached the semi-finals of the Cup Winners' Cup and the UEFA Cup. Their supporters are known for their rebellious spirit.

FK VOJVODINA
The Old Lady
Founded: **1914** • Stadium: **Karađorđe (Novi Sad)**

Founded by students fighting the Austro-Hungarian empire, the club won two titles in the former Yugoslavia. Since 1992, they have been the "eternal third," behind Partizan and Red Star. Their supporters formed their first group in 1937.

FK RADNICKI NIS
Real de Nis
Founded: **1923** • Stadium: **Čair (Niš)**

Originally linked to the workers' movement, the club played twenty-nine seasons in the Yugoslavian first division after 1962. With Dragan Stojković in the squad, they reached the semi-finals of the 1982 UEFA Cup. The club's supporters have been well organized since the 1960s.

FK OBILIC BELGRADE
The Knights
Founded: **1924** • Stadium: **Obilić (Belgrade)**

Named after a Serbian hero of the Middle Ages, Obilić were taken over by the paramilitary leader, Arkan, in 1996. In 1998, they won the league, becoming the only club to break the domination of Partizan and Red Star over the league since the breakup of Yugoslavia.

FK PARTIZAN BELGRADE
The Steamroller
Founded: **1945** • Stadium: **Partizana (Belgrade)**

Founded by Yugoslavian officers after the Second World War, they became the first club from Eastern Europe to play in a European final (1966). A rival of Red Star in the "eternal derby," Partizan Belgrade are the most successful of Serbian clubs, with fifteen titles to their credit.

FK SPARTAK SUBOTICA
The Blue Pigeons
Founded: **1945** • Stadium: **Stade Municipal (Subotica)**

Named after the nickname of a war hero, the club played sixteen seasons in the top flight of the former Yugoslavia. Twice runners-up in the cup, they reached the second round of the Europa League in 2011—their first participation. Nemanja Vidić played here before going abroad.

NK ZAGREB
The Poets

Founded: **1903** • Stadium: **Kranjčevićeva (Zagreb)**

In 1991, during the war with Serbia, NK Zagreb participated with seven other clubs in the first "free championship" of Croatia. In 2002, they became the first and only club to date to break the dominance of Hajduk Split and Dinamo Zagreb on the Croatian league.

NK SLAVEN BELUPO
The Pharmacists

Founded: **1907** • Stadium: **Gradski (Koprivnica)**

The club was founded by students, and underwent numerous name changes before being named after their current sponsor, a pharmaceutical firm. Present in the first division since 1997, the club finished second in 2008, and have since played regularly in the Europa League.

HAJDUK SPLIT
The Pride of Dalmatia

Founded: **1911** • Stadium: **Poljud (Split)**

Founded by students, the club won nine Yugoslavian league titles and six Croatian league titles. Since 1950 they have had the support of Torcida Split—the oldest group of "ultra" fans in Europe—who helped the team survive a serious financial crisis in 2012.

DINAMO ZAGREB
The Blues

Founded: **1945** • Stadium: **Maksimir (Zagreb)**

Dinamo Zagreb, founded by the communist government in 1945, were closely linked to the nationalist camp during the war in the former Yugoslavia. Since 1992, they have dominated the Croatian league, winning seventeen national titles, and maintaining their "Eternal Derby" against Hajduk Split.

HNK RIJEKA
Rijeka Whites

Founded: **1946** • Stadium: **Rujevica (Rijeka)**

A cup-winning specialist (two Yugoslavian, three Croatian), HNK Rijeka have been among the best in the Croatian league since 1992. They play the Adriatic Derby against Hajduk Split. Their supporters specialize in painting murals to honour the team's glory.

NK OSIJEK
The White-Blues

Founded: **1947** • Stadium: **Gradski vrt (Osijek)**

Having played in the first division during the last fifteen years of the Yugoslavian championship, NK Osijek entered the Croatian league, where they have finished no higher than third place. Their supporters, the "Kohorta," were the first Croatians to travel to Serbia after independence.

NK CELJE
The Counts
Founded: **1919** • Stadium: **Arena Petrol (Celje)**

Celje never played in the top flight of the Yugoslavian league, but they are one of three clubs that have been present in the Slovenian league since its establishment in 1991. They have already contested eight finals of the Slovenian Cup since 1993, winning once, in 2005. The club contest the "Styrian derby" with Maribor.

FC KOPER
The Canaries
Founded: **1920** • Stadium: **Bonifika (Koper)**

Koper have played in the Slovenian first division since its founding in 1991. In the early 2000s they were saved from serious financial difficulties by their supporters, and then a Serbian businessman. They went on to win the Slovenian cup in 2006, 2007, and 2015, and were crowned league champions in 2010.

NK DOMZALE
The Brigands
Founded: **1921** • Stadium: **Domžale Sports Park (Domžale)**

Relegated following the first season of the Slovenian league, in 1991–1992, the club returned to the top flight in 2000. Since then, they have been a consistent participant in the league, winning the title twice (2007, 2008), and coming second on three occasions.

ND GORICA
The Roses
Founded: **1947** • Stadium: **Športni Park Nova Gorica (Nova Gorica)**

A regular of the lower divisions of the former Yugoslavia, Gorica have played in the Slovenian first division since the 1991 season. Four-time league champions and three-time cup winners, they field many Italian players, and contest the "coastal derby" with Koper.

NK MARIBOR
The Pride of Styria
Founded: **1960** • Stadium: **Ljudski Vrt (Maribor)**

After yo-yoing between the various divisions of the former Yugoslavia, Maribor have become dominant in Slovenia since independence in 1991, winning thirteen league titles. They are the club of the middle-classes, and are also most popular in the country.

NK OLIMPIJA LJUBLJANA
The Dragons
Founded: **2005** • Stadium: **Stožice (Ljubljana)**

Based in the capital, the club moved up from the fifth to the first division in just four years. Olimpija are the continuation of NK Bežigrad (which folded in 2005), of which they retain the supporters. They remain the national and "historical" rivals of Maribor in the "eternal derby."

HSK ZRINJSKI MOSTAR
The Noblemen

Founded: **1905** • Stadium: **Stadion pod Bijelim Brijegom (Mostar)**

Zrinjski Mostar are the oldest football club in Bosnia and Herzegovina. Banned after World War Two (because of their strong identification with the Croatian community), the club reformed after independence, in 1992. These great rivals of Velež have since become one of the most successful clubs in the country, with three league championships and one cup.

FK ŽELJEZNIČAR
The Railway Workers

Founded: **1921** • Stadium: **Grbavica (Sarajevo)**

Founded by railway workers, the club won the Yugoslavian league championship in 1972. Since independence, Željezničar have overtaken their rivals, FC Sarajevo, to dominate Bosnian football, winning a record six league titles and five cups.

FK VELEŽ MOSTAR
The Natives

Founded: **1922** • Stadium: **Vrapčići (Mostar)**

The most popular club in Herzegovina won two Yugoslav Cups with the striker Vahid Halilhodžić on the team. Their supporters, the "Red Army," may be fewer in number than in the past, but they still welcome members from all of Bosnia's different ethnic groups.

FK SARAJEVO
The Giants

Founded: **1946** • Stadium: **Asim Ferhatović Hase (Sarajevo)**

Before independence, the club rivalled the major teams of the Yugoslavian league, which they won twice (1967, 1985). Now Bosnia's second team, behind Željezničar, they could well see their fortunes rise again following their buyout by a Malaysian businessman.

FK BUDUĆNOST PODGORICA
The Blue and Whites

Founded: **1924** • Stadium: **pod Goricom (Podgorica)**

Budućnost, who play in the capital, have long been the standard-bearer of Montenegrin football, having spent twenty-six seasons in the Yugoslav first division, starting in 1946. They were also the first club of AC Milan star Dejan Savićević. Since independence, they have won the title twice.

FK SUTJESKA
The Blues

Founded: **1927** • Stadium: **Gradski Nikšić (Nikšić)**

Sutjeska were one of only two clubs in the country to play in the first division under the former Yugoslavia. Since independence, they have played in the top flight every season, and have won the title twice (2013, 2014). Their greatest rivals are Budućnost.

FK VARDAR SKOPJE
The Red and Blacks

Founded: **1947** • Stadium: **Philip II Arena (Skopje)**

Under the former Yugoslavia, the club won one cup (1961), as well as one league title in 1987 but their ranking was downgraded following a controversial legal decision (in favour of FK Partizan) that was not recognized by UEFA. Vardar are seven-time league champions since independence.

FK HORIZONT TURNOVO
Turnovians

Founded: **1950** • Stadium: **Kukuš (Turnovo)**

Based in a village of less than 1,000 inhabitants, Horizont Turnovo have been sponsored by a sports betting company since 2008, the year they were promoted to the first division. In 2013, the club finished third in the league championship before qualifying for the second round of the Europa League.

KF TIRANA
The White and Blues

Founded: **1920** • Stadium: **Qemal Stafa (Tirana)**

KF Tirana hold twenty-four league titles, and have dominated Albanian football since the national championship was founded, in 1930. The club has also played in seventy-one European matches. Their most important match of the season is the Tirana derby against Partizan.

DINAMO TIRANA
The Blue Submarine

Founded: **1950** • Stadium: **Selman Stërmasi (Tirana)**

Founded by the Interior Ministry, Dinamo Tirana are the youngest of the major Albanian clubs. They won the league/cup double in their first season. Seventeen other titles would follow. Relegated to the second division in 2012, they are supported by a group of "ultra" fans called the Blue Boys.

KF PRISHTINA
The Blue and Whites

Founded: **1922** • Stadium: **Prishtina City (Prishtina)**

After having played in the Albanian league in the 1940s, then in the Yugoslavian first division during the 1980s–1990s, this club from the Kosovan capital has become the most successful in the country since independence, winning seven titles following the creation of the league in 1999.

KF BESA PEJË
Shqiponjat

Founded: **1923** • Stadium: **Shahin Haxhiislami (Pejë)**

In the 1990s, KF Besa Pejë were outside the Yugoslav football league, and so played in competitions between Kosovan teams. Since independence, and with funding from a brewery, they have won the league championship three years in a row (2005, 2006, 2007).

"We saw a style of play, a system of play that we had never seen before. None of these players meant anything to us. We didn't know about Puskás. All these fantastic players, they were men from Mars as far as we were concerned."
Sir Bobby Robson.

BUDAPEST HONVÉD
Mighty Honvéd

Founded: **1909** • Stadium: **Bozsik József Stadion (Budapest)**

Honvéd formed the backbone of the Hungary team that took Olympic gold in 1952 and who were World Cup runners-up in 1954. Affiliated with the Hungarian army, Honvéd were considered one of the best clubs in the world in the mid-1950s, just before the invention of the European Cup. In 1956, when the city of Budapest was overrun by Soviet tanks, the team found themselves abroad. After extending a tour to Brazil, where they triumphed, several players, including the stars Kocsis, Czibor, and Puskás, opted for a definitive exile. The club effectively had to start over. They found success again by reaching the quarter-finals of the 1966 Champions Cup, and then the quarter-finals of the 1979 UEFA Cup—after eliminating Ajax—and dominated the domestic scene in the 1980s.

13 League Titles

7 National Cups

May 30, 1960
Honvéd receive Ferencvaros.

Star players: József Bozsik, László Budai, Zoltán Czibor, Gyula Grosics, Sándor Kocsis, Gyula Lóránt, Ferenc Puskás, Antal Nagy, Lajos Tichy, Lajos Kocsis, László Dajka, Lajos Détári, Márton Esterházy, Imre Garaba, Sándor Gujdár, István Kocsis, József Varga.

Honours: League: 1949–50, 1950, 1952, 1954, 1955, 1980, 1984, 1985, 1986, 1988, 1989, 1991, 1993; National Cup: 1926, 1964, 1985, 1989, 1996, 2007, 2009.

ÚJPEST FC
Purples
Founded: **1885** • Stadium: **Szusza Ferenc (Budapest)**

In 102 years spent in the first division, Újpest —who were linked to the Ministry of the Interior during the Cold War— have won the national title twenty-one times, and were runners-up in the 1969 UEFA Cup. They are one of the most popular clubs in Hungary, along with their great rivals, Ferencvárosi.

MTK BUDAPEST
The Blue and Whites
Founded: **1888** • Stadium: **Hidegkuti Nándor (Budapest)**

Founded by a group of aristocrats, MTK, who were also called Voros Lobogo during the glory years of the 1950s, are giants of Hungarian football. Twenty-three-time league champions between 1904 and 2008, they were also runners-up in the 1964 Cup Winners' Cup.

FERENCVÁROSI TC
The Green Eagles
Founded: **1899** • Stadium: **Groupama Arena (Budapest)**

This club—the first president of which affirmed it would become "great"—is one of the most popular in Hungary. Twenty-eight time champion, and winner of the 1965 UEFA Cup, Ferencvárosi has fielded such giants of Hungarian football as Florian Albert— 1967 European Footballer of the Year.

DEBRECENI VASUTAS SC
Loki
Founded: **1902** • Stadium: **Nagyerdei (Debrecen)**

For many years, this club founded by railway workers led a modest existence. Since the 2000s, however, they have become one of the most successful clubs in the country— thanks to their player training initiatives— winning seven titles between 2005 and 2014.

GYORI ETO FC
The Green and Whites
Founded: **1904** • Stadium: **ETO Park (Győr)**

This club was established by the members of a factory choir. They won four titles between 1963 and 2013, as well as four cups, and contested the semi-finals of the 1965 Champions Cup. They maintain a strong regional rivalry with Szombathelyi Haladás.

VASAS SC
The Red and Blues
Founded: **1911** • Stadium: **Rudolf-Illovszky (Budapest)**

Founded by metalworkers, the club dominated Hungarian football from the 1960s, taking six titles between 1957 and 1977, and winning the semi-finals of the 1958 European Cup. Vasas' most famous fan was Janos Kadar, the head of state from 1956 to 1988.

SZOMBATHELYI HALADÁS
Hali

Founded: **1919** • Stadium: **Rohonci uti (Szombathelyi)**

Hungary's yo-yo kings, Haladás have experienced twenty-seven relegations to the second division since they were founded, despite playing fifty-one seasons in the first division. They have contested three Hungarian Cup finals, and competed twice in major European cups.

VIDEOTON FC
Vidi

Founded: **1941** • Stadium: **Sóstói (Székesfehérvár)**

Founded by workers from an arms factory, the club caused a stir in 1985 by reaching the final of the UEFA Cup. In 2011, they won their first national title, an exploit they repeated in 2015. The club can count the Prime Minister, Viktor Orban, among its fans.

SLAVIA PRAGUE
The Stitched Ones

Founded: **1892** • Stadium: **Eden Arena (Prague)**

Founded by medical students, the club became popular by winning thirteen Czechoslovakian league titles between 1925 and 1947. Since the establishment of the Czech league in 1993, the club has won three titles. Their strip, which was designed by the sister of one of the players, has remained unchanged since 1896.

SPARTA PRAGUE
Iron Sparta

Founded: **1893** • Stadium: **Generali Arena (Prague)**

Sparta is the country's most popular club, with a working-class fan base. They have won thirty-three national league titles, and since 1896 have played the Pražský S derby against Slavia. Sparta have been a semi-finalist in both the European Cup (1992) and UEFA Cup Winners' Cup (1973).

BOHEMIANS 1905
Kangaroos

Founded: **1905** • Stadium: **Ďolíček (Prague)**

The club earned their nickname from having returned from an Australian tour in 1927 with two live kangaroos—which they donated to the Prague zoo. Czechoslovakian champions in 1983, the Bohemians were saved from relegation to the third division in 2005 thanks to their supporters. They remain very popular.

VIKTORIA PLZEN
Viktorka

Founded: **1911** • Stadium: **Doosan (Plzeň)**

Viktoria Plzeň have the uncommon stat of having known twenty-two relegations in their history. They were also the first club of Pavel Nedvěd—the 2003 European Footballer of the Year. Viktoria Plzeň were Czech league champions in 2011, 2013, and 2015, and have twice played in the group stage of the Champions League.

FC ZBROJOVKA BRNO
The Pistol

Founded: **1913** • Stadium: **Městský (Brno)**

The club regularly played in the Czechoslovakian first division—winning the league championship in 1978 They then spent nineteen seasons in the upper echelons of the Czech league, drawing huge crowds when they played in the Za Lužánkami stadium.

BANÍK OSTRAVA
The Steel Heart of the Republic

Founded: **1922** • Stadium: **Bazaly (Ostrava)**

Founded by coal miners, the club built their own pitch with help from volunteers. Three-time Czechoslovakian champions, Baník finally won the Czech title in 2004. Their supporters are among the most fervent in the country and their biggest rivals are Sparta.

DUKLA PRAGUE
The Soldiers

Founded: **1948** • Stadium: **Juliska (Prague)**

Formerly an army club, Dukla initially became known thanks to Josef Masopust—named 1962 European Footballer of the Year. They were league champions of Czechoslovakia eleven times, were relegated in 1994, and moved to Příbram in 1997. An amateur club resuscitated the name in 2001 and entered the first division in 2011.

FC SLOVAN LIBEREC
The Blue and Whites

Founded: **1958** • Stadium: **Stadion u Nisy (Liberec)**

FC Slovan Liberec were formed from the merger of two rival Liberec teams. They had to wait for the partition of Czechoslovakia to play in the first division. The first club from outside Prague to win the Czech league championship, they hold three national titles and one Czech Cup.

FC PETRZALKA AKADÉMIA
Engerau

Founded: **1898** • Stadium: **FC Petržalka Akadémia (Bratislava)**

The oldest club in Bratislava, they have had more name changes (sixteen) than national titles (two). It was under the name Artmedia, that they qualified for the group stage of the 2005 Champions League, after having eliminated Celtic.

MSK ZILINA
The Shoshons

Founded: **1908** • Stadium: **pod Dubňom (Žilina)**

The club played in the top league of the former Czechoslovakia for thirty seasons, but had to wait for Slovakian independence to start winning trophies: six league championships and one cup since 1993. In 2011, they played in the group stage of the Champions League.

SK SLOVAN BRATISLAVA
Kings of Bratislava
Founded: **1919** • Stadium: **Pasienky (Bratislava)**

Founded by a police officer, Slovan were one of the best clubs in the former Czechoslovakia, with eight titles. In 1969, they won the Cup Winners' Cup, beating FC Barcelona. Since independence, they have been the country's most successful club, with eight titles. Their great rivals are Trnava.

FC SPARTAK TRNAVA
The White Angels
Founded: **1923** • Stadium: **Antona Malatinského (Trnava)**

Spartak used to be linked to the steelmaking industry, and they were very successful in the former Czechoslovakia, winning five league titles, five cups, and reaching one semi-final of the Champions League. The club's supporters are known for being the most loyal and the most numerous in Slovakia.

FK INTER BRATISLAVA
Yellow Blacks
Founded: **1940** • Stadium: **ŠKP Inter Dúbravka (Bratislava)**

Inter Bratislava were a stronghold of the former Czechoslovakia, although they only won the league once (1959). Since independence, they were league champions twice (2000, 2001), before their license was sold for financial reasons. The club was re-established in 2010 and they now play in the third division.

FC VSS KOSICE
VSS
Founded: **1952** • Stadium: **TJ Lokomotíva (Košice)**

Runners-up in the 1971 Czechoslovakian championship, VSS have won two titles since independence—and their buyout by a steel firm. In 1997, they were the first Slovakian club to play in the group stage of the Champions League. Their great rivals are Tatran Prešov.

WISLA KRAKOW
The White Star
Founded: **1906** • Stadium: **Henryk Reyman (Krakow)**

The third most successful club in the country, with thirteen league championship titles, they are supported as far away as Chicago—home of the largest Polish community outside Poland. They contest a derby nicknamed the "Holy War" against KS Cracovia.

RTS WIDZEW LÓDZ
The Red Army
Founded: **1910** • Stadium: **Widzewa (Łódź)**

Four-time league champions, the club reached the semi-finals of the 1983 Champions League—they were beaten by Juventus, to where their star player, Zbigniew Boniek, had moved one year before. These successes earned the club considerable popularity. Their main rivals are Legia.

POLAND

LEGIA WARSAW
The Legionnaires

Founded: **1916** • Stadium: **Polish Army Stadium (Warsaw)**

Founded by legionnaires during the First World War, Legia have won the championship ten times, and reached the semi-finals of the 1970 Champions League. Popular in Warsaw, though not in the rest of the country, they maintain strong rivalries with the other clubs.

KS RUCH CHORZÓW
The Metallurgists

Founded: **1920** • Stadium: **Miejski (Chorzów)**

The joint most successful club in the country, with fourteen league titles (on a par with Górnik Zabrze), Ruch Chorzów have spent seventy-three seasons in the first division—of which they are one of the founding members. Their stadium has a clock given to the club in 1929 by a Swiss watchmaker.

LECH POZNAN
The Railwaymen

Founded: **1922** • Stadium: **Inea (Poznan)**

Historically linked to the railroads, the club started out in the tenth division, then reached the top flight in 1948. Seven-time league champions and five-time winners of the cup, Lech was where the future Bayern Munich star Robert Lewandowski first played football.

GÓRNIK ZABRZE
Tricolour

Founded: **1948** • Stadium: **Ernest Pohl (Zabrze)**

Górnik, who hold the joint record for league champion-ships with fourteen titles, are the only club in the country to have played a European final—the 1970 Cup Winners' Cup against Manchester City. Big rivals of Legia, they contest the Silesian derby against Ruch Chorzów.

FC ALANIA VLADIKAVKAZ
Alanian Snow Leopards

Founded: **1921** • Stadium: **Republican Spartak (Vladikavkaz)**

Alania were playing in the Soviet first division when the USSR collapsed, after which this club from North Ossetia soon found their place in the new Russian league, which they won in 1995. Although they have yo-yoed since 2005, they were runners-up in the 2011 Cup, and played in the 2012 Europa League.

DYNAMO MOSCOW
Cops

Founded: **1923** • Stadium: **Khimki (Moscow)**

Twelve-time champions of the Soviet Union, when Dynamo were the police club, they became the first Muscovite club to play in a European final—the 1972 Cup Winners' Cup. Never relegated since 1936, they fielded the goalkeeper Lev Yachine, who was 1963 European Footballer of the Year.

RUSSIA

FC LOKOMOTIV MOSCOW
La Loco
Founded: **1923** • Stadium: **Lokomotiv (Moscow)**

Founded as part of the Soviet-era Ministry of Transport, the club found success after the collapse of the USSR. Regularly runners-up, or placed third, they won the title in 2002 and 2004, as well as playing two Cup Winners' Cup semi-finals. Their stadium draws some of the biggest crowds in Moscow.

FC TORPEDO MOSCOW
The White and Reds
Founded: **1924** • Stadium: **Saturn (Moscow)**

Established within a truck factory, Torpedo were one of the Moscow big four during the Soviet period, winning three league titles and seven cups. There followed a period of complex ups and downs, before their amateur branch managed to work their way up from the fourth division, reaching the top flight in 2014.

FC ROTOR VOLGOGRAD
Blue Cyan
Founded: **1929** • Stadium: **Zenit (Volgograd)**

Founded in a tractor factory in the former Stalingrad, Rotor grew to become one of the best clubs in Russia in the mid-1990s finishing runners up in the league in 1993 and 1997. However, the club's fortunes rapidly declined in the 2000s and in 2015 a team under new management started competing in the amateur Russian football league.

FC ROSTOV
The Tractors
Founded: **1930** • Stadium: **Olimp-2 (Rostov)**

Rostov often played in the Soviet first division, and have been a regular of the Russian league since 1992. They lost the 2003 cup final, but won it in 2014. In 2012, they signed David Bentley, the first English footballer to play in the Russian championship.

FC RUBIN KAZAN
The Tatars
Founded: **1958** • Stadium: **Kazan (Kazan)**

This representative of the Tatarstan region became a consistent fixture of the Russian championship—which they joined in 2003—winning two titles (2008, 2009). In Europe, the club beat FC Barcelona at Camp Nou in 2009, as well as Inter Milan and Atlético Madrid.

FC ANZHI MAKHACHKALA
Dagestans
Founded: **1991** • Stadium: **Anzhi (Kaspiysk)**

Promoted to the first division in 1999, Anzhi were bought by a billionaire in 2011, and recruited Roberto Carlos and Samuel Eto'o. In 2013, they finished runners-up in the Russian Cup, then decided to focus on training young players. They maintain a strong rivalry with the Moscow clubs.

★★★★

"We were soccer aficionados spoiling for a fight. We were eager to come out on the pitch and play another game. The stadium became our second home." **Nikolai Starostin, Spartak's founder.**

SPARTAK MOSCOW
The Meat

Founded. **1922** • Stadium: **Otkrytiye Arena (Moscow)**

The most successful club during the Soviet period, they were created outside of the ruling state, and were sponsored by a food production factory, which earned them the nickname of "Meat." Renamed in 1934 after Spartacus, the slave who defied Rome, they became the most popular club in the country, regularly filling the huge Luzhniki stadium. Semi-finalists in three European Cups, they have beaten Real Madrid, Liverpool, and Ajax. Although Spartak's oldest rival is Dynamo, they now contest with CSKA the most hotly anticipated derby in their new stadium, which opened in 2014.

21 League Titles

13 National Cups

September 19, 2012
Rômulo beats Valdes, as Spartak give Barça a scare at the Camp Nou.

Star players: Igor Netto, Rinat Dasayev, Vagiz Khidiyatullin, Valery Karpin, Igor Shalimov, Viktor Onopko, Yuryi Nikiforov, Dmitri Alenichev, Pavel Pogrebnyak, Roman Pavlyuchenko, Aleksandr Mostovoi, Nemanja Vidic, Stipe Pletikosa, Kim Källström, Emmanuel Emenike.

Honours: League: (USSR) 1936, 1938, 1939, 1952, 1953, 1956, 1958, 1962, 1969, 1979, 1987, 1989, (Russia) 1992, 1993, 1994, 1996, 1997, 1998, 1999, 2000, 2001; National Cup (USSR) 1938, 1939, 1946, 1947, 1950, 1958, 1963, 1965, 1971, 1992, (Russia) 1994, 1998, 2003.

"It's fun to be at the C-S-K-A!"
(Supporters' chant).

CSKA MOSCOW

The Horses

Founded: **1911** · Stadium: **Arena Khimki (Moscow)**

Founded as part of the army, the club's first period of glory ran from 1946 to 1951, when they won five titles, until Stalin relieved the "lieutenants team" of its players, on the pretext that they weren't real soldiers. Since the end of the USSR, in 1992, they have played in the Russian first division, winning five titles between 2003 and 2014. Even better, in 2005 they became the first Russian club to win a European competition, the Europa League, after eliminating Benfica, Parma, and Sporting Portugal, among others. In 2010, they reached the quarter-finals of the Champions League, after having knocked out Celtic and FC Seville. Among their other great continental performances are victories over FC Barcelona in 1992, and over Inter Milan in 2011.

12 League Titles

12 National Cups

May 18, 2005
CSKA win their
first European title.

Star players: Grigory Fedotov, Wsewolod Bobrov, Albert Shesternyov, Vladimir Fedotov, Sergei Fokin, Dmitri Kuznetsov, Ilshat Faizulin, Sergei Semak, Ivica Olic, Igor Akinfeev, Vasili Berezutski, Miloš Krasić, Tomáš Necid, Vágner Love, João Alves de Assis Silva "Jô," Ahmed Musa.

Honours: League: (USSR) 1946, 1947, 1948, 1950, 1951, 1970, 1991 (Russia) 2003, 2005, 2006, 2013, 2014; National Cup (USSR) 1945, 1948, 1951, 1955, 1991 (Russia) 2002, 2005, 2006, 2008, 2009, 2011, 2013; UEFA Cup 2005.

RUSSIA

"The fans want to see stars, not players in decline, but those at their peak, and on the rise." **Vladimir Putin, in 2010, regarding Zenit's signing of Brazilian striker Hulk.**

FC ZENIT SAINT PETERSBURG

The Blue-White-Sky Blues

Founded: **1925**

Stadium: **Petrovsky (Saint Petersburg)**

Connected to the famous camera manufacturer Lomo during the Soviet period, the club won just one title under their former name, Zenit Leningrad. In 1967, they were saved from relegation by the regime, even though they finished last in the league. Zenit would only reach the top flight after they were taken over by Gazprom in 2005. Four-time league champions since 2007, they won the 2008 Europa League after eliminating Marseille, Leverkusen, and Bayern, then dominated Manchester United in the UEFA Super Cup. They have no local rivals, and are the most popular club in Russia. Vladimir Putin is one of their supporters. In 2016, Zenit will move to a new stadium with a capacity of 65,000.

5 League Titles

3 National Cups

May 14, 2008
Zenith finally win the UEFA Cup, three years after CSKA.

Star players: Roman Berezovsky, Andrey Arshavin, Anatoliy Tymoshchuk, Pavel Pogrebnyak, Viktor Fayzulin, Martin Škrtel, Sergei Semak, Bruno Alves, Givanildo Vieira de Sousa "Hulk", Ezequiel Garay, Daniel Miguel Alves Gomes, Aleksandr Anyukov, Aleksandr Kerzhakov.

Honours: League: (USSR) 1984 (Russia) 2007, 2010, 2012, 2015; National Cup: (USSR) 1944 (Russia) 1999, 2010; UEFA Cup: 2008.

"When we talk about tactical evolution, the first thing we have in mind is to strive for new courses of action that will not allow the opponent to adapt to our style of play."
Valery Lobanowski.

DYNAMO KIEV

Bilo-Syni

Founded: **1927** • Stadium: **Valeriy Lobanovskyi Dynamo (Kiev)**

Present in the Soviet first division, and then the Ukranian first division since 1936; twenty-seven-time league champions, twice winners of the Cup Winners' Cup, three-time semi-finalists in the European Cup/Champions League (1977, 1987, 1999), Dynamo Kiev have built their success on the loyalty of their players. One such former player was Valeriy Lobanovskyi, who was made a Hero of Ukraine after leading the club to their two European victories. Another was the greatest Soviet player in history, Oleg Blokhin, who wore the Kiev shirt for nineteen seasons, and scored 266 goals. Then there's the goalkeeper, Oleksandr Shovkovskiy, who joined the team in 1993 and is still there in 2015, aged forty. Finally there is Andriy Shevchenko, who returned, ten years after leaving, to the club where he started his career. It is thanks to these men, and many others, that Dynamo Kiev was the greatest club in the USSR, and continues, since the independence of Ukraine, to be the greatest club in Eastern Europe.

27 League Titles

20 National Cups

2 European Cup Winners' Cups

Oleksandr Shovkovskiy
This Ukrainian goalkeeper played more than six hundred games while wearing the Dynamo shirt.

The number of trophies won by Dynamo while the club was managed by Valery Lobanovski.

266

23

12

The number of goals scored by Oleg Blokhine while he was playing for Kiev.

Dynamo have removed the number twelve from their strip in honour of their supporters—a practice followed by many other clubs.

Andriy Shevchenko
Winning the 2004 Ballon d'Or during his years at AC Milan, this great talent was already exceptional when he was at Dynamo Kiev, the club where he first played.

ONE CLUB, TWO FOOTBALLER OF THE YEAR AWARDS

Dynamo Kiev are members of a little known but very select club: those who have had several players voted Footballer of the Year while wearing their colours. There are nine of them, all European. Dynamo Kiev's are Oleg Blokhin (1975) and Igor Belanov (1986). In both cases, the award recognizes not just individual distinction, but also a style of play based on counter-attacking—a rigorous application of the technique developed by Valeriy Lobanovskyi to punish a vulnerable defense.

March 17, 1976
After receiving the Ballon d'Or, Oleg Blokhine walks onto the pitch at Geoffroy-Guichard stadium to face Saint-Étienne during the European Cup.

Star players: József Szabó, Valeriy Lobanovskyi, Andriy Biba, Volodymyr Muntyan, Yevhen Rudakov, Oleg Blokhin, Anatoliy Demyanenko, Igor Belanov, Vasyl Rats, Oleksandr Zavarov, Oleksiy Mykhaylychenko, Andriy Shevchenko, Serhiy Rebrov, Oleksandr Shovkovskiy, Maksim Shatskikh, Andriy Yarmolenko.

Honours: League: (USSR) 1961, 1966, 1967, 1968, 1971, 1974, 1975, 1977, 1980, 1981, 1985, 1986, 1990, (Ukraine) 1993, 1994, 1995, 1996, 1997, 1998, 1999, 2000, 2001, 2003, 2004, 2007, 2009, 2015; National Cup (USSR): 1954, 1964, 1966, 1974, 1978, 1982, 1985, 1987, 1990; National Cup (Ukraine): 1993, 1996, 1998, 1999, 2000, 2003, 2005, 2006, 2007, 2014, 2015; European Cup Winners' Cup: 1975, 1986.

"Shakhtar is like the Brazil B side." **Luis Figo.**

FK SHAKHTAR DONETSK

The Miners

Founded: **1936**
Stadium: **Donbass (Donetsk)**

Initially composed of miners from the Donbass region, the club played forty-four seasons in the Soviet top flight, finishing second in 1975 and 1979. Things have changed since Ukraine's independence, and Shakhtar have made up ground on the great Dynamo Kiev, and even overtaken them in the last fifteen years. During the 2008–2009 season, the club made a splash by beating FC Barcelona at the Camp Nou in the Champions League. Having qualified for the UEFA Cup, they managed to win the trophy, allowing themselves the luxury along the way of eliminating Dynamo Kiev in the semi-finals. Their secret? The millions injected by the club president, Rinat Akhmetov—the richest man in Ukraine—which have allowed the club to build their own 52,000-capacity stadium, and to buy many foreign players, particularly Brazilians.

9 League Titles

13 National Cups

May 20, 2009
Manager Lucescu, president Akhmetov and captain Srna triumph in the UEFA Cup.

Star players: Valeriy Lobanovskyi, Anatoliy Tymoschuk, Darijo Srna, Willian, Elano, Fernandinho, Stipe Pletikosa, Ravzan Rat, Ciprian Marica, Francelino Matuzalém da Silva, Zvonimir Vukić, Henrikh Mkhitaryan, Mariusz Lewandowski, Julius Aghahowa, Brandão, Douglas Costa de Souza.

Honours: League: 2002, 2005, 2006, 2008, 2010, 2011, 2012, 2013, 2014; National Cup (USSR): 1961, 1962, 1980, 1983; National Cup (Ukraine): 1995, 1997, 2001, 2002, 2004, 2008, 2011, 2012, 2013; UEFA Cup: 2009.

FC DNIPRO DNIPROPETROVSK
Warriors of Light

Founded: **1918** • Stadium: **Dnipro Arena (Dnipropetrovsk)**

Founded within a machine manufacturing plant, the club won two league titles during the Soviet period. Since independence in 1992, they have picked up a string of third places. In 2015, they reached the final of the Europa League.

FC ARSENAL KIEV
The Cannoneers

Founded: **1925** • Stadium: **Kolos (Kiev)**

This club formed within a Kiev arms factory played in the Soviet second division before becoming the B team of Dynamo Kiev in 1964. Reformed in 2001, they took over from CSKA Borysfen Kiev—who were promoted to the first division in 1996. As of 2014, they had played twenty-four derbies against their rival, Dynamo.

FC METALIST KHARKIV
The Weasels

Founded: **1925** • Stadium: **OSC Metalist (Kharkov)**

Originally sponsored by a locomotive factory, the club played fourteen seasons in the Soviet first division, and won one USSR Cup in 1988. In the Ukrainian league, they finished third from 2007 to 2014, and reached the quarter-finals of the Europa League in 2012.

FC CHORNOMORETS ODESSA
The Sailors

Founded: **1936** • Stadium: **Chornomorets (Odessa)**

Present in the Soviet first division for twenty-four seasons from 1965, the club finished third in 1974 and are placed thirteenth in the USSR's historic rankings. Since independence, they have finished the league as runners-up twice, and third three times, and have won the cup on two occasions.

SC TAVRIYA SIMFEROPOL
Crimeans

Founded: **1958** • Stadium: **RSC Lokomotiv (Simferopol)**

Tavriya were one of the founding members of the Ukrainian first division in 1992, winning the first season. In 2014, they were one of four clubs never to have been relegated. That same year, following the conflict in the Crimea, they made a request to play in Russia.

FC KARPATY LVIV
The Lions

Founded: **1963** • Stadium: **Ukraina (Lviv)**

The club stands out in the history of the USSR for having managed, in 1969, to become the only second division club ever to win the cup, before joining the Soviet top flight in the 1970s. They have played in twenty of the first twenty-two seasons of the Ukrainian league.

DINAMO MINSK
The Blue and Whites
Founded: **1927** • Stadium: **Traktor (Minsk)**

The only Belarusian club to play in the Soviet league, which they won in 1982, Dinamo won the first five seasons of the Belarusian league, starting in 1992. Despite various ups and downs, their supporters follow the team wherever they play.

BATE BORISOV
The Yellow and Blues
Founded: **1996** • Stadium: **Borisov Arena (Borisov)**

BATE have historical connections to the local automobile industry and in recent years have won eleven titles in fifteen seasons, becoming the country's leading club. They have qualified four times from the group stage of the UEFA Champions League, even beating Bayern Munich in 2013.

FC ZIMBRU CHISINAU
The Yellow and Greens
Founded: **1947** • Stadium: **Zimbru (Chisinau)**

The club racked up eleven seasons in the Soviet first division before independence. Starting in 1992, they won eight out of the first nine seasons of the Moldovian championship. A fallow period followed, before they regained the cup in 2014 from their rivals, Sheriff Tiraspol.

FC SHERIFF TIRASPOL
The Yellow and Blacks
Founded: **1997** • Stadium: **Bolshaya Sportivnaya Arena (Tiraspol)**

Founded by Sheriff—the second largest company in the Transnistria region—the club soon became masters of the league championship, winning thirteen titles between 2001 and 2014. Although they are proud representatives of Moldova, they rely on many South American players.

DINAMO TBILISI
The Blue and Whites
Founded: **1925** • Stadium: **Boris Paichadze (Tbilisi)**

The club played in the Soviet first division from 1936 to 1989, was twice champion of the USSR, and won the 1981 European Cup Winners' Cup. Dinamo have dominated the Georgian league since 1990, earning fifteen titles, and remaining a strong national symbol.

TORPEDO KUTAISI
The Torpedos
Founded: **1946** • Stadium: **Givi Kiladze (Kutaisi)**

Torpedo were founded at a car factory in Georgia's second-biggest city. They played in the Georgian league before entering the Soviet first division in 1962. Since independence, the club have won three national titles.

KAZAKHSTAN

FC KAIRAT
The People's Team
Founded: **1954** • Stadium: **Almaty Central (Almaty)**

The best Kazakh club in the USSR, Kairat played in the Soviet first division for twenty-four seasons. Funded by the national railway company, they won two Kazakh league championships before experiencing bankruptcy and relegation. In 2009, the club returned to the first division.

FC SHAKHTER KARAGANDY
The Miners
Founded: **1958** • Stadium: **Shakhter (Karagandy)**

Located in a mining region, the club played in the Soviet second division in the 1960s. Twice national league champions since independence, and the best performing Kazakh club on the European scene, Shakhter Karagandy sacrifice a sheep the day before a match.

FC IRTYSH PAVLODAR
The Blues
Founded: **1965** • Stadium: **Pavlodar Central (Pavlodar)**

Irtysh Pavlodar have been league champions five times, and have also won the national cup. They have been consistent performers at the top level since the establishment of the league in 1992. In March 2015, striker Alan Gatagov's amazing goal against Ordabasy from a scorpion kick went viral around the world.

FC AKTOBE
The Red and Whites
Founded: **1967** • Stadium: **Aktobe Central (Aktobe)**

FC Aktobe were flying high when the USSR collapsed, so they took advantage of Kazakhstan's independence to enter the first division. They have won the league championship five times, starting in 2005, and have been runners-up twice. In 2008, the club won the Kazakhstan Cup.

SKONTO FC
The Reds
Founded: **1991** • Stadium: **Skonto (Riga)**

Winner of the first national league championship, in 1991, Skonto have achieved an exploit unique in Europe by taking fourteen league titles in a row. In the final stage of Euro 2004, all of the Latvian national team were either current or former players of Skonto FC.

FK VENTSPILS
The Yellow and Blues
Founded: **1997** • Stadium: **Ventspils Olimpiskais (Riga)**

Formed from the merger of FK Nafta and FK Venta—a club that had some success in the 1960s—Ventspils have overtaken Skonto Riga in the hierarchy of Latvian football, winning the league championship six times since 2006. In 2009, Ventspils became the first club in the country to play in the group stage of the Europa League.

LATVIA

LEVSKI SOFIA
The People's Club
Founded: **1914** • Stadium: **Georgi Asparuhov (Sofia)**

Levski Sofia were founded by a group of students, and have always been the main rival of CSKA, against whom they have played over 130 "Eternal Derbies." They have won the league twenty-six times. In 2006, Levski became the first Bulgarian club to play in the group stage of the UEFA Champions League.

LOKOMOTIV PLOVDIV
The Smurfs
Founded: **1936** • Stadium: **Lokomotiv (Plovdiv)**

Lokomotiv may have only won the league championship once, in 2004, but the club, which was founded by railway workers in Plovdiv (the country's second-largest city), provides the main opposition to the teams from the capital, Sofia. This has long made Lokomotiv very popular in Bulgaria.

LUDOGORETS RAZGRAD
The Eagles
Founded: **1945** • Stadium: **Ludogorets Arena (Razgrad)**

Ever since Ludogorets Razgrad was bought by a Bulgarian businessman (who was then a member of CSKA Sofia's supervisory board) in 2010, this club from the little town of Razgrad has maintained a good success rate, winning four successive victories since 2012—the year they entered the first division.

CSKA SOFIA
Charisma
Founded: **1948** • Stadium: **Balgarska Armia (Sofia)**

Originally founded by army officers, the club dominated Bulgarian football for sixty years, winning the league championship thirty-one times between 1948 and 2008. With nearly eight hundred supporters' clubs around the world, CSKA Sofia are also the most popular team in Bulgaria.

FC ARARAT YEREVAN
The White Eagles
Founded: **1935** • Stadium: **Hrazdan (Yerevan)**

The club played in the USSR league championship starting in the 1940s. In 1973 they won the league/cup double. During that same period they regularly progressed through the early rounds of various European cups. Since 1991, Ararat Yerevan have only won the Armenian league once.

FC PYUNIK
The Phoenix
Founded: **1992** • Stadium: **Yerevan Football Academy Stadium (Yerevan)**

Pyunik were founded after independence, and won the first-ever national league championship in 1995, going on to win the same title ten times in succession between 2001 and 2010. Their success has made them the great rivals of Ararat in the hearts of Yerevan football fans.

NEFTCHI PFK
Oil Workers
Founded: **1937** • Stadium: **Bakcell Arena (Baku)**

These pioneers of Azeri football have links to the petroleum industry, and are the most popular of the capital's clubs, having won the most titles of any team in the country, with eight league championships and six cups. In 2012, Neftchi qualified for the group stage of the Europa League for the first time.

QARABAG FK
The Horsemen
Founded: **1951** • Stadium: **Tofiq Bahramov (Baku)**

Qarabağ FK have played in the Azeri league since they were founded in 1992, and have won the title twice (1993, 2014). Although their home city is Baku, where they play in the capital's largest stadium, this very popular club represents the people of Nagorno-Karabakh, an area disputed by Armenia and Azerbaijan.

ALTAY SK
Great Altay
Founded: **1914** • Stadium: **Alsancak (Izmir)**

Based in Izmir, Altay took over the stadium of Panionios—Greece's oldest club—after the latter's departure in 1922. Altay was the first team to put an end to Galatasaray's reign in the national cup, winning it in 1967, and again in 1980.

KASIMPAŞA SK
The Apaches
Founded: **1921** • Stadium: **Recep Tayyip Erdoğan (Istanbul)**

Kasımpaşa, who played their first match in the street against English soldiers, were one of the pioneers of the professional game. Promoted to the first division in 1959, they have played thirteen seasons in the top flight. Their stadium bears the name of the Turkish prime minister, who comes from the Kasımpaşa neighbourhood.

BURSASPOR
Green Crocodiles
Founded: **1963** • Stadium: **Bursa Atatürk (Bursa)**

In 2010, the club caused a splash by becoming the fifth club to win the national league title. The club share a deep friendship with Ankaragücü, and their supporters often come to cheer the other team at matches. Bursaspor have had their own TV station since 2009.

TRABZONSPOR
Black Sea Storm
Founded: **1967** • Stadium: **Hüseyin Avni Aker (Trabzon)**

Trabzonspor were promoted to the top flight in 1974, and have never been relegated. League champions in their first season, they have racked up six titles and eight cups. They are the fourth biggest Turkish club, behind the big three from Istanbul. In 2012, Trabzonspor beat Inter Milan in the Champions League.

"When you come to Galatasaray, you're told 'Welcome to hell.' During the derbies against Fenerbahçe, you tremble from beginning to end. Even though I've coached and played in several countries, this was a whole other world."

Eric Gerets, Galatasaray coach, 2005–2007.

GALATASARAY SK

The Lions of the Bosphorus

Founded: **1905**

Stadium: **Türk Telekom Arena (Istanbul)**

This club from the European bank of the Bosphorus gets their name from the high school whose students founded it, while their colours come from a fifteenth century Turkish legend. They are the biggest club in Turkey, despite harsh local competition from Beşiktaş and Fenerbahçe—their greatest rivals, against whom they have played over 370 "intercontinental derbies." In 2015, their twentieth league title made it the most successful club in the country. But it is in European cups that the club have distinguished themselves the most. The first Turkish club to take part in the Cup Winners' Cup, in 1956, they were also the first to reach the semi-finals, in 1989, then the first to win a continental trophy: the 2000 UEFA Cup—beating Arsenal.

20 League Titles

16 National Cups

1 UEFA Cup

May 31, 2015
Galatasaray become champions of Turkey for the twentieth time in their history.

Star players: Fatih Terim, Rüdiger Abramczik, Gheorghe Hagi, Claudio Taffarel, Mario Jardel, Franck Ribéry, Hakan Sükur, Fatih Terim, Frank de Boer, Milan Baroš, Servet Çetin, Ümit Davala, Rigobert Song, Lincoln, Arda Turan, Fernando Muslera, Didier Drogba, Hamit Altıntop, Wesley Sneijder.

Honours: League: 1962, 1963, 1969, 1971, 1972, 1973, 1987, 1988, 1993, 1994, 1997, 1998, 1999, 2000, 2002, 2006, 2008, 2012, 2013, 2015; National Cup: 1963, 1964, 1965, 1966, 1973, 1976, 1982, 1985, 1991, 1993, 1996, 1999, 2000, 2005, 2014, 2015; UEFA Cup: 2000.

"Even if you beat Barcelona in the European Cup, it's not the same as beating Galatasaray! This match is special."
Ridvan Dilmen.

TURKEY

FENERBAHÇE SK

The Yellow Canaries
Founded: **1907** • Stadium: **Şükrü-Saracoğlu (Istanbul)**

Based on Istanbul's Asian bank, and historically considered the embodiment of the working class, Fenerbahçe are the most popular club of the capital and the country. They even counted Atatürk—the father of modern Turkey—among their supporters. With nineteen national titles, they lag just one title behind their eternal rivals, Galatasaray. Their performances at European level have improved these last few years, thanks to the work of coaches such as Zico. In 2008, they reached the quarter-finals of the Champions League—in a campaign where they beat Inter Milan, PSV Eindhoven, Seville and Chelsea—and the semi-finals of the 2013 Europa League—with victories over Marseille, Mönchengladbach, and Lazio.

19
League Titles

6
National Cups

March 4, 2008
Fenerbahce prevail over Sevilla FC and go through to the Champions League quarter-final.

Star players: Toni Schumacher, Emil Kostadinov, Jay-Jay Okocha, Murat Yakin, Pierre van Hooijdonk, Mamadou Niang, Diego Lugano, Daniel González Güiza, Mateja Kežman, Kennet Andersson, Ali Günes, Stephen Appiah, Nicolas Anelka, Roberto Carlos, Tuncay Sanli, Rüstü Recber, Serhiy Rebrov.

Honours: League: 1959, 1961, 1964, 1965, 1968, 1970, 1974, 1975, 1978, 1983, 1985, 1989, 1996, 2001, 2004, 2005, 2007, 2011, 2014; National Cup: 1968, 1974, 1979, 1983, 2012, 2013.

"I do know the Beşiktaş fans made the loudest noise I have ever heard. They never stopped the whole night." **Sir Alex Ferguson.**

BEŞIKTAŞ JK
The Black Eagles

Founded: **1903**
Stadium: **Vodafone (Istanbul)**

Beşiktaş are the oldest sports club in Turkey. They represented the country in a match against Greece, thus earning them the right to display the national flag on their insignia—currently the only club permitted to do so. Winner of the first two seasons of the current national league—and the first champions to remain unbeaten for an entire season (1992)—they now have thirteen titles, and are part of the trio that dominate Turkish football, alongside Galatasaray and Fenerbahçe. ⚽ The noisiest supporters in the world: Beşiktaş' supporters are particularly fervent. Capable of arriving at the stadium seven hours before a match, and of singing for ninety minutes without interruption, in 2008 they beat their own record for the decibel level recorded at a stadium, when they played Liverpool at home.

13 League Titles

9 National Cups

May 30, 2009
Beşiktaş win the league and cup double.

Star players: Şeref Görkey, Hakkı Yeten, Mersad Kovačević, Metin Tekin, Feyyaz Uçar, Ali Gültiken, Eyjólfur Gjafar Sverrisson, Stefan Kuntz, Daniel Amokachi, Nihat Kaveci, Kleberson, Yordan Letchkov, Gökhan Zan, John Carew, Rüstü Recber, Sergen Yalçin, Ahmed Hassan, Ricardo Quaresma.

Honours: League: 1957, 1958, 1960, 1966, 1967, 1982, 1986, 1990, 1991, 1992, 1995, 2003, 2009; National Cup: 1975, 1989, 1990, 1994, 1998, 2006, 2007, 2009.

"They tremble when they hear your name, Olympiacos /
They still recall your name, Santos de Pelé / Olympia,
Olympia, Olympiacos / The best and the greatest club of all."
Olympiacos anthem, in memory of a victory over Santos in 1961.

OLYMPIACOS FC

The Legend

Founded: **1925** • Stadium: **Georgios Karaiskakis (Athens)**

Founded in Piraeus, a port city within the Athens urban area, by the Andrianopoulos family, six brothers of which wore the team's colours, Olympiacos very soon acquired the nickname "Legend." With six league titles between 1931 and 1938, the club established themselves as the greatest in Greece, and would remain so, having racked up forty-two league titles and twenty-seven cups. On the European scene, they have played two quarter-finals—the 1993 Cup Winners' Cup and the 1999 Champions League. One tragically notable event in the club's history was the Karaiskakis Stadium disaster of February 8, 1981, when twenty-one supporters lost their lives in a stampede while leaving a match. The club's initial fan base was drawn from port workers, and Olympiacos remain very popular today—ensuring that the "derby of the eternal enemies," against Panathinaikos, is always fiercely contested. Up until 2003, the club played in a stadium built in 1895 for the first modern Olympic Games.

42 League Titles

27 National Cups

April 19, 2015
Olympiacos celebrate their
forty-second league title.

Star players: Rivaldo, Dennis Rommedahl, Predrag Đorđević, Thanassis Bebis, Giovanni, Christian Karembeu, Antonios Nikopolidis, Giorgos Sideris, Savvas Theodoridis, Giorgos Darivas, Nery Castillo, Alexandros Alexandris, Nikos Anastopoulos, Oleh Protasov, Darko Kovačević, Grigoris Georgatos.

Honours: League: 1931, 1933, 1934, 1936, 1937, 1938, 1947, 1948, 1951, 1954, 1955, 1956, 1957, 1958, 1959, 1966, 1967, 1973, 1974, 1975, 1980, 1981, 1982, 1983, 1987, 1997, 1998, 1999, 2000, 2001, 2002, 2003, 2005, 2006, 2007, 2008, 2009, 2011, 2012, 2013, 2014, 2015; National Cup: 1947, 1951, 1952, 1953, 1954, 1957, 1958, 1959, 1960, 1961, 1963, 1965, 1968, 1971, 1973, 1975, 1981, 1990, 1992, 1999, 2005, 2006, 2008, 2009, 2012, 2013, 2015.

GREECE

> "It's more than football to the fans, it's almost like a religion."
> Luke Steele, Panathinaikos' goalkeeper, 2014.

PANATHINAIKOS

The Great Club

Founded: **1908** • Stadium: **Apóstolos-Nikolaïdis (Athens)**

This is the oldest of the capital's three major clubs. Founded by the Kalafatis brothers, they dominated Greek football before the arrival of Olympiacos. In 1930, the club became the first national league champions to come from Athens, and they have accumulated twenty league titles and eighteen cups. On the European scene, they are by far the most successful of the Greek clubs. In 1971—and managed by the legendary Ferenc Puskas—Panathinaikos reached the final of the UEFA Champions League, where they were beaten by Johan Cruyff's Ajax. In 1985 and 1986, "Pana" reached the semi-finals of this same competition. Traditionally supported by the Athenian middle-classes, they are now the most popular in the region, and count Greek politician Alexis Tsipras among their supporters.

20 League
Titles

18 National
Cups

May 2, 2010
Djibril Cissé and Panathinaikos celebrate winning the league and cup double.

Star players: Giorgos Kalafatis, Krzysztof Warzycha, Antonis Antoniadis, Giorgos Karagounis, Dimitrios Domazos, Gilberto Silva, Djibril Cissé, Velimir Zajec, Aljoša Asanović, Igor Bišćan, Angelos Basinas, Józef Wandzik, Antonios Nikopolidis, Dimitrios Salpingidis, Kostas Katsouranis, Sotiris Ninis.

Honours: League: 1930, 1949, 1953, 1960, 1961, 1962, 1964, 1965, 1969, 1970, 1972, 1977, 1984, 1986, 1990, 1991, 1995, 1996, 2004, 2010; National Cup: 1940, 1948, 1955, 1967, 1969, 1977, 1982, 1984, 1986, 1988, 1989, 1991, 1993, 1994, 1995, 2004, 2010, 2014.

"This is a symbolic gesture. It will give the fans of AEK the satisfaction that they helped in that procedure, the same way that the refugees from [Constantinople/Istanbul] built AEK's first stadium." **Aggeliki Arkadi, AEK's spokeswoman, about the naming of the new stadium, Saint-Sophia.**

AEK ATHENS
Double-Headed Eagle

Founded: **1924**
Stadium: **Olympic (Athens)**

Founded by Greek refugees from Constantinople—the "K" in the name stands for "Konstantinoupoleos"—AEK have been league champions eleven times, and won the cup on fourteen occasions. One of the three top Greek clubs, they have played 175 derbies against Panathinaikos and 154 against Olympiacos. They were semi-finalists in the 1977 UEFA Cup, and also played in the quarter-finals of the 1969 Champions League and the 1997 and 1998 Cup Winners' Cup. In 2002, the club got through the group stage of the Champions League unbeaten, after playing Real Madrid and AS Rome. AEK are the third most popular club in Greece, particularly with descendants of refugees from Constantinople. 2017 will see the opening of the Saint Sophia stadium, named after the Greek cathedral in Constantinople.

11 League Titles

14 National Cups

November 21, 2006
AEK defeat AC Milan (1-0) during the group phase of the Champions League.

Star players: Mimis Papaioannou, Nikos Liberopoulos, Dusan Bajevic, Kostas Nestoridis, Thomas Mavros, Vasilis Dimitriadis, Ismael Blanco, Kleanthis Maropoulos, Andreas Stamatiadis, Stelios Manolas, Alexis Alexandris, Demis Nikolaidis, Vassilios Tsiartas, Lakis Nikolaou, Michalis Kasapis, Elias Atmatsidis.

Honours: League: 1939, 1940, 1963, 1968, 1971, 1978, 1979, 1989, 1992, 1993, 1994; National Cup: 1932, 1939, 1949, 1950, 1956, 1964, 1966, 1978, 1983, 1996, 1997, 2000, 2002, 2011.

PANIONIOS
Panthers

Founded: **1890** • Stadium: **Nea Smyrni (Athens)**

The oldest of Greek clubs, they refused to merge with Apollon after the two clubs were moved from Smyrna to Athens in 1922. With fifty seasons in the first division behind them, their best results were being runners-up in 1951 and 1971. They have also won two Greek Cups.

APOLLON SMYRNI
Light Brigade

Founded: **1891** • Stadium: **Georgios Kamaras (Athens)**

Founded in Smyrna, a Greek-speaking city in Turkey, the club moved to Athens in 1922. They enjoy popularity not only for the quality of their football, but also for their youth training academy. In the 1960s and 1990s, they regularly managed to finish near the top of the league, and also played in the UEFA Cup.

PANACHAIKI G.E.
Lady of the Peloponnese

Founded: **1891** • Stadium: **Pampeloponnisiako (Patras)**

The club played twenty-six seasons in the first division between 1969 and 2003, using a mixture of local, English, and Italian players. In 1973, they were the first club outside Athens or Thessaloniki to play in the UEFA Cup, eliminating the Austrian club, Grazer AK in the first round.

IRAKLIS 1908 FC
The Elder

Founded: **1908** • Stadium: **Kaftanzoglio (Thessaloniki)**

As the oldest of Thessaloniki's three major clubs, and the only one to have never been champions, Iraklis 1908 have played fifty-one seasons in the first division, and won the cup in 1976. Relegated to the fourth division in 2011 owing to licensing irregularities, they then merged with Pontioi Katerini and started over.

A.C. ARIS THESSALONIKI
God of War

Founded: **1914** • Stadium: **Kleanthis Vikelidis (Thessaloniki)**

Named after the Greek god of war, Aris have won the league championship three times, and taken one cup. They are one of the five most popular clubs in the country, and in 2006 they allowed supporters to buy shares—a move which sadly didn't prevent them from dropping down to the third division.

ETHNIKOS PIRAEUS
The Blue and Whites

Founded: **1923** • Stadium: **Hellinikon (Athens)**

Winner of the cup in 1933, the club competed with the top teams until the 1980s, before being relegated in 1989, after more than thirty seasons in the top flight. Their historic rivals are Olympiacos—both clubs having been formed from the split of AFC Piraeus.

OFI CRETE
The Club

Founded: **1925** • Stadium: **Theodoros Vardinogiannis (Heraklion)**

As the island's leading club, OFI Crete played thirty-one consecutive seasons in the top flight from 1979 to 2009, and won the cup in 1987. The Greek dictatorship of the 1970s exacerbated the rivalry with Ergotelis as a result of their policy of only allowing one club from each region to play in each division.

PAOK FC
Two-Headed Eagle

Founded: **1926** • Stadium: **Toumba (Thessaloniki)**

Founded by Greeks who had fled Turkey, the PAOK are the country's most successful after the three Athens clubs, with two league titles and four cups. They have played in the first division from the very start, and enjoy a brisk rivalry with Olympiacos.

AE LARISSA FC
Queen of Thessaly

Founded: **1964** • Stadium: **AEL FC Arena (Larissa)**

AEL were formed from the merger of four Larissa clubs. In 1988, they were the first club—and only one to date—outside Athens or Thessaloniki to win the league championship. They have also won two cups. They were obliged to give up their professional status in 2013.

SKODA XANTHI FC
Queen of Thrace

Founded: **1967** • Stadium: **Skoda Xanthi Arena (Xanthi)**

Xanthi were promoted to the first division in 1989, and adopted their sponsor's name in 1991—a first in Greece. They have qualified for the UEFA Cup several times, some say because the club is under the protection of the philosopher Democritus, who was born in Thrace.

ANORTHOSIS FAMAGUSTA
The Great Lady

Founded: **1911** • Stadium: **Antonis Papadopoulos (Larnaca)**

Anorthosis are the oldest Cypriot club, and were forced to move to Larnaca after the conflict with Turkey in 1974. Thirteen-time champions, in 2008–2009 the club became the first in the country to qualify for the group stage of the Champions League.

APOEL NICOSIA
The Legend

Founded: **1926** • Stadium: **GSP (Nicosia)**

APOEL have been the most popular Cypriot club since the 1930s, holding a record twenty-four national titles. They are the country's only club to have participated in the 1974 Greek championship. In 2012, they reached the quarter-finals of the Champions League.

AEL LIMASSOL
Lions

Founded: **1930** • Stadium: **Tsirion (Limassol)**

A founding member of the Cypriot League in 1934, the club won their fifth championship in 1968, but then had to wait forty-four years to take their sixth title, in 2012. They have also won six national cups. The club's great local rival is Apollon—founded in 1954 with several of AEL's players.

AC OMONIA NICOSIA
Shamrock Bearers

Founded: **1948** • Stadium: **GSP (Nicosia)**

Founded after a politically-motivated split within Apoel Nicosia, Omonia maintain a fierce rivalry with their neighbours. After dominating in the 1970s–1980s, the club won their twentieth national title in 2010. They have also won fourteen Cypriot Cups.

MACCABI HAIFA
The Greens

Founded: **1913** • Stadium: **Sammy Ofer (Haifa)**

The most popular club in Israel, Maccabi Haifa began their rise when they recruited players from Austria Wien in 1939. Twelve-time champions, in 2002 they became the first team in the country to play in the group stage of the Champions League. Their big rivals are Hapoel Haifa.

HAPOEL TEL AVIV FC
The Workers

Founded: **1919** • Stadium: **Bloomfield (Tel Aviv)**

Affiliated to a union—"Hapoel" means "worker"—the club was for a long time linked to the Labour Party. Thirteen-time champions, they won the 1967 Asian Club Championship. In Europe, they took part in the group stage of the 2010 Champions League.

HAPOEL HAIFA
The Sharks

Founded: **1924** • Stadium: **Ofer (Haifa)**

Despite a rather limited honours record—one league championship title and seven cups—Hapoel Haifa are very popular among the working classes of Haifa, where they have developed a great rivalry with Maccabi Haifa. They have played in European competitions five times.

BEITAR JERUSALEM
Lions from the capital

Founded: **1936** • Stadium: **Teddy (Jerusalem)**

Historically linked to the Zionist movement, Beitar are six-time league champions and seven-time winners of the cup. As one of the most popular clubs in Israel, they can count on some particularly excitable supporters, earning their stadium the nickname of "hell."

ISRAEL

"I'm not in danger. I am the danger." **A banner made by Maccabi Tel Aviv fans in 2014 that quotes the TV show Breaking Bad.**

MACCABI TEL AVIV FC

The Yellows

Founded: **1906**
Stadium: **Bloomfield (Tel Aviv)**

The oldest and most successful Israeli team before the creation of the league championship, the club won some of the first national tournaments in 1923 and 1929. Holder of a record twenty-one national titles, far ahead of Hapoel Tel Aviv and Maccabi Haifa, Maccabi Tel Aviv also shone during the first seasons of the AFC Champions League, which they have won twice, before taking part in UEFA competitions in 1992, managed by Avraham Grant. In 2004, the club played in the group stage of the Champions League, beating Ajax. During the 2013-2014 Europa League, Maccabi beat Frankfurt and Bordeaux. A middle-class club, they share the top spot for popularity with their great rivals, Hapoel Tel-Aviv.

21 League Titles

23 National Cups

October 3, 2013
Maccabi are victorious (2-1) in Bordeaux during the Europa League.

Star players: Itzik Shnior, Avraham Bendori, Yosef Goldstein, Tzvika Stodinski, Yehoshua Glazer, Rafi Levi, Dror Bar Nur, Yossef Merimovich, Menachem Bello, Avi Nimni, Zvi Rosen, Rahamim Talbi, Giora Spiegel, Shiran Yeini, Benny Tabak, Moti Ivanir, Alon Natan, Eli Driks, Nir Klinger, Carlos Garcia.

Honours: League: 1936, 1937, 1942, 1947, 1950, 1952, 1954, 1956, 1958, 1968, 1970, 1972, 1977, 1979, 1992, 1995, 1996, 2003, 2013, 2014, 2015; National Cup: 1929, 1930, 1933, 1941, 1946, 1947, 1954, 1955, 1958, 1959, 1964, 1965, 1967, 1970, 1977, 1987, 1988, 1994, 1996, 2001, 2002, 2005, 2015; AFC Champions League: 1969, 1971.

"Playing for Real Madrid is like touching the sky."
Juanito, Real Madrid player 1977–1987.

REAL MADRID

The Meringues

Founded: **1902** · Stadium: **Santiago Bernabéu (Madrid)**

Founded as Madrid FC, the club became "Real" in 1920 by royal decree. They found initial success in the Copa del Rey (King's Cup), then in the league. Reaching their peak in the 1950s, they took advantage of the creation of the European Cup to establish themselves as the greatest club in the world. With ten European Cup/Champions League titles won over five different decades, Real Madrid are a superlative club. Their records include being the first to have scored more than one thousand goals in European competition. Although they have never neglected their youth academy, the club is known for having attracted some of the greatest players of all time. In the 1950s-1960s, Real Madrid counted Di Stefano, Kopa, and Puskás among their ranks. During their second golden age, marked by three Champions League titles (between 1998 and 2002), the club fielded Zidane, Ronaldo, and Beckham— who were soon nicknamed "Los Galacticos." Luis Figo, another star of the team, made a different comparison: "We were like the Beatles."

32 League Titles

19 National Cups

10 Champions League / European Cups

Francisco Gento
He played a major role in the first six European titles of Real Madrid between 1956 and 1966.

The amount of money, in millions of euros, paid by Real Madrid to sign Cristiano Ronaldo and Gareth Bale: 94 million euros each.

Raul Gonzalez
He is Real's second top scorer after Cristiano Ronaldo and holds the record for games played for the club: 741.

The number of players who received the Ballon d'Or when they were playing for Real: Di Stéfano, Kopa, Figo, Ronaldo, Cannavaro, Cristiano Ronaldo.

The number of goals scored by Cristiano Ronaldo while he was playing for Real during the 2014-15 season.

6

188

61

They wrote the history of the White House
1. Alfredo di Stéfano (1953-1964); 2. Raymond Kopa (1956-1959);
3. Ferenc Puskas (1958-1966); 4. Michel (1982-1996);
5. Emilio Butragueno (1984-1995); 6. Manuel Sanchis (1989-2003);
7. Fernando Hierro (1989-2003); 8. Roberto Carlos (1996-2007);
9. Iker Casillas (1999-2015); 10. Zinédine Zidane (2001-2006);
11. Ronaldo (2002-2007); 12. Sergio Ramos (since 2005);
13. Cristiano Ronaldo (since 2009).

SANTIAGO BERNABÉU, REAL'S ETERNAL FATHER

If there was just one person whose name should be associated with Real Madrid, it would be Santiago Bernabéu. He played for the team, and was part of the squad that won the 1917 Copa del Rey. Ten years later, he joined the club's management, becoming club president in 1943. Under Bernabéu, Real, who had only been Spanish league champions twice, took a leap forward. Their new boss professionalized the club, and had a training centre built, along with a 75,000-capacity stadium—increased to 125,000 in 1954, one year before the stadium was renamed after their president. Sure of his club's strength, Bernabéu lobbied for the creation of the European Cup, of which Real won the first five competitions. Under his presidency, the club won sixteen league titles and became the greatest club in Spain, and arguably the world. "I'll leave the day the *socios* say 'Bernabéu, out,'" he declared. Bernabéu died in 1978, still at the head of the club, and 100,000 people filed past his coffin in the temporary chapel set up in the stadium.

"LOS GALACTICOS" IN THE STANDS, TOO

Since the 1950s, Real have found admirers across the world. The presence of Beckham, married to a singer from the Spice Girls, in the 2000s, even gave the club a glamorous edge in the eyes of some of the biggest stars. Famous supporters of Real include Julio Iglesias, who was once goalkeeper for the club's youth team. Another celebrity from the music world with a soft spot for "The Meringues" is Jennifer Lopez, while Shakira, married to Gerard Piqué, centre-back for Barça, also supports Real. Among actors, both Antonio Banderas and Penelope Cruz are fans of "The Whites." As for sportspeople, Rafael Nadal also supports "Casa Blanca," despite being from the Balearics, not to mention the fact that his uncle, Miguel Angel, played for Barcelona.

THE CRAZIEST LIGA

Of the thirty-two Ligas won by Real—a record—the victory of 2007 was undoubtedly the craziest. On June 9, 2007, there remained eighteen seconds left to play on the last day of the league championship, and Barcelona were all set to take their third successive title. Barça were leading Español 2–1 in Barcelona's Camp Nou stadium, while in Zaragoza, Real were 2–1 down to the home team. But Madrid, who were on equal points with the Catalans before kick-off, couldn't allow themselves a worse result than their rivals if they wanted to win the title. In the ninetieth minute of the game, Van Nistelrooy equalized for Real, while Raúl Tamudo also scored for Español, thus equalizing against Barça. Eighteen seconds later, both matches finished, and Real were triumphant.

May 24, 2014
As Cristiano Ronaldo seals victory (4-1), Real become champions of Europe for the tenth time.

Star players: Ricardo Zamora, Alfredo di Stefano, Francisco Gento, Ferenc Puskás, Pirri, Michel, Emilio Butragueño, Jorge Valdano, Manuel Sanchis, Camacho, Hugo Sanchez, Ivan Zamorano, Fernando Hierro, Fernando Morientes, Raul, Roberto Carlos, Zinedine Zidane, Ronaldo, Luis Figo, Iker Casillas, Sergio Ramos, Cristiano Ronaldo, Gareth Bale.

Honours: League: 1932, 1933, 1954, 1955, 1957, 1958, 1961, 1962, 1963, 1964, 1965, 1967, 1968, 1969, 1972, 1975, 1976, 1978, 1979, 1980, 1986, 1987, 1988, 1989, 1990, 1995, 1997, 2001, 2003, 2007, 2008, 2012; National Cup: 1905, 1906, 1907, 1908, 1917, 1934, 1936, 1946, 1947, 1962, 1970, 1974, 1975, 1980, 1982, 1989, 1993, 2011, 2014; European Cup/Champions League: 1956, 1957, 1958, 1959, 1960, 1966, 1998, 2000, 2002, 2014; UEFA Cup: 1985, 1986; Intercontinental Cup: 1960, 1998, 2002; FIFA Club World Cup: 2014.

"If we lose, we'll always be the best team in the world. If we win, we'll be eternal." **Pep Guardiola, before the 2009 FIFA Club World Cup final against Estudiantes.**

FC BARCELONA

Blaugranes

Founded: **1899** • Stadium: **Camp Nou (Barcelona)**

Founded by the Swiss footballer Hans Gamper, who gave the new club the colours of his first club, FC Basel, Barcelona are synonymous with beautiful football, victories, and Catalan identity. On match nights, Barça's 98,000-capacity stadium—the largest in Europe—is decked out in the colours of Catalonia, defying Madrid, the Spanish capital, and Real, their eternal rivals. Holders of the record for number of European matches played—over 500—Barça have never missed a season of continental competition. Paradoxically, it was not until 1992 that the club triumphed in the Champions League, but once underway, nothing could stop them: Barcelona won four more trophies between 2006 and 2015. Their 144,000 *socios* elect the club president, and give their club considerable popular support. Barça have achieved many great things, earning them the nickname "Mès que un club" (more than a club), given by one of their former presidents.

23 League Titles

27 National Cups

5 Champions League Titles

Pep Guardiola
When he managed the Blaugrana, they won four titles in only one year (2009): La Liga, Copa del Rey, Champions League, Club World Cup.

The number of points obtained by Barça in the league during the 2012-13 season.

100

The number of games played by Xavi for Barça.

767

The number of successive victories by Barcelona in 2010-2011.

16

Ronald Koeman
He scored the only goal during the final against Sampdoria, giving Barcelona its first Champions League title.

SPAIN

LIONEL MESSI, CHILD OF BARCELONA

Of all the players who have matured at Barcelona, Lionel Messi is without a doubt the greatest. The first footballer to be named European Footballer of the year four times, he has been involved in four of the five Champions Leagues the club has won. Above all, he dusted off a number of old records that were thought unbeatable: number of goals in the Liga (186 as of May 23, 2015); greatest number of Liga goals in one season (fifty in 2012); and of course highest goal scorer in the club's history (412 as of May 23, 2015). Yet Messi's arrival was a gamble for Barça. Afflicted by growth hormone deficiency as a child, the boy left his native Argentina for Barcelona aged thirteen. Barça paid for him to have expensive medical treatment. Shy off the pitch, he shone very brightly when playing with the youth and reserve teams. In 2004, aged seventeen, he played his first match with the first team, and the rest is history.

June 6, 2015
Lionel Messi lifts his fourth Champions League trophy, also the fifth in Barça's history.

THE CLUB WITH TEN FOOTBALLER OF THE YEAR TROPHIES

Three Ballon d'Or winners
Johan Cruyff (left),
Hristo Stoichkov (centre),
and Ronaldinho (right).

With six players who have won a total of ten Footballer of the Year trophies between them, FC Barcelona are ahead of Real Madrid, AC Milan, and Juventus. The first was Luis Suárez, in 1960. The Dutch genius, Johan Cruyff, was rewarded twice (1973 and 1974). The Bulgarian striker, Hristo Stoichkov, received the Ballon d'Or in 1994, while the Brazilians, Rivaldo and Ronaldinho, were crowned respectively in 1999 and 2005. Finally, the Argentinian, Lionel Messi, made history by becoming the first player in the world to win the award four years in a row, in 2009, 2010, 2011, and 2012.

A UNIQUE STYLE

Since the early 1990s, Barcelona have been synonymous with beautiful football and efficiency. Five European championship titles and a characteristic style have made the Catalan club the most popular in Europe, with sixty million fans. At the origin of this style of play is one man, Johan Cruyff, who, after having enchanted Camp Nou as a forward and attacking midfielder between 1973 and 1978, turned his hand to coaching, and guided the first Blaugrana squad to victory in the 1992 Champions League. The Dutch master summed up his philosophy in a single phrase: "There is only one ball, so you need to have it." For over twenty years now, this has created a ballet in which Barça players drive their adversaries mad with their technical control, set-pieces, and short-ball play that's always moving forward. As Sir Alex Ferguson said: "It wasn't really Messi who was the problem. It was Iniesta and Xavi. They can keep the ball all night long."

Twelve titles between them
Messi, Xavi and Iniesta (from left to right) each won four Champions League titles while playing for Barça (2006, 2009, 2011, 2015).

Star players: Ricardo Zamora, Ladislao Kubala, Luis Suárez, Johan Cruyff, Diego Maradona, Gary Lineker, José Maria Bakero, Pep Guardiola, Ronald Koeman, Hristo Stoichkov, Romario, Michael Laudrup, Rivaldo, Ronaldo, Ronaldinho, Carles Puyol, Lionel Messi, Xavi Hernández, Samuel Eto'o, Andrés Iniesta, Neymar, Luis Suarez.

Honours: League: 1929, 1945, 1948, 1949, 1952, 1953, 1959, 1960, 1974, 1985, 1991, 1992, 1993, 1994,1998, 1999, 2005, 2006, 2009, 2010, 2011, 2013, 2015; National Cup: 1910, 1912, 1913, 1920, 1922, 1925, 1926, 1928, 1942, 1951, 1952, 1953, 1957, 1959, 1963, 1968, 1971, 1978, 1981, 1983, 1988, 1990, 1997, 1998, 2009, 2012, 2015; Champions League: 1992, 2006, 2009, 2011, 2015; European Cup Winners' Cup: 1979, 1982, 1989, 1997; UEFA Cup: 1958, 1960, 1966; FIFA Club World Cup: 2009, 2011.

"Thank you to the mothers who gave birth to these Atléti players." **Diego Simeone, Atlético coach, following the team's 3–1 win over Chelsea in the 2014 Champions League.**

ATLÉTICO MADRID
The Indians

Founded: **1903**
Stadium: **Vicente Calderon (Madrid)**

Founded by Basque students living in Madrid, the club initially took the name (Athletic) and the colours (blue and white) of Bilbao, before receiving red and white striped shirts that a former player and member of the board borrowed from Southampton for the two sister clubs. It was these stripes, a traditional pattern on Spanish mattresses, that earned Atlético—their official name since 1947—the nickname "Mattress Makers." They are the third most successful club in Spain when it comes to league titles, and they have a superb European record: one victory and two runners-up places in the Cup Winners' Cup, two victories in the UEFA Cup, and two runners-up places in the Champions League—the first in 1974 against Bayern, the second in 2014 against Real Madrid, after having knocked out FC Barcelona and Chelsea. Unlike their aristocratic rivals, Atlético long found their supporters in the capital's working-classes. The club is the third most supported in Spain, recording a record number of members in 2000—rising from 23,742 to 42,229, even though they were playing in the second division.

10 League Titles

10 National Cups

9 European Finals

The cost, in millions of euros, of Radamel Falcao's transfer from Atlético to AS Monaco in 2013.

60

Fernando Torres
His first club was Atlético, to which he returned in 2015 after playing in England and Italy.

The number of games played by Adelardo while he was wearing the red and white shirt (1959–1976).

511

172

The number of goals scored by Luis Aragonés while he was playing for Atlético Madrid (1964-1974).

May 12, 2010
Atlético Forlán and Simão win the Europa League.

COURAGE AND HEART

Atlético's supporters praise their team's commitment and their anthem speaks of "courage and heart" *(coraje y corazon)*, words that have become a true motto for the club. Away from Calderón stadium, you can hear this anthem around the Neptune fountain in the centre of Madrid, where the "*Colchoneros*" supporters gather on victory nights.

Yo me voy al Manzanares,
al estadio Vicente Calderon,
donde acuden a millares,
los que gustan del fútbol de emocion
Porque luchan como hermanos
Defendiendo sus colores
Con un juego noble y sano
Derrochando coraje y corazon
Atleti, Atleti, Atlético de Madrid

(I'm going to Manzanares
To the Vicente Calderón stadium
Where thousands gather
Those who love passionate football
For they strive like brothers
Defending their colours
Playing nobly and cleanly
With courage and heart
Atleti, Atleti, Atlético de Madrid)

May 18, 2014
The players of Atlético greet their supporters in Plaza de Neptuno, Madrid after the club win their tenth league title.

Star players: Adelardo, Luis Aragones, José Garate, Adrián Escudero, Joaquín Peiró, Rubén Cano, Javier Irureta, Luis Pereira, Hugo Sanchez, Paolo Futre, Bernd Schuster, Kiko, Diego Simeone, Fernando Torres, Diego Forlan, Radamel Falcao, Sergio Agüero, Juanfran, Raúl García, Koke, Antoine Griezmann.

Honours: League: 1940, 1941, 1950, 1951, 1966, 1970, 1973, 1977, 1996, 2014; National Cup: 1960, 1961, 1965, 1972, 1976, 1985, 1991, 1992, 1996, 2013; European Cup Winners' Cup: 1962; Europa League: 2010, 2012; Intercontinental Cup: 1974.

"Mestalla asks who we are, and we say who we are: we are the strength of Valencia, and no one will stop us. We travel the world, proud of your name. Valencia is our champion." **Chant of the Mestalla Stadium's north stand (Curva Nord).**

VALENCIA CF

The Bats

Founded: **1919** • Stadium: **Mestalla (Valence)**

Somewhat overshadowed by Real Madrid and FC Barcelona, Valencia have nonetheless made a splash on the European scene, winning four European titles, and having been runners-up on three occasions, including the Champions League in 2000 and 2001. The club's glory days came under the reign of several top coaches: Alfredo Di Stefano, Claudio Ranieri, and Rafael Benitez. Valencia are the fourth most popular club in Spain, with some 750 supporters clubs, and a following considered to be among the best in Spain, so much so that Zaragoza used the chants of Valencian supporters during their 2015 campaign.

6 League Titles

7 National Cups

4 European Titles

May 19, 2004
Valencia win the UEFA Cup after defeating Olympique de Marseille (2-0) in the final.

Star players: Eduardo Cubells, Antonio Puchades, Juan Carlos Quincones, Manuel Mestre, Ignacio Eizaguirre, Mario Kempes, Ricardo Arias, Luboslav Penev, Predrag Mijatovic, Fernando Gómez, Claudio López, Gaizka Mendieta, Amadeo Carboni, Santiago Cañizares, David Villa, David Silva.

Honours: League: 1942, 1944, 1947, 1971, 2002, 2004; National Cup: 1941, 1949, 1954, 1967, 1979, 1999, 2008; UEFA Cup Winners' Cup: 1980; UEFA Cup: 1962, 1963, 2004.

"Maintaining their uniqueness after the Bosman ruling was an act of heroic resistance for Athletic."
Luis Miguel Hinojal, journalist for *El País*.

ATHLETIC BILBAO
The Lions

Founded: **1898** • Stadium: **San Mamés (Bilbao)**

Athletic Bilbao are one of the only teams, along with Real Madrid and FC Barcelona, to have never been relegated since the start of La Liga. The club made a name for themselves by only hiring players with a strong link to the Basque Country, either by birth or through having chosen to train there—making it a first-rate training club. José Antonio Aguirre, president of the Basque government during the Spanish Civil War, played for the team. The last club to keep their shirt free from any advertising—until 2008—they make decisions in consultation with their 44,000 *socios*, such as that regarding the building of their new stadium, which opened in 2013. The fifth most supported club in Spain, Athletic were runners-up in two seasons of the Europa League (1977, 2012).

8 League Titles

23 National Cups

August 17, 2015
Athletic win the Spanish Super Cup by thrashing the great Barça (4-0; 1 1).

Star players: Rafael Moreno ("Pichichi"), Victorio Unamuno, Francisco Gárate, Agustín Gainza, Rafael Iriondo, Telmo Zarra, José Ángel Iribar, Ángel María Villar, Andoni Goikoetxea, Manuel Sarabia, Andoni Zubizarreta, Rafael Alkorta, Julen Guerrero, Joseba Etxeberría, Fernando Llorente, Ismael Urzaiz.

Honours: League: 1930, 1931, 1934, 1936, 1943, 1956, 1983, 1984; National Cup: 1902, 1903, 1904, 1910, 1911, 1914, 1915, 1916, 1921, 1923, 1930, 1931, 1932, 1933, 1943, 1944, 1945, 1950, 1955, 1956, 1958, 1969, 1973, 1984.

RC RECREATIVO DE HUELVA
The Doyen
Founded: **1889** • Stadium: **Nuevo Colombino (Huelva)**

Founded by two Scots, Recreativo de Huelva are the oldest Spanish football club still in existence, and had King Alfonso XIII as honorary president. In 1978, the club made their debut in the first division, racking up five seasons in the top flight. In 2003, they were runners-up in the Copa del Rey.

RCD ESPAÑOL
The Parakeets
Founded: **1900** • Stadium: **Cornellà-El Prat (Barcelona)**

The first club in Barcelona to open their doors to Spanish players, they have spent a total of eighty-one seasons in the first division. An old rival of FC Barcelona, the club holds the record for the largest margin of victory in the Catalan derby: 6–0 in 1951. They were twice runners-up in the Europa League.

MÁLAGA CF
The Anchovies
Founded: **1904** • Stadium: **La Rosaleda (Malaga)**

Promoted to the first division in 1949, Málaga have pulled off some coups, such as their 6–0 defeat of Real Madrid in 1953, or their 6–2 thrashing of the same Real in 1983. Major rivals of Granada, Málaga played in the quarter-finals of the 2013 Champions League.

REAL SPORTING DE GIJÓN
Sportinguistas
Founded: **1905** • Stadium: **El Molinón (Gijòn)**

The club's day of glory came in 1979, when they achieved second place in La Liga. In 1981 and 1982, they were runners-up in the Copa del Rey. Sporting de Gijón have been playing in their stadium—the oldest in Spanish professional football—for a hundred years. They are a regional rival of Real Oviedo.

SEVILLE FC
Sevillistas
Founded: **1905** • Stadium: **Ramón Sánchez Pizjuán (Seville)**

The oldest club in Seville, they are also the most successful, with one Liga title, five Copas del Rey, and a record four victories in the Europa League. Seville were Diego Maradona's last European club, playing there for one year, in 1993. They have the oldest group of "ultra" fans in Spain, the Biris Norte.

RC DEPORTIVO LA CORUÑA
The Turks
Founded: **1906** • Stadium: **Riazor (La Coruña)**

These rivals of Celta Vigo entered the first division in 1949, but it wasn't until 1993 that they hit the big time again, finishing runners-up in the league. With such players as Bebeto and Roy Makaay, they have rivalled both Real and Barca. Champions in 2000, they were also semi-finalists in the 2004 Champions League.

REAL BETIS BALOMPIÉ
Big Greens

Founded: **1907** • Stadium: **Benito Villamarín (Seville)**

The club, whose name, "Balompié," is the original Spanish word for "football," were champions in 1935, and winners of the Copa del Rey in 1977 and 2005. The sixth most popular club in Spain, far ahead of their rivals, Sevilla FC, they have over 500 supporters clubs.

LEVANTE UD
The Frogs

Founded: **1909** • Stadium: **Ciutat de València (Valencia)**

For most of its history, this club has lived in the shadows of CF Valencia. In 1981, Levante hit the headlines when they recruited Johan Cruyff, despite the club only playing in the second division. Having re-signed themselves to yo-yoing between the first and second divisions in the 2000s, they finally got to play in a European competition in 2012.

REAL SOCIEDAD DE FÙTBOL
White and Blue

Founded: **1909** • Stadium: **Anoeta (Saint Sebastián)**

Winner of the Copa del Rey in their first year of existence, Real Sociedad's heyday came in the years 1981 to 1983, when they won two league titles and semi-finals of the European Cup. Up until 1989, the club only signed Basque players.

REAL UNIÓN
The White and Black

Founded: **1915** • Stadium: **Gal (Irun)**

Real Unión are proud to have beaten Boca Juniors on the latter's 1925 Spanish tour, and they were a founding member of the Spanish Liga in 1928. Four-time winners of the Copa del Rey, they caused a stir in 2008, when they eliminated Real Madrid from the cup despite only being in the third division.

RCD MALLORCA
Els Barralets

Founded: **1916** • Stadium: **Iberostar (Palma)**

Originally called the "Alfonso XIII Football Club," in honour of the King of Spain, the club has spent twenty-seven seasons in the first division. Runner-up in the 1999 UEFA Cup Winners' Cup, Mallorca won the 2003 Copa del Rey, with striker Samuel Eto'o—who first made his mark on world football at the club.

CA OSASUNA
The Reds

Founded: **1920** • Stadium: **El Sadar (Pamplona)**

Osasuna (which means "health/strength/vigour" in Basque) are one of the ten most popular clubs in Spain, and one of four clubs in La Liga that are owned by their *socios*. They were runners-up in the 2005 Copa del Rey, and reached the semi-finals of the 2007 Europa League.

DEPORTIVO ALAVÉS
The Glorious

Founded: **1921** • Stadium: **Mendizorroza (Vitoria-Gasteiz)**

Deportivo Alavés, from the capital of the Basque Country, have played eleven seasons in the first division. In 2001, they contested an epic UEFA Cup final against Liverpool, losing 5–4. They more recently founded an educational charity in collaboration with Baskonia, the city's major basketball club.

RC CELTA DE VIGO
The Celtics

Founded: **1923** • Stadium: **Balaídos (Vigo)**

Formed from the merger of two of the town's clubs, Celta de Vigo are the ninth most popular club in Spain, ahead of their Galician rival, Deportivo. They have racked up fifty seasons in the top flight, in addition to being runners-up three times in the Copa del Rey, and three-time quarter-finalists in the UEFA Cup.

VILLAREAL CF
The Yellow Submarine

Founded: **1923** • Stadium: **El Madrigal (Villarreal)**

Promoted to the top flight in 1998, the club became a stronghold of Spanish football in the 2000s. The Argentinian attacking midfielder Riquelme helped them to the semi-finals of both the 2004 Europa League and the 2006 Champions League.

RAYO VALLECANO DE MADRID
The Red Sashes

Founded: **1924** • Stadium: **Campo de Fútbol de Vallecas (Madrid)**

This club started out playing in a workers' league. Following an agreement with Atlético Madrid in 1950, the club added a red diagonal stripe to their previously all-white strip—considered to be too close to that of Real Madrid. As the third club of Madrid, Rayo Vallecano have played fifteen seasons in the first division.

GRANADA CF
El Graná

Founded: **1931** • Stadium: **Los Cármenes (Granada)**

Granada have spent twenty-one seasons in the top flight, and were once runners-up in the Copa del Rey. In 1987, to celebrate the transfer of their brother Lalo to Granada, Diego and Hugo Maradona played a friendly match in the club's colours.

REAL ZARAGOZA
The Aragonese

Founded: **1932** • Stadium: **La Romareda (Zaragoza)**

Six-time winners of the Copa del Rey, Real Zaragoza have won two European trophies: the 1964 UEFA Cup and the Cup Winners' Cup—after knocking out Chelsea and Arsenal. They have played fifty-eight seasons in the first division. In 2014, they were the tenth most popular club in Spain.

SD EIBAR
The Gunners
Founded: **1940** • Stadium: **Ipurua (Eibar)**

The club wears the colours of FC Barcelona, having received the latter's shirts as a gift when they were starting out. Regulars of the second division, Xabi Alonso's former club was promoted to the first division in 2014, and now host Real Madrid and other Spanish giants in their 6,000-capacity stadium.

GETAFE CF
The Deep Blues
Founded: **1946** • Stadium: **Coliseum Alfonso Pérez (Madrid)**

In 2004, Getafe became the fourth club in the Madrid region to enter the first division. They even won their first match at home, against Real Madrid. Two Copa del Rey finals and participation in the Europa League have cemented their popularity.

ASSOCIAÇÃO ACADÉMICA DE COIMBRA Mágica Briosa
Founded: **1887** • Stadium: **Cidade de Coimbra (Coimbra)**

The oldest club in Portugal, Académica were established in a university town, and mainly fielded students until the 1970s. They have won the cup twice, and been runner-up three times. Their "ultra" group Mancha Negra was founded in 1985.

BOAVISTA FC
The Black Panthers
Founded: **1903** • Stadium: **Estádio do Bessa Século XXI (Porto)**

Founded by two young Englishmen, Boavista are one of only two clubs outside Portugal's big three to have won the league championship (in 2001). In 2003, they were knocked out of the semi-finals of the UEFA Cup, thus avoiding a showdown with their neighbours and friends, FC Porto, in the final.

CS MARÍTIMO
The Lions of Madeira
Founded: **1910** • Stadium: **Estádio dos Barreiros (Funchal)**

This working-class club from the capital of the island of Madeira won the league title in 1926—which at the time was played by direct elimination—and have twice been runners-up in the cup. Present in the first division for thirty years, their main local rivals are Nacional.

CD NACIONAL
The Nationalists
Founded: **1910** • Stadium: **Estádio de Madeira (Funchal)**

Founded the same year as their Madeiran rivals, Marítimo, the club started out in the first division in 1988. Since 2004, they have participated in five Europa Leagues. Cristiano Ronaldo was playing for the Nacional youth team when Sporting CP noticed him.

SC FARENSE
The Lions of Faro
Founded: **1910** • Stadium: **Estádio Algarve (Faro)**

The oldest club in the Algarve, Farense became the second subsidiary of Sporting Portugal in 1922. They have been a regular presence in the first division from the 1970s to the 2000s, and are encouraged by several supporters' clubs, including the South Side Boys, founded in 1994.

VITÓRIA FC
Victorians
Founded: **1910** • Stadium: **Estádio do Bonfim (Setúbal)**

This institution of Portuguese football was baptized with the cry "Victory shall be ours." The club played in the first division during the inaugural season in 1934, and then for a further sixty-six seasons to date. In Europe, Vitória have beaten several major names, including Liverpool and Inter Milan.

CF OS BELENENSES
Christ's Cross
Founded: **1919** • Stadium: **Estádio do Restelo (Lisbon)**

Belenenses were the first club to break the domination of the big three by winning the league title in 1946. They have many supporters throughout the country and in the former Portuguese colonies, including Amalia Rodrigues, the late famous Portuguese singer.

SPORTING CLUBE DE BRAGA
The Archbishops
Founded: **1921** • Stadium: **Municipal de Braga (Braga)**

Over the last ten years, Braga have finished towards the top of the league. In 2011, they contested the Europa League final against Porto. They are known for their 30,000-capacity stadium, which has the peculiarity of being built on a former quarry.

SC BEIRA MAR
Gold and Black
Founded: **1922** • Stadium: **Municipal de Aveiro (Aveiro)**

Founded in a fishing neighbourhood one New Year's Eve, the club's anthem includes the words: "With the sea as godfather, Beira-Mar has inherited his courage." Winners of the cup in 1999, they are known for having recruited the legendary Eusebio upon his return from America in 1976.

VITÓRIA SC
Conquistadores
Founded: **1922** • Stadium: **D. Alfonso Henriques (Guimarães)**

In the course of seventy-one seasons spent in the first division, Vitória have finished third on four occasions, and they won the cup in 2013. They have the highest average attendance in the league after the big three, and play the Minho derby against Braga.

"We want this club to be a big club, as big as the best in Europe." **José Alvalade, founder of Sporting CP.**

SPORTING CLUBE DE PORTUGAL

The Lions

Founded: **1906**
Stadium: **José Alvalade (Lisbon)**

Established to take part in a local festival, Sporting CP were officially founded four years later. They got their definitive colours by borrowing the horizontal stripes from their rugby team. The club dominated in the 1940s-1950s. On September 4, 1955, they played Partizan Belgrade at home for the very first European Cup match in history, and scored the very first goal in the competition. In 1964, SCP won the Cup Winners' Cup after beating Manchester United 4-1 in the quarter-finals, and then 5-0 in the return leg. The third biggest club in Portugal, they were runners-up in the 2005 UEFA Cup, and remain Benfica's great Lisboan rival. They are also known for the quality of their youth academy, which has produced such players as Luis Figo and Cristiano Ronaldo.

18
League Titles

16
National Cups

August 9, 2015
Sporting CP celebrate with the Portuguese Super Cup after their victory (1-0) against Benfica.

Star players: Jesús Correia, Manuel Vasques, Fernando Peyroteo, Jose Travassos, Albano, Alvaro Cardoso, Joao Martins, Juca, Joaquim Carvalho, Osvaldo da Silva, Hilario Conceiçao, Héctor Yazalde, Vitor Damas, Manuel Fernandes, Ricardo Sa Pinto, Pedro Barbosa, Luis Figo, Mario Jardel.

Honours: League: 1941, 1944, 1947, 1948, 1949, 1951, 1952, 1953, 1954, 1958, 1962, 1966, 1970, 1974, 1980, 1982, 2000, 2002; National Cup: 1941, 1945, 1946, 1948, 1954, 1963, 1971, 1973, 1974, 1978, 1982, 1995, 2002, 2007, 2008, 2015; European Cup Winners' Cup: 1964.

"Sporting have money. We have passion. For the moment, money trumps passion. In the future, passion will beat money."
Luís Carlos de Faria Leal, president of Benfica (1906–1907)

S.L. BENFICA The Eagles

Founded: **1904** • Stadium: **Estadio da Luz (Lisbon)**

The club had difficult beginnings, with their rivals, Sporting, attracting the best players. But a fresh start came for the Eagles when, in 1954, they moved to the Luz stadium—then the largest in Europe, and capable of holding 135,000 spectators. In 1961, they put paid to Real Madrid's reign as European Cup champions, and repeated the feat the following year, with the backing of Eusebio. Benfica would contest five European Cup finals up until 1990, as well as three Europa League finals—the last in 2013 and 2014. They are also the most successful multi-sports club in the world (22,000 trophies), as well as the most popular, with 235,000 *socios*—a world record—and fourteen million supporters across the globe.

34 League Titles

25 National Cups

2 European Cups

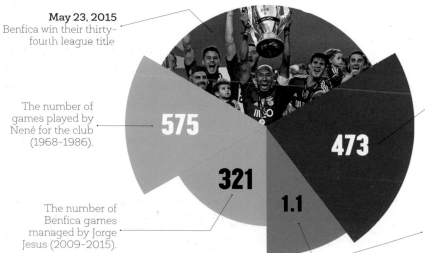

May 23, 2015
Benfica win their thirty-fourth league title

The number of goals scored by Eusébio for Benfica.

The number of games played by Nené for the club (1968-1986).

575

473

321

1.1

The average number of goals scored per match (440 in total) by Eusébio while he was playing for the Eagles.

The number of Benfica games managed by Jorge Jesus (2009-2015).

THE EAGLE OF VICTORY

The Benfica coat of arms comprises a red and white shield surmounted by an eagle. To bring the tableau to life, a white-headed eagle nicknamed Victory (Vitória) flies over the stadium before each home match, then lands on the club's coat of arms. According to legend, if the eagle manages two circuits of the stadium, then Benfica will win the match.

EUSEBIO, A PANTHER AT THE EAGLES

The arrival in Lisbon of Eusebio, the greatest player in the history of Benfica, was as amazing as his legendary dribbles. Aged fifteen, and rejected for health reasons by a Benfica subsidiary in the capital of Mozambique—where he lived—Eusebio signed with a subsidiary of Sporting. The latter then planned for him to move to Lisbon in late 1960. But a Benfica emissary put the now eighteen-year-old player on board a plane for Lisbon under a false name, and had him sign with the Eagles. A superbly talented striker, Eusebio quickly became known as the "Black Panther." Scorer of 473 goals in 440 matches for Benfica, the 1965 European Footballer of the Year has his own statue at the entrance to the Luz stadium.

Star players: Rogerio, Jose Aguas, Mario Coluna, Jose Augusto, Torres, Eusébio, Antonio Simoes, Manuel Bento, Nené, Diamantino Miranda, Chalana, Carlos Mozer, Rui Costa, Joao Pinto, Michel Preud'Homme, Nuno Gomes, Simao Sabrosa, Óscar Cardozo, Ángel Di María, Fábio Coentrão.

Honours: League: 1936, 1937, 1938, 1942, 1943, 1945, 1950, 1955, 1957, 1960, 1961, 1963, 1964, 1965, 1967, 1968, 1969, 1971, 1972, 1973, 1975, 1976, 1977, 1981, 1983, 1984, 1987, 1989, 1991, 1994, 2005, 2010, 2014, 2015; National Cup: 1940, 1943, 1944, 1949, 1951, 1952, 1953, 1955, 1957, 1959, 1962, 1964, 1969, 1970, 1972, 1980, 1981, 1983, 1985, 1986, 1987, 1993, 1996, 2004, 2014; European Cup: 1961, 1962.

"FC Porto succeed because they plan for the future, they invest in youngsters, buy the best in Portugal, and have an excellent scouting system. They give opportunities to young players." **Arsène Wenger.**

FC PORTO
The Dragons

Founded: **1893** • Stadium: **Estádio do Dragão (Porto)**

Founded by a wine merchant who had discovered football during a trip to England, Porto were slow to find success. Their national titles were even quite rare until the 1980s. Although they took longer than Benfica to hit their stride, the Dragons are now the benchmark for Portuguese football throughout Europe. Unlucky runners-up in the 1984 Cup Winners' Cup—when they lost to Juventus—they snatched a surprising victory in the 1987 competition, beating Bayern Munich. Indeed the victory remains famous for the goal scored by Rabah Madjer with a deft back-heel. In 2003 and 2004, an exceptional squad coached by José Mourinho took Porto back to the top, first winning the UEFA Cup, then eliminating Manchester United in the last sixteen the following season to go on and win the Champions League. Porto are the second most popular club in the country and with 120,000 members, they have the fifth highest number of *socios* in the world.

27 League Titles

16 National Cups

2 Champions League / European Cups

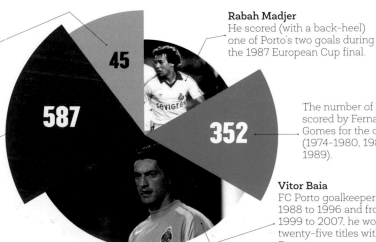

The cost, in millions of euros, of James Rodríguez's transfer from FC Porto to AS Monaco in 2013.

45

587

The number of games played by João Pinto while he was wearing the Porto shirt (1981-1997).

Rabah Madjer
He scored (with a back-heel) one of Porto's two goals during the 1987 European Cup final.

352
The number of goals scored by Fernando Gomes for the club (1974-1980, 1982-1989).

Vitor Baia
FC Porto goalkeeper from 1988 to 1996 and from 1999 to 2007, he won twenty-five titles with the Dragons.

A BLAZING ATMOSPHERE

Formed in 1986 to bring some life to the ageing Das Antas stadium, the Super Dragons supporters group (Super Dragões) now have over 10,000 members, making them the largest "ultra" group in Portugal, and one of the largest in the world. Represented by over 100 subsidiaries in various countries, the Super Dragons are the main group in the "Dragon" stadium—opened in 2004, and owned by the club.

Quando sobes ao relvado / Teras a curva sempre ao teu lado / 90 minutos sem parar de cantar / Nos vivemos para te amar / Porto! Porto!
(Climbing to the summit / You'll always have the terraces by your side / Singing for ninety minutes without stopping / We live only to love you / Porto! Porto!)

May 26, 2004
After a victory (3-0) in the final against Monaco, the Dragons become champions of Europe for the second time.

Star players: Pinga, Costuras, Correia Dias, António Araújo, Azumir, Oliveira, Fernando Gomes, Paulinho Santos, Frasco, Jorge Costa, Rabah Madjer, Paulo Futre, Domingos Paciência, Mario Jardel, Zé Carlos, Maniche, Ricardo Carvalho, Benni McCarthy, Deco, Vitor Baia, João Pinto, Hulk, Radamel Falcao.

Honours: League: 1935, 1939, 1940, 1956, 1959, 1978, 1979, 1985, 1986, 1988, 1990, 1992, 1993, 1995, 1996, 1997, 1998, 1999, 2003, 2004, 2006, 2007, 2008, 2009, 2011, 2012, 2013; National Cup: 1956, 1958, 1968, 1977, 1984, 1988, 1991, 1994, 1998, 2000, 2001, 2003, 2006, 2009, 2010, 2011; European Cup/Champions League: 1987, 2004; UEFA Cup 2003, 2011; Intercontinental Cup: 1987, 2004.

THE AMERICAS

"David Beckham brought recognition around the world. He helped elevate the quality of the league. Obviously he helped elevate the focus on the league. And the league's growth during that period of time was unprecedented." **Bruce Arena, LA Galaxy coach.**

LOS ANGELES GALAXY

Los Galácticos

Founded: **1995** • Stadium: **StubHub Center (Carson)**

LA Galaxy hold the record for victories in the MLS (five), and were the first American team to reach the final of the CONCACAF Champions League, in 1997, going on to win the title in 2000. In order to achieve such results, they have relied upon such dependable assets of the American squad as Alexi Lalas, Cobi Jones, and Landon Donovan, as well as young players who have come up through their academy. They have also brought in stars from Europe. From 2007 to 2012, David Beckham helped the club achieve worldwide fame. The Irish striker Robbie Keane has been their key player since 2011 and Steven Gerrard arrived in 2015. Ever since Chivas USA folded, Los Galácticos' rivals have been San José Earthquake.

5 League Titles

2 National Cups

Star players: Jorge Campos, Cobi Jones, Alexi Lalas, Eduardo Hurtado, Mauricio Cienfuegos, Kevin Hartman, Simon Elliott, Ezra Hendrickson, Carlos Ruiz, Herculez Gomez, Landon Donovan, David Beckham, Chris Klein, Edson Buddle, Robbie Keane.

Honours: League: 2002, 2005, 2011, 2012, 2014; National Cup: 2001, 2005; CONCACAF Champions League 2000.

December 7, 2014
Landon Donovan (left)
and Robbie Keane celebrate
Galaxy's fifth league title.

USA

"Some teams talk about home-field advantage—they sleep in their beds, and they don't have to travel. We truly have a home-field advantage. It's an atmosphere that gives us an edge." **Ben Olsen, DC United coach, talking about the fans.**

DC UNITED
Black-and-Red

Founded: **1995** Stadium: **RFK (Washington, DC)**

Heir to Johan Cruyff's Washington Diplomats, DC United were one of the founders of the MLS. Three-time champions during the league's first four seasons, they were the first American club to win the CONCACAF Champions League (1998), and the Copa Interamericana (1998)—beating Vasco da Gama. They owe their early successes to a mix of international stars—Marco Etcheverry, Jaime Moreno—and local ones—John Harkes, Eddie Pope, Jeff Agoos—all under the watch of head coach, Bruce Arena who managed the club from 1996 to 1998. In 2004, DC United launched the professional career of Freddy Adu—aged just fourteen. Their supporters—many of whom are of South American origin—are renowned for being the most loyal in the country. A film was even made about them, called *Muerte O Gloria*.

4 League Titles

3 National Cups

Freddy Adu
Adu started his professional career with DC United at the age of fourteen.

Star players: Marco Etcheverry, Christian Gomez, John Harkes, Jeff Agoos, Freddy Adu, Roy Lassiter, Ryan Nelsen, Eddie Pope, Hristo Stoichkov, Earnie Stewart, Jaime Moreno, Raul Diaz Arce, Bobby Convey, Ben Olsen, Marcelo Gallardo.

Honours: League: 1996, 1997, 1999, 2004; National Cup: 1996, 2008, 2013; CONCACAF Champions League: 1998.

"The Red Bull fans taunted their rivals with a banner reading: "The Big Apple, red to the core since day one," before applying the final insult with a multistory *tifo* depicting Dopey the dwarf in City blue, labelled "Man City Lite" and bearing the legend, "20 years late and a stadium short.""

espnfc.com, after the first derby between NY Red Bulls and NYC FC.

NEW YORK RED BULLS

Red Bulls

Founded: **1995**
Stadium: **Red Bull Arena (New York)**

The New York Red Bulls were called the New York Metrostars until they were bought by the Red Bull energy drink brand in 2006. The club followed in the footsteps of the New York Cosmos by hiring huge stars—such as Lothar Matthäus, as well as French world champions Youri Djorkaeff and Thierry Henry. The list of coaches is just as impressive, since it includes Carlos Queiroz, Carlos Alberto Parreira, Bora Milutinović, and Bruce Arena. On four occasions, the Red Bulls have finished top of the Eastern Conference, and twice they have been awarded the Supporters' Shield, which goes to the team with the most points at the end of the season. They were runners up in the MLS Cup in 2008. The Red Bulls have drawn on strong support since their first season when they played at Giants Stadium, with an average attendance of 24,000. Since 2010, they have their own 25,000-capacity stadium.

4 Eastern Conference Titles

2 Supporters' Shields

Thierry Henry
The second highest scorer in the history of the club.

Star players: Tim Howard, Tony Meola, Tab Ramos, Clint Mathis, Eddie Pope, Roberto Donadoni, Lothar Matthäus, Adolfo Valencia, Youri Djorkaeff, Amado Guevara, Juan Pablo Ángel, Thierry Henry, Rafael Márquez, Jan Gunnar Solli, Tim Ream, Bradley Wright-Phillips, Tim Cahill.

USA

"At North Carolina, I was in an empowering environment where it was OK to really care about the result, and demand of yourself and expect yourself to be better every single day." **Mia Hamm.**

NORTH CAROLINA TAR HEELS

Tar Heels

Founded: **1977** • Stadium: **Fetzer Field (Chapel Hill)**

Founded by female students, the University of North Carolina team have dominated the NCAA championship since the very beginning. They have won twenty-one titles in thirty-two seasons, and all with the same coach—Anson Dorrance, who fell in love with football as a child in Africa and Europe. The Tar Heels provided nine players, or former team players, to the national team squad that won the Women's World Cup in 1991. This included Mia Hamm, largely considered to be the best female player to have ever played the game, and an emblem of American women's football. The 2015 World Cup winning squad featured six North Carolina players. Their main rivals in the NCAA are Notre Dame, and these matches draw the biggest crowds.

21
League Titles

Star players: April Heinrichs, Shannon Higgins, Kristine Lilly, Mia Hamm, Tisha Venturini, Cindy Parlow, Cat Reddick, Yael Averbuch, Tobin Heath, Meghan Klingenberg, Lori Chalupny, Heather O'Reilly, Ashlyn Harris, Whitney Engen, Crystal Dunn, Casey Nogueira, Amber Brooks, Kealia Ohai.

Honours: League: 1982, 1983, 1984, 1986, 1987, 1988, 1989, 1990, 1991, 1992, 1993, 1994, 1996, 1997, 1999, 2000, 2003, 2006, 2008, 2009, 2012.

Mia Hamm
An icon of women's soccer who led the Tar Heels from 1989 to 1993.

SAN JOSÉ EARTHQUAKES
Quakes

Founded: **1994** • Stadium: **Avaya (San José)**

The first club to have joined the MLS (1996), San José have their roots in the team established in 1974, which had George Best in its ranks. Twice winners of the league, in 2001 and 2003, they contest the California Clasico with the LA Galaxy.

SPORTING KANSAS CITY
Wizards

Founded: **1995** • Stadium: **Sporting Park (Kansas City)**

Sporting Kansas City were called Kansas City Wizards for a long time, and were one of the founders of the MLS. Twice league champions, in 2000 and 2013, they reached the semi-finals of the CONCACAF Champions League in 2002. Since the 2014 season, they have drawn on average 20,000 spectators to matches.

NEW ENGLAND REVOLUTION
The Revs

Founded: **1995** • Stadium: **Gillette (Foxborough)**

New England Revolution, based in the Boston region, were one of the founding members of the MLS. Five-time winners of the final stage of the Eastern Conference, they have been runners-up in the MLS Cup on five occasions. Their main rivals are the New York Red Bulls and Chicago Fire.

SEATTLE SOUNDERS FC
Rave Green

Founded: **1995** • Stadium: **CenturyLink Field (Seattle)**

Heir to the eponymous club founded in 1994, they have played in the MLS since 2009, and won the regular season of the Western Conference in 2014. Very popular, they have the best average attendance in the league, and involve their supporters in club decisions.

COLORADO RAPIDS
The Rapids

Founded: **1996** • Stadium: **Dick's Sporting Goods Park (Commerce City)**

The Colorado Rapids, who are based in a Denver suburb, are founding members of the MLS. They have fielded Carlos Valderrama, contested the 1997 league final, and won the title (2010). As far as their supporters are concerned, the one match not to lose is the Rocky Mountain Cup—played against Real Salt Lake.

CHICAGO FIRE
Men in Red

Founded: **1997** • Stadium: **Toyota Park (Chicago)**

In 1998, the Chicago Fire made their debut by winning the league/cup double, fielding several players of Polish origin—Chicago has a strong Polish community. Their enthusiastic travelling public were 5,000 strong when the team played the Mexicans of Cuauhtémoc Blanco in 2007.

USA

REAL SALT LAKE
Royals

Founded: **2004** • Stadium: **Rio Tinto (Salt Lake City)**

A consistent force in the MLS since their first season in 2005, the club won the title in 2009, and reached the national final in 2013. In 2011, they were also runners-up in the CONCACAF Champions League. In 2014, the club's average attendance exceeded 20,000 spectators.

HOUSTON DYNAMO
Orange Crush

Founded: **2005** • Stadium: **BBVA Compass (Houston)**

In their early years, the club, one of whose owners is the former world boxing champion Oscar de La Hoya, won the Western Conference in 2006 and 2007, and reached the semi-finals of the 2007 CONCACAF Champions League. They contest the Texas derby with FC Dallas.

PORTLAND TIMBERS
The Timbers

Founded: **2009** • Stadium: **Providence Park (Portland)**

Promoted to the MLS in 2011, the club quickly found its feet, finishing first in the Western Conference in 2013. They are the historic rivals of the Seattle Sounders—located in the neighbouring state—and have both a reserve team and a youth academy.

NEW YORK COSMOS
The Cosmos

Founded: **2010** • Stadium: **Shuart (Hempstead)**

Heir to Pelé's club of the 1970s, they have played in the NASL—the North American second division—since 2013. Winners of the fall championship in 2013, and the spring championship in 2015, the Cosmos signed the Spanish players Marcos Senna and Raùl in 2013 and 2015 respectively.

ORLANDO CITY SC
Lions

Founded: **2010** • Stadium: **Citrus Bowl (Orlando)**

Sponsored by Disney World, Orlando City made their debut in the MLS in 2015, after having won two USL titles. The arrival of the Brazilian midfielder Kaka created a massive surge in attendance, with several matches played at full capacity, in front of 60,000 spectators.

NEW YORK CITY FC
NYC FC

Founded: **2013** • Stadium: **Yankee Stadium (New York)**

NYC FC were founded by the owners of Manchester City, and are the only MLS franchise in New York City. During their first season, in 2015, they went all out, signing the likes of David Villa, Frank Lampard, and Andrea Pirlo, setting themselves up as major rivals of the Red Bulls.

TORONTO CROATIA
The Croats

Founded: **1956** • Stadium: **Centennial Park (Toronto)**

Originally called the Toronto Metros, the club joined the old NASL in 1971, then merged with a club founded by the Croatian community, becoming the Toronto Metros-Croatia. In 1976, Toronto Metros became the first Canadian club to win the NASL championship, helped by the Portuguese legend Eusebio.

IMPACT MONTRÉAL
The Blue-White-Black

Founded: **1992** • Stadium: **Saputo (Montréal)**

With origins in the Italian community, the club joined Major League Soccer (MLS) in 2012 and signed Italian internationals Marco Di Vaio and Alessandro Nesta. The club own their own stadium and draw crowds of 60,000 for gala matches.

TORONTO FC
Reds

Founded: **2006** • Stadium: **BMO Field (Toronto)**

The main rival of Impact Montreal, Toronto FC were the first Canadian club to play in the MLS, attracting top players such as the German midfielder Torsten Frings and the English striker Jermaine Defoe. In 2012, the club reached the semi-finals of the CONCACAF Champions League.

VANCOUVER WHITECAPS
Caps

Founded: **2009** • Stadium: **BC Place (Vancouver)**

The current team inherited the name of a club that won the second-division North American Soccer League (NASL) in 1974, then joined the United Soccer League (USL), and finally the MLS in 2011. In 2014, Vancouver qualified for the MLS playoffs for the second time—a first for a Canadian team.

FC EDMONTON
The Rabbits

Founded: **2010** • Stadium: **Clarke (Edmonton)**

FC Edmonton play in the NASL and are considered among the major Canadian football clubs. They parti-cipate in the qualifying competition for professional Canadian teams to play in the CONCACAF Champions League.

OTTAWA FURY
The Fury

Founded: **2011** • Stadium: **TD Place (Ottawa)**

Ottawa Fury are the youngest of the professional Canadian teams. The club maintain a rivalry with FC Edmonton, who they play against in the NASL. Despite only being around for four years, Ottawa Fury already have three groups of "ultras": Bytown Boys, Stony Monday Riot, and Fury Ultras.

PEMBROKE HAMILTON CLUB
The Zebras

Founded: **1876** • Stadium: **PHC Field (Warwick)**

Formed from a yachting club, PHC are the most successful football club in Bermuda, with nine league championships and ten cups. They are proud to have their own stadium, as well as a charitable foundation that assists young athletes.

NORTH VILLAGE RAMS
The Rams

Founded: **1957** • Stadium: **Bernard Park (Pembroke)**

With eight league titles and ten cups, the Rams are heavyweights of Bermudian football. The club also have a strong community focus, and since 2014 have run a joint programme with Glasgow Rangers to develop young football talent on the island.

LYFORD CAY FC
Ospreys

Founded: **1989** • Stadium: **Roscow A. L. Davies Soccer Field (Nassau)**

Lyford Cay FC grew out of a school-based football programme, eventually becoming a major club in Bahamian football. In 2014, the club won the national league title, putting an end to a five-year domination of the league by Bears FC, and in 2015, they became the first Bahamian club to play in the CFU Club Championship.

BEARS FC
Bears

Founded: **1996** • Stadium: **Thomas Robinson (Nassau)**

Bears FC have links to the financial industry, and they dominated the league on New Providence, the archipelago's largest island. They then joined the Bahamas National Championship, winning the first five competitions. The Bears have also set up a youth training centre.

CHESHIRE HALL FC
Cheshire

Founded: **1999** • Stadium: **TCIFA National Academy (Providenciales)**

The club played and won their first season in the league in 2012, before repeating the performance in 2013. They have continued their excellent form finishing second and third in 2014 and 2015.

AFC ACADEMY
The Academy

Founded: **2007** • Stadium: **TCIFA National Academy (Providenciales)**

Rising stars of football in the archipelago, AFC Academy won their first league title in 2010, followed by two others in 2014 and 2015, thereby equalling the record for league victories held by PWC Athletic—who are now inactive.

BODDEN TOWN FC
The Dean of the Cayman

Founded: **1970** • Stadium: **Bodden Town (Bodden Town)**

Bodden Town were established in the former capital, and are the oldest Cayman Islands football club currently in operation. They did not win the league championship until 2013, an exploit they repeated in 2014. Bodden Town have also won three Cayman Islands cups (2001, 2009, 2013).

SCHOLARS INTERNATIONAL SC
The Greatest

Founded: **1977** • Stadium: **T. E. McField Sports Centre (George Town)**

With eight league titles and four cups, this club from West Bay is the most successful in the history of Cayman Islands football. At an international level, the club succeeded in reaching the second round of the 1991 CONCACAF Champions' Cup.

VIOLETTE ATHLETIC CLUB
The Old Tiger

Founded: **1918** • Stadium: **Sylvio Cator (Port-au-Prince)**

Six-time league champions, the club won their first title in 1939, and their most recent in 1999. In 1984, they became the second club in the country to win the CONCACAF Champions' Cup. Violette are based in the capital, and their great historic national rivals are Racing Club Haïtien.

RACING CLUB HAÏTIEN
The Old Lion

Founded: **1923** • Stadium: **Sylvio Cator (Port-au-Prince)**

Racing Club Haïtien from the capital Port-au-Prince hold the record for league championship victories, with eleven titles. In 1963 they were the first club in the country to win the CONCACAF Champions' Cup. They are the most popular club in Haiti and their motto is: "Racing and then the rest."

MOCA FC
The Cradle of Dominican Football

Founded: **1971** • Stadium: **Don Bosco Moca (Moca)**

Initially called Don Bosco, Moca have been the most successful club in the country over the past forty years, with eleven league titles. Despite a lack of infrastructure, this historic cradle of Dominican football now play in the new professional league—established in 2015.

BAUGER FC
The School

Founded: **1989** • Stadium: **Olímpico Félix Sánchez (Santo Domingo)**

Founded by an Argentinian, after whom they are named, the club was initially the country's first football school. Although they have never won a national title, Bauger are now one of the major teams to have joined the Dominican Republic's first professional league.

CRIOLLOS DE CAGUAS FC
Creoles

Founded: **1981** • Stadium: **Asociación Central de Balompié de Puerto Rico (Caguas)**

After having played in various local leagues, and contested a friendly match in England, the club joined the Puerto Rico Soccer League in 2014. The club asked their supporters to choose the colour of their new strip, and they won the title in their first season.

PUERTO RICO BAYAMÓN FC
The Cowboys

Founded: **1999** • Stadium: **Juan Ramón Loubriel (Bayamón)**

Champions in 2009, and twice winners of the CFU Champions League, Bayamón FC are famous for the atmosphere in their stadium, dubbed "the Mecca" of Puerto Rican football. In 2016, their professional squad will join the NASL, under the name Puerto Rico FC.

HELENITES SOCCER CLUB
The Blue-Whites

Founded: **1990** • Stadium: **Grove Place (Grove Place)**

This club, based on the island of Saint Croix, is flying high. After losing three finals in the St. Thomas League between 1998 and 2005, they have won the national championship four times, becoming the most successful club in the archipelago.

POSITIVE VIBES SCC
The Greens

Founded: **2000** • Stadium: **Lionel Roberts (Saint Thomas)**

The club hold a record seven victories in the regional league, and have won the national championship twice, in 2005 and 2008, and been runners-up on seven other occasions. Their main local rivals are New Vibes.

SUGAR BOYS
The Blues

Founded: **2003** • Stadium: **Virgin Gorda Recreation Ground (Virgin Gorda)**

This club from Virgin Gorda has regularly finished near the top of the league in recent years. In 2012 and 2013, the club won the pre-season Wendol Williams Cup, beating Islanders FC.

ISLANDERS FC
The Islanders

Founded: **2009** • Stadium: **A. O. Shirley Recreation Ground (Tortola)**

In an archipelago where each main island has long organized its own league championship, Islanders FC have largely dominated ever since the best teams started playing against each other. They have won the major league five times between 2010 and 2014.

FC VILLA CLARA
The Centre Express

Founded: **1978** • Stadium: **Augusto Cesar Sandino (Santa Clara)**

Villa Clara have played regularly at the highest level, winning the national league championship thirteen times between 1980 and 2013. Despite making few appearances in international competitions, they are the most prominent club in Cuban football.

FC PINAR DEL RIO
Pinar

Founded: **1978** • Stadium: **La Bombonera (Pinar del Río)**

Pinar have one of the best records in Cuban football, with seven league titles. The club have twice been runner-up in the CONCACAF Champions' Cup (1989, 1990), and are the island's top team as regards performances in international competitions.

SANTOS FC
The Brazilians

Founded: **1964** • Stadium: **Bell Chung (Kingston)**

Named in honour of the famous Brazilian club, the team dominated Jamaican football until 1980, winning five league titles. Their day of glory came in 1975 when they beat Pelé's New York Cosmos in the National Stadium.

TIVOLI GARDENS FC
T.G.

Founded: **1970** • Stadium: **Edward Seaga Sports Complex (Kingston)**

Co-holder of the record for most league titles, with five won between 1983 and 2011, Tivoli Gardens are very popular—they drew close to 124,000 spectators for one cup match in 1987. Their current president is a former prime minister, and they have a strong youth academy.

HARBOUR VIEW
Stars of the East

Founded: **1974** • Stadium: **Harbour View (Kingston)**

Harbour View are one of the most successful clubs in Jamaican football, both nationally—they have won four league titles—and internationally—they won the CFU Club Championship in 2004 (against Tivoli Gardens) and 2007 (against Joe Public).

PORTMORE UNITED FC
Courage and Strength

Founded: **1983** • Stadium: **Ferdi Neita Sports Complex (Portmore)**

This club from Portmore, in the Kingston suburbs, is a stronghold of Jamaican football, with five league titles (won between 1993 and 2012), four national cups, and one CFU Club Championship victory (2005).

SUNSET HOMES ATTACKERS
Attackers

Founded: **1978** • Stadium: **Ronald Webster Park (The Valley)**

Four-time league champions (1999, 2008, 2009, 2013), Sunset Homes Attackers FC are sponsored and coached by a local architecture entrepreneur, and are always prepared to travel to play teams from Saint Martin, Saint-Barthélemy, or Guadeloupe.

ROARING LIONS FC
The Lions

Founded: **1982** • Stadium: **Ronald Webster Park (The Valley)**

Roaring Lions FC are the club of the Stoney Ground neighbourhood of Anguilla's capital, The Valley. They hold the most number of titles in Anguilla's first division, having won the league five times, most recently in 2009–2010. They have yet to compete in the CONCACAF.

NEWTOWN UNITED
The Reds

Founded: **1962** • Stadium: **Newtown Playing Field (Basseterre)**

Established in the capital of the archipelago, under the name Zip Side Football Team, the club has become the most successful in the country by winning the league sixteen times since 1981. In 1994, they managed to reach the third round of the CONCACAF Champions League.

GARDEN HOTSPURS FC
Spurs

Founded: **1962** • Stadium: **Warner Park (Basseterre)**

Four-time winners of the league championship, Garden Hotspurs are known for their initiatives to develop football among young people and women, as well as for their social action—they organize cancer-awareness campaigns, and activities to celebrate Fathers' Day.

ROYAL MONTSERRAT POLICE FORCE FC Police

Founded: **around 1970** • Stadium: **Blakes Estate (Brades)**

Winner of four out of the five seasons of the league contested between 1995 and 2004, this club (founded by the local police) is the best in a country that is ranked last in the world by FIFA. Montserrat's national team played "the other final," in 2002, a friendly match against Bhutan, ranked second to last, which became a documentary film.

IDEAL SC
Ideal

Founded: **1975** Stadium: **Brades Park (Brades)**

The only club to have succeeded in breaking Royal Montserrat Police Force's domination of the local league championship, in 2004. Ideal are also the sole club to date to have played in an international competition: the 2004 CFU Champions Cup.

ANGUILLA

SAINT KITTS AND NEVIS

MONTSERRAT

BASSA SPORTS CLUB
All Saints

Founded: **1985** • Stadium: **All Saints (Antigua)**

Bassa Sports Club's five victories in the Antigua and Barbuda first division have made them the most successful football club in the country. They have also won the Antigua and Barbuda FA Cup twice, and reached the quarter-finals of the Caribbean Football Union Club Championship twice.

SAP FC
Spirited

Founded: **1986** • Stadium: **Antigua Recreation Ground (St John's)**

With "Spirit, Attitude, Performance" as their motto, the club claims that they could not fail to scale the heights of local football. SAP FC won their first league title in 1989, repeating this success twice since (2006, 2009). They have also achieved some impressive results at Caribbean level.

HARLEM UNITED FC
United Lions

Founded: **1970** • Stadium: **Windsor Park (Roseau)**

Harlem United are the most successful club on the island. They were crowned champions in 1970—their first season—and have won a total of twenty league titles to date. Based in the Newtown neighbourhood of Roseau, the capital, the club have the advantage of watching every league match as they all take place at their Windsor Park Stadium.

BATH ESTATE FC
Bath Estate

Founded: **1982** • Stadium: **Windsor Park (Roseau)**

Based in Roseau, just like their rivals Harlem United, the club won their first championship title in 2008. This success was followed by three more titles (2009, 2010, 2013). Bath Estate also won the 2013 Creole Cup, beating the league champions of Guadeloupe, Martinique, and Saint Lucia.

NORTHERN UNITED ALL STARS
All Stars

Founded: **1985** • Stadium: **Mindoo Phillip Park (Castries)**

Based in Gros Islet, to the north of the island, Northern United are one of the best-performing clubs in the league championship these last few years, having won the title in 2005 and 2010. At an international level, they reached the semi-finals of the 2005 CFU Club Championship.

BIG PLAYERS FC
Big Ballers

Founded: **1993** • Stadium: **Marchand Grounds (Castries)**

Big Players are the descendants of a club originally founded by schoolchildren, and they are inspired by the Brazilian style of play. Their motto, "Play to win," is fitting as they lifted the league trophy in 2013. They have become one of the most popular teams in the capital.

WEYMOUTH WALES
Purples

Founded: **1960** • Stadium: **Barbados National Stadium (Bridgetown)**

The club dominated Barbadian football from the 1960s to the 1980s, winning a number of league and cup titles under several different names. In 2012, they tasted success again, by taking their sixteenth national championship. Weymouth Wales have also won the Barbados FA Cup eight times.

BARBADOS DEFENCE FORCE
Barbados Army

Founded: **1979** • Stadium: **Barbados National Stadium (Bridgetown)**

The club is the Barbados Defence Forces' sporting arm, providing opportunities for top Barbadian athletes. The "Barbados Army" play in the Barbados Premier Division, and have won the league title five times, most recently in 2013, 2014, and 2015, making them currently the island's top team.

CARIB HURRICANE FC
Hurricanes

Founded: **1983** • Stadium: **Aloton George Park (Victoria)**

Based in Victoria, a little town on Grenada's west coast, Carib Hurricane FC were one of the founders of the Grenadan league in 1983. They have since won the league championship three times (2003, 2006, 2008) and have never been relegated to the second division.

QUEEN'S PARK RANGERS SC
Rangers

Founded: **1983** • Stadium: **National Cricket (St. George's)**

This club, from Grenada's capital, St. George's, pay homage in name and colours to their English namesake. They entered the first division in 1986, where they have remained ever since. Three-time national league champions, the club have also played in the Caribbean Cup.

DEFENCE FORCE FC
Teleron Boys

Founded: **1972** • Stadium: **Hasely Crawford (Port of Spain)**

Composed largely of players from the army, Defense Force have been a dominating presence in national football ever since it was founded, winning the league twenty-two times. They played in four CONCACAF Champions League finals between 1978 and 1988, and have won the title twice.

W CONNECTION FC
Savonetta Boys

Founded: **1999** • Stadium: **Manny Ramjohn (San Fernando)**

Founded to play in the new professional league, W Connection have won five titles, becoming Defence Force's biggest rivals. They have been victorious in the CFU Champions League on five occasions, and in 2007 they beat the Mexicans of Chivas in the CONCACAF Champions League.

BARBADOS

GRENADA

TRINIDAD AND TOBAGO

SV DAKOTA
The Bees
Founded: **1947** • Stadium: **Guillermo P. Trinidad (Oranjestad)**

The club that represents the Aruban capital, Oranjestad, has won a record fifteen titles in the Aruban league, even though their last victory dates from 1995. Dakota also made it into the second round of the CONCACAF Champions' Cup in 1983. Their great local rivals are Racing Club Aruba.

SV ESTRELLA
Orange Star
Founded: **1957** • Stadium: **Guillermo P. Trinidad (Oranjestad)**

Estrella are based in Santa Cruz and are one of only two Aruban clubs to have won the Netherlands Antilles Championship. They have also won the Aruban League twelve times, and reached the final round of the CONCACAF Champions' Cup once.

JONG COLOMBIA
The Sharks of Boka Sami
Founded: **1951** • Stadium: **Ergilio Hato (Willemstad)**

Jong Colombia, from the town of Sint Michiel, have made their mark on Curaçaoan football by reaching the finals of the CONCACAF Champions' Cup (1967, 1979) and winning the national league title twelve times. Jong Colombia's historic rival is Jong Holland, based in the capital.

CS DEPORTIVO BARBER
The Barbers
Founded: **1953** • Stadium: **Ergilio Hato (Willemstad)**

CSD Barber have dominated Curaçaoan football since 2002. They have won the Netherlands Antilles Championships eight times, and the Curaçao League five times. In 2005, the club reached the semi-finals of the CFU Club Championship, their best international performance.

JUVENTUS FC
Suga boyz
Founded: **1978** • Stadium: **Orange Walk People's Stadium (Orange Walk)**

Five-time champions of Belize between 1996 and 2005, Juventus FC are also the only club in the country to have played in the CONCACAF Cup Winners' Cup. Since 2006, Juventus's local rivals have been San Felipe Barcelona.

BELMOPAN BANDITS FSC
Bandits
Founded: **1986** • Stadium: **Isidro Beaton (Belmopan)**

Since 2012, this club from Belize's capital have been tremendously successful, winning four of the six seasons of the new league. Two of their players became famous for having refused bribes while playing for the national team.

"América doesn't go to Guadalajara to win—that's routine. We come here to change the long-distance dialling code. As all my friends know, to call Guadalajara, you need to dial 2-0, 2-0, 2-0."
Fernando Marcos, América coach, 1957–1961.

CF AMÉRICA

The Eagles

Founded: **1916** · Stadium: **Estadio Azteca (Mexico City)**

With a first team composed entirely of Mexicans, at a time when other clubs were signing international players, América had to await until 1959, and a buyout by a TV magnate, to reach the big time. By paying dearly to purchase foreign stars, the club took on the role of the "bad guy" against their great rivals, Chivas, and became the most successful club not only in the country but also the CONCACAF zone. This has made them both the most popular and divisive team in Mexico. The great club from the capital possesses another asset: their 115,000-capacity Azteca stadium—the stage for two World Cup finals.

12
League Titles

5
National Cups

Christian Benitez
The striker played for América from 2011 to 2013, and finished each season as the top scorer in the Mexican league.

Star players: José Alves Zague, Carlos Reinoso, Enrique Borja, Alfredo Tena, Cristóbal Ortega, Luis Roberto Alves Zague, Juan Antonio Luna, Cuauhtémoc Blanco, Raúl Rodrigo Lara, Pável Pardo, Duilio Davino, Germán Villa, Guillermo Ochoa, Salvador Cabañas.

Honours: League: 1966, 1971, 1976, 1984, 1985, 1985, 1988, 1989, 2002-I, 2005-II, 2013-II, 2014-II; National Cup: 1954, 1955, 1964, 1965, 1974; CONCACAF Champions League: 1977, 1987, 1990, 1992, 2001, 2006, 2015.

"They get goose bumps just at the sight of us." **Advertisement by "Chivas" Guadalajara before a clàsico against América, April 2009.**

CD GUADALAJARA
The Goats

Founded: **1906**
Stadium: **Omnilife (Guadalajara)**

Founded by a Belgian, and initially composed of construction workers, Guadalajara —who have called themselves "Chivas" (goats) since 1949—are one of the most popular clubs in Mexico, and across the Mexican diaspora. This is partly because of their successful record, but also because, unlike their rivals, América, they have always refused to sign foreign players, and consequently have produced some of the greatest Mexican footballers. They have never been relegated since the establishment of the league in 1943, and in 2010 they spoiled their wonderful fans—the most inventive in the country, through their *tifos* deployed in the stands—by reaching the final of the Copa Libertadores against Internacional Porto Alegre.

11 League Titles

2 National Cups

July 31, 2014
Aldo de Nigris' Chivas plays Bayern Munich as the German club tours the Americas.

Star players: Jaime Gómez, Salvador Reyes, Javier De la Torre, Guillermo Sepúlveda, Juan Jasso, Isidoro Díaz, Crescencio Gutiérrez, Javier Valdivia, Raúl Gómez, Ricardo Pérez, Eduardo de la Torre, Ramón Ramírez, Héctor Alberto Coyote, Ramon Morales, Carlos Vela, Javier Hernàndez, Omar Bravo.

Honours: League: 1957 1959 1960 1961 1962 1964 1965 1970 1987, 1997-II, 2006-I; National Cup: 1963, 1970; CONCACAF Champions League: 1962.

CF PACHUCA
The Gophers

Founded: **1895** • Stadium: **Hidalgo (Pachuca)**

Five-time champions of Mexico, Pachuca have an unusual string of international successes. Four-time winners of the CONCACAF Champions League, they are also the only club in the world to have won a trophy—the 2006 Copa Sudamericana—outside of their confederation.

CLUB DEPORTIVO ALBINEGROS DE ORIZABA The White and Blacks

Founded: **1898** • Stadium: **Socum (Orizaba)**

Orizaba were born in the jute fields where the country's first football matches were played. Mexico's first amateur champion, in 1902, they were promoted to the professional premier league, but now play in the second division.

CLUB ATLAS
The Foxes

Founded: **1916** • Stadium: **Jalisco (Guadalajara)**

Founded by Mexican students returned from England, earning them the nickname of "bourgeois club," they play the Clásico Tapatío against Chivas. They are one of the teams most regularly present since the start of the league, and won the title in 1951.

CF ATLANTE
The Iron Colts

Founded: **1916** • Stadium: **Andres Quintana Roo (Cancun)**

Founded by workers from a poor neighbourhood of Mexico City, the club became "the people's team" in the 1930s. Since then, they have changed city five times, eventually basing themselves in Cancún in 2007. Five times league champions, they have won the CONCACAF Champions League twice.

DEPORTIVO TOLUCA FC
The Sausagers

Founded: **1917** • Stadium: **Nemesio Diez (Toluca)**

Founded on a farm, Toluca joined the first division in 1953, and have never looked back. With ten league titles, they are the most successful club in the country after América and Chivas. Their supporters celebrate each goal by taking off their tops.

CLUB NECAXA
The Electricians

Founded: **1923** • Stadium: **Victoria (Aguascalientes)**

Founded by an electric company in Mexico City, Necaxa were the first in the country to host a foreign club, in 1927. Three times champions in the 1990s, and winners of the 1999 CONCACAF Champions League, they moved to Aguascalientes in 2003.

CA MONARCAS MORELIA
The Monarchy
Founded: **1924** • Stadium: **Morelos (Morelia)**

Professional since 1950 and present in the first division for over thirty years, the club reached their peak in 2000, when they took a national title, then followed up with a quarter-final in the Copa Libertadores (2002) and two finals of the CONCACAF Champions League (2002, 2003).

CRUZ AZUL FC
The Machine
Founded: **1927** • Stadium: **Azul (Mexico City)**

Founded by a cement manufacturer, the club moved to Mexico City in 1971 at the height of its heyday, when they won most of their eight national titles. Winner of six CONCACAF Champions Leagues, they are the most popular club in the country after América and Chivas.

CLUB LEÓN FC
The Green Bellies
Founded: **1943** • Stadium: **León (León)**

Established to enable the state of Guanajuato to have a representative in the new league, Léon are one of the most successful clubs in Mexico, with seven titles won between 1948 and 2014. They were also runners-up in the 1993 CONCACAF Champions League.

TIBURONES ROJOS DE VERACRUZ   The Red Sharks
Founded: **1943** • Stadium: **Luis "Pirata" Fuente (Veracruz)**

Created from the merger of two local clubs, Veracruz took part in the first season of the professional league in 1943, and soon won two league titles (1946, 1950). A great rival of Puebla, they tasted glory again in 2004 with the arrival of Cuauhtémoc Blanco.

PUEBLA FC
The Sweet Potatoers
Founded: **1944** • Stadium: **Cuauhtémoc (Puebla)**

Founded by textile factories, Puebla were runners-up in the league and won the Mexican Cup in their first season. Twice winners of the league championship (1983, 1990), they also won the 1991 CONCACAF Champions League.

CF MONTERREY
The Striped Ones
Founded: **1945** • Stadium: **BBVA Bancomer (Monterrey)**

The club's early days were marred by a bus accident that caused the death of several players, but they would go on to win four national titles and the CONCACAF Champions League three times. Very popular, this great rival of Tigres regularly draw 20,000 spectators to their training sessions.

QUERÉTARO FC
The White Roosters

Founded: **1950** • Stadium: **Corregidora (Santiago de Querétaro)**

When they were established in 1950, the club won a local tournament to earn their ticket to the second division, but they would not play in the first division until 1990. In 2015, they achieved some fame after placing second and for having signed the Brazilian Ballon d'Or winner Ronaldinho.

CLUB UNIVERSIDAD NACIONAL
The Cougars

Founded: **1954** • Stadium: **Olimpico Universitario (Mexico City)**

The Cougars are one of the four most popular clubs in the country, and the second most popular in Mexico City. Champions seven times, they have won the CONCACAF Champions League on three occasions. Hugo Sanchez, the greatest Mexican player ever, started out at the club.

TIGRES UANL
The Tigers

Founded: **1960** • Stadium: **Universitario (Monterrey)**

Three-time league champions, Tigres rely on a fan base considered to be one of the best in Mexico. Not only do the supporters fill the Universitario stadium—nicknamed "The Volcano"—for each match, but they have been known to fill even their rival's stadiums.

CLUB SANTOS LAGUNA
The Warriors

Founded: **1983** • Stadium: **Corona (Torreón)**

Santos Laguna have never been relegated since entering the first division in 1989. The club have won the league title five times, were twice runners-up in the CONCACAF Champions League, and sum up their rapid rise to success with a slogan: "Little time, lots of history." They have links to Glasgow Celtic.

CHIAPAS FÚTBOL CLUB
Jaguars

Founded: **2002** • Stadium: **Victor Manuel Reyna (Tuxtla Gutiérrez)**

Founded in 2002 in Chiapas—which didn't have a first division team—the club qualified for the Copa Libertadores two years in a row (2010, 2011), reaching the quarter-finals on both occasions. They moved to Querétaro in 2013.

CLUB TIJUANA
The Aztec Dogs

Founded: **2007** • Stadium: **Caliente (Tijuana)**

Established recently to serve as a subsidiary of Querétaro, the club became the first in Tijuana to enter the first division, in 2011, then to win the league championship, in 2012. The club had to enlarge their 22,000-capacity stadium, which even after expansion is always full.

GUATEMALA

CLUB XELAJÚ MC
Los Superchivos
Founded: **1928** • Stadium: **Mario Camposeco (Quetzaltenango)**

Having been promoted to the first division in 1957, Xelajú have won five national titles, making them the most successful club outside the capital. They have also drawn the most spectators over the last few years, and play an eagerly awaited regional derby against Deportivo Suchitepéquez.

CLUB SOCIAL Y DEPORTIVO MUNICIPAL Darling of the Fans
Founded: **1936** • Stadium: **Manuel Felipe Carrera (Guatemala City)**

Founded by municipal workers of Guatemala City, Municipal have won twenty-nine titles since the start of the league—from which they have never been relegated. Winner of the 1974 CONCACAF Champions' Cup, they are very popular and describe themselves as "the greatest club in the country."

AURORA FC
The Soldiers
Founded: **1945** • Stadium: **Estadio del Ejército (Guatemala City)**

Owned by the army, Aurora were founded by a lieutenant colonel nicknamed Zorro. They are the country's third most successful club, with eight national titles—the last of which was won in 1993. They were runners-up in the 1994 CONCACAF Cup Winners' Cup. In 2005, they were relegated to the second division.

COMUNICACIONES FÚTBOL CLUB The Creams
Founded: **1949** • Stadium: **Cementos Progreso (Guatemala City)**

Founded with the support of the Minister of Communications, the club has won one CONCACAF Champions' Cup (1978), and has been runner-up twice, in addition to wining thirty national titles.

EL SALVADOR

CD ÁGUILA
The Feathered
Founded: **1926** • Stadium: **Juan Francisco Barraza (San Miguel)**

The second most successful Salvadorian club, with fifteen league championships and one CONCACAF Champions' Cup (1976), Águila are the most popular in the country, even in the capital. They contest the Superclasico nacional against their great rivals, Deportivo FAS.

CLUB DEPORTIVO FAS
Tigers
Founded: **1947** • Stadium: **Óscar Alberto Quiteño (Santa Ana)**

This club from Santa Ana, the cradle of Salvadorian football, has the best record in the national competition, having won seventeen league titles. They also won the 1979 CONCACAF Champions' Cup. The club's stadium is named after a former goalkeeper, who died of a heart attack during a match in 1963.

ALIANZA FC
The White Elephants
Founded: **1958** • Stadium: **Cuscatlán (San Salvador)**

Founded by the workers of a local brewing company, Alianza bought the licence of another club for a nominal sum, so allowing them to enter the first division. Ten-time champions, they play the San Salvador derby against Atlético Marte, and the "clasico of hate" against Deportivo FAS.

AD ISIDRO METAPÁN
The Jaguars
Founded: **2000** • Stadium: **Jorge Calero Suárez (San Salvador)**

Born of the merger between Metapán FC and CD Isidro Menéndez, the club entered the first division in 2000. In 2007, they hit the big time, winning the first of their ten national titles (opening and closing season tournaments combined).

CLUB DEPORTIVO OLIMPIA
The Most Popular
Founded: **1912** • Stadium: **Tiburcio Carias Andino (Tegucigalpa)**

The most popular club in the country, Olimpia dominate Honduran football, having won twenty-nine league titles and two CONCACAF Champions' Cups. In 2001, they were the first Central American club to qualify for the FIFA Club World Cup, which was sadly eventually cancelled.

CLUB DEPORTIVO MARATHÓN
The Green Monster
Founded: **1925** • Stadium: **Yankel Rosenthal (San Pedro Sula)**

Marathón, from the country's second-largest city, have won eight league championship titles. The first Honduran club to own their own stadium, they maintain a fierce rivalry with Olimpia in the Clásico Nacional.

CLUB DEPORTIVO MOTAGUA
Blue Cyclone
Founded: **1928** • Stadium: **Tiburcio Carías Andino (Tegucigalpa)**

Motagua were founded by a religious institution. With thirteen league titles, they are the second most successful club in the country after their local rival, Olimpia, against whom they play the Superclásico up to six times a year. This very popular club has been in the first division for eighty-four years.

REAL CD ESPAÑA
The Coalmen
Founded: **1929** • Stadium: **Francisco Morazan (San Pedro Sula)**

The most successful club outside the capital, with eleven league championships, Real España's great local rivals are Club Deportivo Marathón. In 1977, King Juan Carlos of Spain agreed to be the honorary chairman of the club, which meant they became the only true "Real" ('Royal') in the Americas.

DIRIANGÉN FC
Caciques
Founded: **1917** • Stadium: **Cacique Diriangén (Diriamba)**

The club's first training pitch was a field used to dry coffee. They have played in the first division ever since the league was established in 1931. Diriangén hold the record for Nicaraguan league championships—twenty-six titles.

REAL ESTELÍ FC
The Train of the North
Founded: **1961** • Stadium: **Independencia (Estelí)**

Winner of thirteen titles since 1991, Real Estelí have become the number one rivals of Diriangén, against whom they play a hotly-contested derby. They have also forged an international reputation by playing in the group stage of the CONCACAF Champions League on several occasions.

REAL MADRIZ FC
Los Merenguese
Founded: **vers 1980** • Stadium: **Solidaridad "Augusto Cesar Mendoza" (Somoto)**

After many years spent yo-yoing between the second and third divisions, the club—who represent the Madriz department in the west of the country—entered the top-flight in 1999. They contest the Duelo de Realezas against Real Estelí. Their local rivals are Deportivo Ocotal.

DEPORTIVO WALTER FERRETTI
Los Sandinistas
Founded: **1987** • Stadium: **Olímpico del IND Managua (Managua)**

Based in the capital, and affiliated with the police, the club take their name from the Sandinista guerrilla movement of the 1980s. Five-time winners of the opening tournament in recent years, they are one of the few clubs to rival Diriangén and Estelí.

CS CARTAGINÉS
The Foggers
Founded: **1906** • Stadium: **José Rafael Fello Meza Ivankovich (Cartago)**

CS Cartaginés are the oldest Costa Rican football club. They were founded by a Canadian, and won three national titles during the first years of their existence (1923, 1936, 1940). Later, Cartaginés shone in international competitions, winning the 1994 CONCACAF Champions' Cup.

LD ALAJUELENSE
La Liga
Founded: **1919** • Stadium: **Alejandro Morera Soto (Alajuela)**

Alajuelense were one of the original seven teams who formed the national league, and they are the most popular club in the country, having won twenty-nine national titles and two CONCACAF Champions' Cups. The club maintain a firm rivalry with Deportivo Saprissa, against whom they play the Clásico of Costa Rica.

CS HEREDIANO
The Team
Founded: **1921** • Stadium: **Eladio Rosabal Cordero (Heredia)**

Founded the same year that the league was created, Herediano won the first national league championship, going on to win twenty-three more to date, making them the third most successful team in the country. They play a fiercely contested derby against Cartaginés, the oldest team in Costa Rican football.

DEPORTIVO SAPRISSA
The Monster
Founded: **1935** • Stadium: **Ricardo Saprissa (Tibás)**

Deportivo Saprissa were the first club in South America to undertake a world tour, in 1959. They are also the most successful Costa Rican club, with thirty-one league championships and three CONCACAF Champions' Cups. Many of Saprissa's players come from their own youth academy.

CD PLAZA AMADOR
The Lions
Founded: **1955** • Stadium: **Maracaná (Panama City)**

CD Plaza Amador have been a continual presence in the league from the very start, winning the first season in 1988, and securing another four titles. Their great rivals are Tauro FC, but they also maintain a major rivalry with their neighbours, Chorillo FC, against whom they play the *Clásico del Pueblo*.

SAN FRANCISCO FC
The Monks
Founded: **1971** • Stadium: **Agustín "Muquita" Sánchez (La Chorrera)**

Present since the start of the championship (in 1988) under the name La Previsora, the club have been champions nine times, making them the third most successful in the country. They are the most popular club in their region, where they play the *Gran Derby de La Chorrera* against CA Independiente.

TAURO FC
The Bulls of Pedregal
Founded: **1984** • Stadium: **Rommel Fernández (Panama City)**

Founded in a tannery owned by an Italian, the club took the black-and-white-striped design of Juventus. They are one of the three clubs present since the establishment of the championship, and have won twelve titles. Very popular, they call themselves "THE" club of Panama.

CD ÁRABE UNIDO
The Blue Express
Founded: **1994** • Stadium: **Armando Dely Valdés (Colón)**

Initially called Club Atlético Argentina, they are the country's most successful club, with thirteen league titles. Julio Dely Valdes, the most famous Panamanian player, who played with Nacional Montevideo, Paris Saint-Germain, Cagliari, and Malaga, ended his career here.

"With my Santos team, we halted war. People are so crazy about football, they love football so much, that they stopped fighting to watch Santos play in Africa." **Pelé.**

SANTOS FC
The Fish

Founded: **1912** • Stadium: **Urbano Caldeira (Santos)**

Based in a town around forty miles from São Paulo, Santos FC's great historic rivals are Corinthians. Although the latter had the upper hand during certain periods, under Pelé, Santos became invincible. Between December 29, 1956 and March 13, 1968, "The Fish" remained unbeaten by their adversary during the twenty-two matches they contested. Corinthians suffered the highly personal wrath of Pelé, who had had little love for them ever since one of their defenders nearly injured him before the 1958 World Cup. All in all, "The King" scored fifty goals against Corinthians in forty-eight matches.

8 League Titles

1 National Cup

3 Copa Libertadores

2 Intercontinental Cups

November 19, 1969
Pelé scores his thousandth goal during a game against Vasco de Gama.

The number of games played by Pepe (1954-1969), the second top scorer in the history of the club (405 goals).

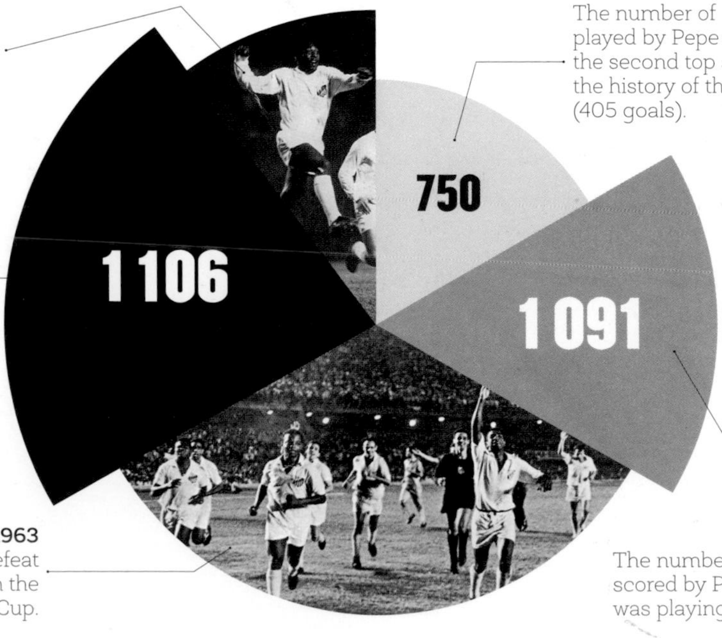

The number of games played by Pelé while he was wearing the black and white shirt.

750

1 106

1 091

October 16, 1963
Santos defeat AC Milan and win the Intercontinental Cup.

The number of goals scored by Pelé while he was playing for Santos.

KING PELÉ'S CLUB

What would Santos be without Pelé? Less than they are, that's for sure. The club that boasts of having "scored the most goals in world football" would not have achieved such a feat without their son and national treasure who scored 1,091 goals in the club's black and white strip between 1956 and 1974. One man who predicted this success was Waldemar de Brito, who brought a fifteen-year-old Pelé to Santos, and prophesized: "this boy will be the greatest footballer in the world."

PLAYMAKERS MAKING THE DIFFERENCE

Santos, who were nearly named Concórdia, África, or Brasil Atlético, had won two Paulista local league titles before 1956, when a man arrived who would change their destiny: Pelé. Thanks to their new king, the club won two Intercontinental Cups. Although Pelé's departure in 1974 was hard to get over, the club managed to regain their former glory, first by winning the national league championship in 2002, under the leadership of Robinho, then by winning the Copa Libertadores in 2011, thanks to a new generation of players led by Neymar.

Robinho
One of the major players in the revival of Santos—Brazilian champions in 2002 and 2004.

THE CLUB THAT STOPS WARS

In 1969, at the pinnacle of their international glory, Santos and Pelé made a tour of Africa. On two occasions, their presence calmed internal conflicts in the countries they visited. First was the Democratic Republic of Congo, where the team had to be protected by the armed forces in order that they might reach neighbouring Congo-Brazzaville. Next was Nigeria, where the Biafran War was raging. On each occasion, the passion for Santos was so great that the fighting ceased, recommencing only after the famous visitors left. This earned Santos a new moniker: "The Club That Stops Wars."

BRAZIL

September 26, 2012
Neymar celebrates winning a final title with Santos (the Recopa Sudamericana), before leaving for Barcelona.

Star players: Pelé, Gilmar, Edu, Carlos Alberto, César Sampaio, Renato, Robinho, Alex, Neymar.

Honours: League: 1961, 1962, 1963, 1964, 1965, 1968, 2002, 2004; National Cup: 2010; Copa Libertadores: 1962, 1963, 2011; Intercontinental Cup: 1962, 1963.

"Being a Corinthian is like diving / Into the ocean of drowning illusion / No matter destiny's design / At each match, it's the heart that plays."
Gilberto Gil, Corinthian.

CORINTHIANS
The People's Club

Founded: **1910** · Stadium: **Arena Corinthians (São Paulo)**

Founded by workers wishing to challenge the hitherto dominant clubs of the upper classes, Corinthians would become the greatest club in São Paulo, both by their results (twenty-seven Paulista titles) and their popularity—they count thirty-five million supporters. The club have remained at the highest world level of the sport, thanks to such exceptional players as Gilmar in the 1950s, Rivelino in the 1970s, and Sócrates in the 1980s. Corinthians are the only club, along with FC Barcelona, to have won the FIFA Club World Cup twice.

5 League Titles

3 National Cups

1 Copa Libertadores

2 FIFA Club World Cups

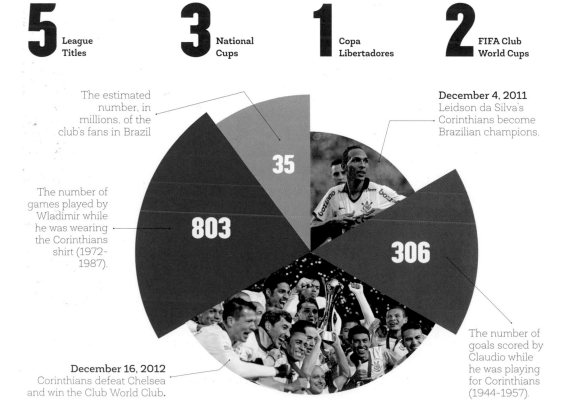

The estimated number, in millions, of the club's fans in Brazil — **35**

December 4, 2011
Leidson da Silva's Corinthians become Brazilian champions.

The number of games played by Wladimir while he was wearing the Corinthians shirt (1972-1987). — **803**

306 — The number of goals scored by Claudio while he was playing for Corinthians (1944-1957).

December 16, 2012
Corinthians defeat Chelsea and win the Club World Club.

SÓCRATES, A CERTAIN PHILOSOPHY OF FOOTBALL

In 1981, inspired by the club's historic charter, which states that "Corinthians will be the team of the people, by the people, and for the people," and as a counterpoint to the military dictatorship, Sócrates and other players instituted "Corinthian Democracy." Henceforth, everything, from contracts to rules of conduct inside or outside the club, was voted on by the players. And apparently it worked: Corinthians were state champions in 1982 and 1983.

Star players: Clàudio, Gilmar, Dida, Zé Maria, Rivelino, Wladimir, Socrates, Ronaldo, Carlos Tevez.

Honours: League: 1990, 1998, 1999, 2005, 2011; Copa Libertadores: 2012; FIFA Club World Cups: 2000, 2012.

"It was everything I had wanted; to end by scoring in my favourite manner: a free kick." **Zico, regarding his departure from Flamengo to play in Japan, in 1990.**

FLAMENGO

Scarlet-Black

Founded: **1895** · Stadium: **Maracana (Rio de Janeiro)**

Flamengo may be the most popular club in Rio, if not Brazil, but this is not just due to their honours. One of only four Brazilian clubs never to have been relegated to the second division, Flamengo achieved worldwide glory by winning the Intercontinental Cup in 1981, with Zico, often called the "White Pelé," playing a key part. But it is through their closeness to the people, in opposition to their great rival, the "bourgeois" Fluminense, that Flamengo have become an untouchable institution. The "Scarlet-Black Nation," as their supporters are known, number nearly forty million across Brazil.

6 League Titles

3 National Cups

1 Copa Libertadores

1 Intercontinental Cup

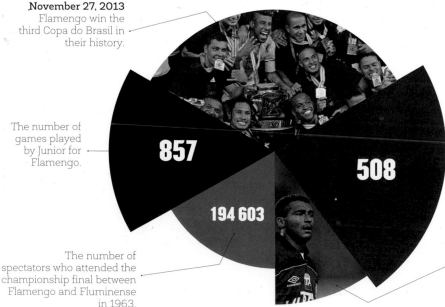

November 27, 2013
Flamengo win the third Copa do Brasil in their history.

The number of goals scored by Zico while he was wearing the Flamengo shirt.

The number of games played by Junior for Flamengo.

857

508

194 603

The number of spectators who attended the championship final between Flamengo and Fluminense in 1963.

Romario
The 1994 world champion scored over one thousand goals in his career including fifty-five goals for his country.

BRAZIL

FIO MARAVILHA

In 1972, the singer Jorge Ben wrote a song that would be heard around the world. It was inspired by a goal scored against Benfica by a popular Flamengo player of the 1960s–1970s, the forward João Batista de Sales, better known as "Fio Maravilha." The nickname stuck after his mother was heard yelling "filho" (son) from the stands. The song was such a hit that soon the Flamengo supporters made a habit of singing it at the Maracanã.

Foi um gol de anjo um verdadeiro gol de placa / Que a magnética agradecida assim cantava
Foi um gol de anjo um verdadeiro gol de placa / Que a magnetica agradecida assim cantava
Fio maravilha, / Nós gostamos de você / Fio maravilha, / Faz mais um pra gente ver.

"It was an angelic goal, a real home run / So magnetic that the grateful sang / It was an angelic goal, a real home run / So magnetic that we sang so gratefully / Wonder son / We like you / Wonder son / Score one more goal for us to see."

Star players: Leonidas da Silva, Mario Zagallo, Zico, Junior, Leandro, Marinho, Carlos Mozer, Leonardo, Aldair, Bebeto, Romario, Julio Cesar, Adriano.

Honours: League: 1980, 1982, 1983, 1987, 1992, 2009; Copa Libertadores: 1981; Intercontinental Cups: 1981.

"Sao Paulo FC changed my life."
Rogerio Ceni, goalkeeper for the club since 1990.

SÃO PAULO FC
Sovereign

Founded: **1930**
Stadium: **Morumbi (São Paulo)**

São Paulo FC have a special place in Brazilian football. They became the most popular club of the country's economic capital in the 1940s after displaying the state colours one match day, despite such an act being banned by the central government. Holder of three world titles, São Paulo FC are in a class of their own in Brazilian football, and the battles they have fought against Corinthians (in the Clássico Majestoso) and against Palmeiras (in the Choque-Rei) are among the greatest derbies in the world.

6 League Titles

3 Copa Libertadores

3 FIFA Club World Cups

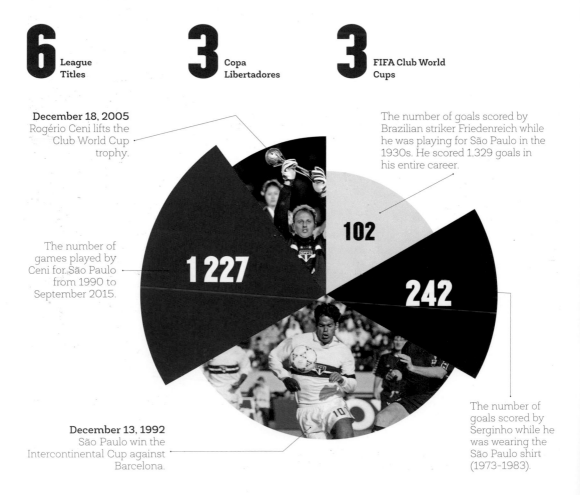

December 18, 2005
Rogério Ceni lifts the Club World Cup trophy.

The number of goals scored by Brazilian striker Friedenreich while he was playing for São Paulo in the 1930s. He scored 1,329 goals in his entire career.

102

The number of games played by Ceni for São Paulo from 1990 to September 2015.

1 227

242

The number of goals scored by Serginho while he was wearing the São Paulo shirt (1973-1983).

December 13, 1992
São Paulo win the Intercontinental Cup against Barcelona.

CENI, GOALKEEPER AND GOAL SCORER

What do attacking midfielder Rai and goalkeeper Rogério Ceni have in common? They each scored almost the same number of goals for São Paulo FC. With a total of 129 goals by mid-2015, Ceni holds the world record for most number of goals scored by a goalie. Since 1997, he has been the official free-kick and penalty taker for São Paulo. His best performance was in 2005, when he scored twenty-one goals. And he is as skilled with his hands as he is with his feet: in 1997, he beat the Brazilian clean-sheet record by racking up a total of 990 minutes without letting in a single goal. Ceni is a true idol of Morumbi stadium, having played over 1,200 matches for São Paulo FC.

March 27, 2011
Rogério Ceni scores from a free kick, his hundredth for São Paulo, during a game against Corinthians.

Star players: Leonidas da Silva, Rogério Ceni, Cafu, Oscar, Diego Lugano, Leonardo, Toninho Cerezo, Kaka, Rai, Careca, Luis Fabiano.

Honours: League: 1977, 1986, 1991, 2006, 2007, 2008; Copa Libertadores: 1992, 1993, 2005; Intercontinental Cup/FIFA Club World Cup: 1992, 1993, 2005.

"This was a normal result. What is abnormal is when Flamengo wins the clássico." **Eurico Miranda, president of Vasco de Gama, after his club's 5–1 victory over Flamengo in 2001.**

VASCO DA GAMA
Giant of the Hill

Founded: **1898**
Stadium: **São Januário (Rio de Janeiro)**

In 1923, Vasco da Gama became the first Brazilian club to win a championship with black and mixed-race players. The club was initially ostracized by the other Rio teams, before being reintegrated into the league. In 1933, when Brazilian football was starting to become professional, the club's position smoothed the way for black and mixed-race players to join all the other clubs. Supported by twenty million fans—making them the second most supported club in Rio, particularly among the working classes—Vasco da Gama maintain a special rivalry with Flamengo, against whom they play the "derby of millions" (of fans) in the legendary Maracanã stadium.

4 League Titles

1 National Cup

Star players: Leonidas Da Silva, Vavà, Tostao, Romario, Roberto Dinamite, Bebeto, Juninho Pernambucano.

Honours: League: 1974, 1989, 1997, 2000; Copa Libertadores: 1998.

May 21, 2007
Romario scores his thousandth goal (off a penalty kick), becoming a true legend.

BRAZIL

"Fighting is the pursuit of power / Pushing my club /
To be champions forever . . ." **Club chant.**

CRUZEIRO EC
The Foxes

Founded: **1921** · Stadium: **Mineirão (Belo Horizonte)**

Cruzeiro EC, the great rivals of Atlético Mineiro, were founded by the Italian community and soon became the most popular club in Minas Gerais. In 1966, they won their first national championship by thrashing Pelé's Santos 6–2 in the final. Following the doldrums of the 1950s, a new style of management saw Cruzeiro introduce a training programme that launched such great players as Ronaldo, who scored forty-four goals in forty-seven games for Cruzeiro between 1993 and 1994. So large is their fan base that Cruzeiro's supporters are dubbed "Blue China." In 2014, the average attendance at Cruzeiro matches was around 30,000, following the completion of the renovated Mineirão stadium.

4 League Titles

4 National Cups

Ronaldo
In 1993, at the age of sixteen, Ronaldo scored his first goals as a professional and Cruzeiro player.

Star players: Tostão, Dirceu Lopes, Zé Carlos, Palhinha, Joãozinho, Ronaldo, Juan Pablo Sorín.

Honours: League: 1966, 2003, 2013, 2014; National Cup: 1993, 1996, 2000, 2003; Copa Libertadores: 1976, 1997.

ESPORTE CLUBE VITÓRIA
Barra's Lion
Founded: **1899** • Stadium: **Manoel Barradas (Salvador)**

Vitória were the first club to be founded solely by Brazilians. Their fortunes improved significantly when they had their own stadium built in 1986, allowing them to beat their local rival EC Bahia in most meetings over the following two decades.

AA PONTE PRETA
She-Monkey
Founded: **1900** • Stadium: **Moisés Lucarelli (Campinas)**

The oldest club in Brazilian football, and the first in South America to sign a black player, Ponte Preta were recognized in 2006 by FIFA as "the first racial democracy in the history of football." In 1974, Pelé played his last match for Santos against Ponte Preta.

FLUMINENSE
Warriors
Founded: **1902** • Stadium: **Maracanã (Rio de Janeiro)**

Fluminense were Rio's first club dedicated 100 percent to football. In 1911, nine of their players left to join Flamengo, beginning the Fla-Flu rivalry that continues to this day. The club has been national champion four times, most recently in 2012.

EC 14 DE JULHO
Frontier Lion
Founded: **1902** • Stadium: **João Martins (Santana do Livramento)**

Founded in a town on the border with Uruguay, the club became the first Brazilian side to win an international tournament (in 1909). It was given its nickname by the players of Penarol Montevideo. The supporters' group, Comando Rubro-Negro, encourages the team in Spanish.

GRÊMIO FOOT-BALL PORTO ALEGRENSE The Tricolores
Founded: **1903** • Stadium: **Arena do Grêmio (Porto Alegre)**

Founded by Italian and German immigrants, Grêmio are the great rivals of Internacional, against whom they have played over forty derbies since their 10–0 victory in 1909. Grêmio were Ronaldinho's first club, and have won two Copas Libertadores (1983, 1995).

AMERICA FC
Devil
Founded: **1904** • Stadium: **Giulite Coutihno (Rio de Janeiro)**

This club, who have produced fifty-seven Brazilian internationals, were Cariocan league champions seven times, and achieved their best national result in 1986 (third place). America have contested more than 300 clàssicos against Flamengo, making them one of Rio's great historic teams.

BOTAFOGO
The Lone Star

Founded: **1904** • Stadium: **Engenhão (Rio de Janeiro)**

Botafogo dominated Cariocan football from the 1930s to the 1960s, a time when the fabulous Garrincha was playing for them, earning the club the nickname "The Glorious One," as well as a commemorative day in the State of Rio's official calendar. Their biggest rivals are Flamengo.

SC RECIFE
The Lion of the North

Founded: **1905** • Stadium: **Ilha do Retiro (Recife)**

Founded by a Brazilian, who discovered football when he was studying at Cambridge (England), the most popular club in Northeast Brazil turned down the opportunity to sign Pelé on a loan deal in 1957, considering him to be too young. Recife were Champions of Brazil in 1987, and have won forty state titles.

ATLÉTICO MINEIRO
Rooster

Founded: **1908** • Stadium: **Independência (Belo Horizonte)**

Founded by students, Atlético Mineiro soon became the leading club of the Minas Gerais region. Champions of Brazil in 1971, the club won the Copa Libertadores in 2013 with Ronaldinho. Their popularity draws more spectators to the stadium than their rivals, Cruzeiro.

CORITIBA FC
White Thigh

Founded: **1909** • Stadium: **Couto Pereira (Curitiba)**

Coritiba Foot Ball Club was founded by German immigrants, hence their nickname of "White Thigh." In 1985, they became the first league champions to come from the state of Paraná, much to the dismay of their rivals, Atlético Paranaense.

SC INTERNACIONAL
The Steamroller

Founded: **1909** • Stadium: **Beira-Rio (Porto Alegre)**

Internacional had their first successes in the 1970s, with three league titles, before winning the Copa Libertadores in 2006 and 2010, and the FIFA Club World Cup in 2006. Above all, they lead Grêmio on wins in their GreNal *clàssico*.

GUARANI FC
The Indian

Founded: **1911** • Stadium: **Brinco de Ouro (Campinas)**

Ponte Preta's rivals had their hour of glory in 1978, when they won the league championship with a team led by Careca, who scored forty-six goals during his time with the club. Guarani's main supporters' clubs, such as Guerreiros da Tribo, have been active for nearly forty years.

PALMEIRAS
Big Green
Founded: **1914** • Stadium: **Allianz Parque (São Paulo)**

Founded by Italian immigrants, the quality of Palmeiras's playing earned them the nickname "The Academy of Football" in the 1960s–1970s, when they dominated Brazilian football. Having returned to the top, Palmeiras—the greatest Paulista rivals of Corinthians—won the Copa Libertadores in 1999.

ABC FUTEBOL CLUBE
The Elephant of Frasqueirão
Founded: **1915** • Stadium: **Frasqueirão (Natal)**

ABC have won the state championship of Rio Grande do Norte fifty-two times, and are the Brazilian club with the most titles. ABC have played more than 510 derbies against their great regional rival, América de Natal. The club boast eleven million fans.

PORTUGUESA
The Fabulous
Founded: **1920** • Stadium: **Canindé (São Paulo)**

Created from the merging of five clubs representing the Portuguese community, Portuguesa had their greatest success in the 1950s, with Djalma Santos. In 1975, the club decided against buying Maradona, then aged fifteen. Portuguesa are now considered to be the fifth most popular Paulista club.

ATLÉTICO PARANAENSE
Hurricane
Founded: **1924** • Stadium: **Arena da Baixada (Curitiba)**

From the very start, the club has contested the Atletiba derby against Coritiba, the region's other major club, becoming a little more popular than their rivals. The team became league champions in 2001, with the striker Adriano leading the attack. In 2005, they reached the final of the Copa Libertadores.

ESPORTE CLUBE BAHIA
Steel Squad
Founded: **1931** • Stadium: **Fonte Nova (Salvador)**

The club have no real rivals in the State of Bahia, which explains their forty-five state championships, as well as their popularity. Bahia have also won two national league titles (1959, 1988) and were the first Brazilian team to play in the Copa Libertadores. They enjoy a local rivalry with Vitòria.

GOIAS EC
Big Emerald Green
Founded: **1943** • Stadium: **Serra Dourada (Goiânia)**

Long criticized for their poor history of results, Goias have played in more league championships than any other club from the State of Goias, and are the only one to have played in a Copa Libertadores. They are now the most popular club in the region.

ROBINHOOD
No Fight, No Crown

Founded: **1945** • Stadium: **André Kamperveen (Paramaribo)**

Established to allow the capital's poor to play football, Robinhood have become an institution, with twenty-three league titles (a record), and four second places in the CONCACAF Champions League. They beat Ajax from Amsterdam in a friendly match in the 1980s.

STICHTING INTER MOENGOTAPOE The Red and Blacks

Founded: **1922** • Stadium: **Ronnie Brunswijkstadion (Moengo)**

Inter Moengotapoe have become the new dominant force in Surinamese football, winning seven league titles between 2007 and 2015. At an international level, the club reached the semi-finals of the 2004 CFU Club Championship. They play the Moengo derby against Notch.

SANTOS FC GEORGETOWN
SFC

Founded: **1964** • Stadium: **Providence (Georgetown)**

Named in honour of the famous Brazilian club, whose black and white colours they wear, Santos Georgetown were the first champions of the Guyanese league, in 1990. With a total of three titles, they are the second most successful club behind Alpha United.

ALPHA UNITED FC
The Hammer

Founded: **2000** • Stadium: **Providence (Georgetown)**

Founded in the early 2000s, the club soon became the most prominent in the history of Guyanese football. Winner of five league titles from 2009, they were the first Guyanese team to represent the country in the CONCACAF Champions League.

CARACAS FC
The Reds from Ávila

Founded: **1967** • Stadium: **Estadio Olímpico de la UCV (Caracas)**

Established merely for leisure play, the club remained amateur until another club, Yamaha FC, were turning professional in 1984 and asked to merge with them in order to use their name. From this merger grew the biggest club in the country and they have subsequently won the league title eleven times.

DEPORTIVO TÁCHIRA FC
The Gold and Blacks

Founded: **1974** • Stadium: **Polideportivo de Pueblo Nuevo (San Cristóbal)**

Eight-time champions, Deportivo Táchira contest the Venezuelan Clasico against Caracas FC. They are also known for their pioneering supporters, Avalancha Sur. Deportivo Táchira's stadium Estadio Polideportivo de Pueblo Nuevo is also referred to as the "holy temple of football."

"Living without Liga is not living." **www.ldu.com.ec**

LDU QUITO
The Meringues

Founded: **1930** • Stadium: **Liga Deportiva Universitaria (Quito)**

Liga Deportiva Universitaria de Quito call themselves "the greatest club in Ecuador." At national level they vie for popularity with Barcelona SC, but they are the best supported club in Quito. They are the only Ecuadorean club to have won the Copa Libertadores, and one of only three teams to have won three different CONMEBOL trophies. ⚽ 2008–2010, the golden age: In 2008, Liga won the Copa Libertadores after beating the Argentinian clubs Estudiantes and San Lorenzo, the Mexican club América and the Brazilian club Fluminense. A FIFA Club World Cup finalist, Liga won the Recopa Sudamericana and the Copa Sudamericana in 2009, and then the Recopa Sudamericana again in 2010. In 2011, the club took the top spot in the brand new CONMEBOL ranking.

July 2, 2008
LDU Quito win the Copa Libertadores, beating Fluminense's Brazilians.

10 League Titles

1 Copa Libertadores

Star players: Neicer Reasco, Paul Ambrossi, Patricio Urrutia, Luis Bolaños, Joffre Guerrón, Alex Escobar, José Francisco Cevallos, Claudio Bieler.

Honours: League: 1969, 1974, 1975, 1990, 1998, 1999, 2003, 2005, 2007, 2010; Copa Libertadores: 2008; Copa Sudamericana: 2009.

CC DEPORTIVO OLMEDO
The Cyclone of the Andes

Founded: **1919** • Stadium: **Olímpico de Riobamba (Riobamba)**

Olmedo are the oldest of Ecuador's professional clubs. In 2000, they became the first club outside Quito and Guayaquil to win the national league championship. The club contest the *Clásico Interandino* against rivals SD Macarà.

BARCELONA SC
The Bullfighters

Founded: **1925** • Stadium: **Monumental Banco Pichincha (Guayaquil)**

Founded by Catalonian immigrants, the club took the colours of FC Barcelona before switching to those of Catalonia. They are the most popular club in the country, the only ones never to have been relegated, and they hold the record for league titles: fourteen since 1951.

EMELEC
The Light Bulb

Founded: **1929** • Stadium: **George Capwell (Guayaquil)**

Founded by employees of the Electric Company of Ecuador, Emelec are among the most successful clubs in Ecuadorean football, and the only ones to have won at least one title in each decade since the creation of the league. They contest the *Clásico del Astillero* against Barcelona SC.

DEPORTIVO QUITO
The Academy

Founded: **1940** • Stadium: **Olímpico Atahualpa (Quito)**

Quito were founded under the name SD Argentina, before being renamed in 1955 and entering the professional league championship. Five-time national champions, and the first Ecuadorean club to play in the Copa Libertadores, they are known for the technical quality of their football.

CD EL NACIONAL
Pure Creoles

Founded: **1964** • Stadium: **stade olympique Atahualpa (Quito)**

Long administered by the army, El Nacional have won thirteen league titles, making them the second most successful Ecuadorean club after Barcelona. They are also the most popular club in Quito after the LDU, and have the peculiarity of only signing Ecuadoreans.

MUSHUC RUNA SC
The Cooperative

Founded: **2003** • Stadium: **Bellavista (Ambato)**

Mushuc Runa are sponsored by a microcredit cooperative who support the representation of indigenous peoples and Ecuadorean farmers on the country's football scene at the highest level. The club have had professional status since 2008, and they entered the first division in 2014.

CLUB ALIANZA LIMA
Aliancistas
Founded: **1901** • Stadium: **Alejandro Villanueva (Lima)**

Twenty-two time league champions, the most popular club in the country was graced with the presence of Teofilo Cubillas, the greatest Peruvian player in history. In 1987, the entire squad and coaching staff were killed in an air crash, forcing the club to finish that season with their youth team, and players loaned from elsewhere.

CLUB UNIVERSITARIO DE DEPORTES   The U
Founded: **1924** • Stadium: **Monumental (Lima)**

Twenty-six time league champions (a record), Universitario were runners-up in the 1972 Copa Libertadores. Supported by the upper echelons of society, they count Nobel Prize winning author Vargas Llosa among their *socios*. The tragic death of one of their more colourful supporters, Misterio, inspired a TV series.

SPORTING CRISTAL
The Brewers
Founded: **1955** • Stadium: **Alberto Gallardo (Lima)**

Founded by a couple of brewers, Sporting Cristal have been in the first division for sixty years. Champions since their first season in the top flight, they were nicknamed "the club born a champion." In all, they have won seventeen league titles, and are the most popular club in the country after Alianza and Universitario.

CD UNIVERSIDAD DE SAN MARTÍN DE PORRES   Santo
Founded: **2004** • Stadium: **Villa Deportiva USMP (Lima)**

Although still a relatively young club, USMP have been league champions three times (2007, 2008, 2010). They were the first Peruvian club to have the status of a public limited company. In February 2012, they withdrew from the league, but were reinstated less than one month later.

THE STRONGEST
The Tigers
Founded: **1908** • Stadium: **Rafael Mendoza Castellón (La Paz)**

Despite suffering hardships during the Chaco War against Paraguay (1932–1935), and losing sixteen of their players in an air crash in 1969, The Strongest have always been able to bounce back. They now dominate Bolivian football.

CLUB ATLETICO BOLIVAR
The Academy
Founded: **1925** • Stadium: **Hernando Siles (La Paz)**

Founded in the year of the hundredth anniversary of independence, the club is named after Simon Bolivar, the country's liberator. Bolivar have won the league title a record nineteen times, and can be proud of having beaten Boca Juniors 3–1 in the group stage of the 2004 Copa Libertadores.

BLOOMING
The Millionaires
Founded: **1946** • Stadium: **Tahuichi Aguilera (Santa Cruz)**

The *clásico cruceño* between Blooming and Oriente Petrolero is the most exciting derby in Bolivia. In 1985, both clubs qualified for the group stage of the Copa Libertadores, where Blooming finished ahead of Oriente, thanks to an 8-0 victory over Deportivo Italia (Venezuela). They have won the league five times.

CLUB JORGE WILSTERMANN
The Aviator
Founded: **1949** • Stadium: **Félix Capriles (Cochabamaba)**

Founded by workers from an aeronautical firm, the club is named after pioneering Bolivian aviator Jorge Wilstermann. Eleven-time league champions, the club reached the semi-finals of the 1981 Copa Libertadores, the best result by a Bolivian club to date.

CD SANTIAGO WANDERERS
Harbour Men
Founded: **1892** • Stadium: **Elias Figueroa Brander (Valparaiso)**

The first club in South America to be totally devoted to football, Santiago Wanderers have won three national titles. Their rivalry with Everton Viña del Mar has given the Panzers, its main supporters' group, plenty of opportunities to show they are among the best in Chile.

UNIÓN ESPAÑOLA
The Red Fury
Founded: **1897** • Stadium: **Santa Laura (Santiago)**

Founding members of the professional league, and the great rivals of Audax Italiano, Unión Española are one of the most successful clubs in Chile, with seven first-division titles. In 1975, the club played in the final of the Copa Libertadores against the Argentines of Independiente.

EVERTON VIÑA DEL MAR
Roulette Players
Founded: **1909** • Stadium: **Sausalito (Viña del Mar)**

The club was founded by English immigrants in Valparaiso, before moving to Viña del Mar, and has won four league titles and one cup, making for one of the most impressive lists of honours for a team outside the capital, Santiago. Everton are Chile's sixth most popular club.

AUDAX ITALIANO
Los Itálicos
Founded: **1910** • Stadium: **Bicentenario de la Florida (Santiago)**

Audax Italiano were formed by Santiago's Italian community, and were one of the founders of the professional league. During their heyday (1940-50), the club played the *Clásico Criollo* against Colo-Colo—at the time, both clubs had only Chilean players.

CD PALESTINO
The Arabs

Founded: **1920** • Stadium: **Estadio Municipal de La Cisterna (Santiago)**

Founded by members of the Arab diaspora, the club has won two Chilean league titles. The second of these victorious campaigns, in 1978, was led by one of the biggest stars of Chilean football, Elias Figueroa. Palestino are, perhaps understandably, very popular in Palestine.

CF UNIVERSIDAD DE CHILE
The Owl

Founded: **1927** • Stadium: **Estadio Nacional (Santiago)**

The second most successful team in Chile, with sixteen league titles, Universidad de Chile enjoy the greatest popularity after Colo-Colo, against whom they contest the *Super Clásico*. The club won the 2011 Copa Sudamericana and are known for playing some of the most beautiful football in South America.

CD UNIVERSIDAD CATÓLICA
The Crusaders

Founded: **1937** • Stadium: **San Carlos de Apoquindo (Santiago)**

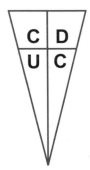

A rival of Universidad de Chile, of which it is an offshoot, the club is renowned for the quality of their youth programme. Ten-time league champions, Universidad Católica reached the finals of the Copa Libertadores in 1993. Despite their middle-class image, the club's fans come from all levels of Chilean society.

HUACHIPATO
The Steelers

Founded: **1947** • Stadium: **CAP (Talcahuano)**

Twice first-division champions (1974, 2012), Huachipato are much more than just a football team. They are a social institution and actively involved in the industrial development of the Bio Bio region, as well as being the country's biggest multi-sports club.

CD COBRELOA
Desert Foxes

Founded: **1977** • Stadium: **Zorros del Desierto (Cobreloa)**

Cobreloa sport an orange strip that evokes the copper mines in the region. The club became Chilean league champions in their third year, and were then finalists in the Copa Libertadores (1981, 1982). Cobreloa's stadium sits at an altitude of 7,500 feet—the club once remained unbeaten at home for five consecutive years.

CLUB DEPORTIVO INCAS DEL SUR   The Incas

Founded: **2013** • Stadium: **Las Rejas (Santiago)**

This club was created to bring together the youth of Chile and Peru—all their players are Chilean but of Peruvian origin. Currently playing in the fourth division, the club was honoured in 2014 with a visit from Michelle Bachelet, the Chilean president.

"Who is Chile? Colo-Colo! Who is Colo-Colo? Chile!" **Club anthem.**

COLO-COLO
The Chief

- Founded: **1925**

Stadium: **Monumental David Arellano (Santiago)**

Colo-Colo are the most successful team in Chilean football. They are named after a sixteenth-century Mapuche chief who fought the Spanish. In the 1920s, their player-founder, Arellano, was credited with popularizing the bicycle kick, dubbed the "Chilena." Colo-Colo hold the national record for most league titles. In 1973, they were the first club in the country to play in a final of the Copa Libertadores, a trophy they won in 1991, after beating Nacional Montevideo, Boca Juniors, and the Paraguayans of Olimpia. Colo-Colo are Chile's most popular club and have been a social phenomenon ever since they were founded. Their superiority is such that one of its alternative nicknames is "The Eternal Champions."

30
League Titles

10
National Cups

1
Copa Libertadores

May 29, 1991
Colo-Colo win the Copa Libertadores, their first continental title.

Star players: David Arellano, Francisco Valdés, Carlos Caszely, Matías Fernández, Humberto Suazo.

Honours: League: 1937, 1939, 1941, 1944, 1947, 1953, 1956, 1960, 1963, 1970, 1972, 1979, 1981, 1983, 1986, 1989, 1990, 1991, 1993, 1996, 1997–II, 1998, 2002–II, 2006–I, 2006–II, 2007–I, 2007–II, 2008–II, 2009–II, 2014–II; National Cup: 1958, 1974, 1981, 1982, 1985, 1988, 1989, 1990, 1994, 1996; Copa Libertadores: 1991.

"Nacional is my life. I am more of a supporter than a player."
Victor Arlstizábal, scorer of 206 goals for Nacional during his four stints with the club.

ATLÉTICO NACIONAL

The Green

Founded: **1947** • Stadium: **Atanasio Girardot (Medellin)**

The club promoted the use of Colombian players from the very start, at a time when many South American stars were playing for Colombian teams. Many of their fourteen league titles have been won by entirely Colombian teams. Nicknamed the "King of Cups," Nacional were the first Colombian club to win the Copa Libertadores, in 1989, thanks in large part to their extraordinary goalkeeper René Higuita. In the 1970s, their fans were the first to come up with *tifos* (choreographed displays in the stands of a stadium) to greet the players as they walked onto the pitch.

14 League Titles

2 National Cups

1 Copa Libertadores

René Higuita
The legendary goalkeeper (far right, standing) won two league titles (1991, 1994) and the Copa Libertadores (1989) with Nacional.

Star players: René Higuita, Andrés Escobar, Víctor Hugo Aristizabal, Faustino Asprilla.

Honours: League: 1954, 1973, 1976, 1981, 1991, 1994, 1999, 2005–I, 2007–I, 2007–II, 2011–I, 2013–I, 2013–II, 2014–I; Copa Libertadores: 1989.

DEPORTIVO CALI
The Green Menace

Founded: **1912** • Stadium: **Deportivo Cali (Cali)**

This club, founded by students, lag behind América Cali in terms of honours. Winner of nine Championships, and twice a finalist in the Copa Libertadores, Deportivo Cali do, however, outstrip their historic rivals when it comes to the number of victories in the *clasico*.

DEPORTIVO INDEPENDIENTE MEDELLIN   The King Of Hearts

Founded: **1913** • Stadium: **Atanasio Girardot (Medellin)**

A pioneer of Colombian football, and with five league championship titles, DIM played their first professional matches in 1948 with Peruvian players of such brilliance that they were nicknamed "The Sun Dance." Around the same time, they began to play the *clásico paisa* against Nacional.

ATLÉTICO JUNIOR
The Sharks

Founded: **1924** • Stadium: **Metropolitano Roberto Meléndez (Baranquilla)**

The club was founded by a mother who wanted her four sons to play football. Over the last four decades, Junior have won seven league titles and in 1994, with Carlos Valderrama at the helm, they played in the semi-finals of Copa Libertadores. Junior's fans are among the most devoted in Colombia.

CÚCUTA DEPORTIVO
The Motilon Wrath

Founded: **1924** • Stadium: **General Santander (Cúcuta)**

Despite spending more than sixty seasons in the first division, the club has won just one national title, in 2006. This was followed by a semi-final in the Copa Libertadores. Cúcuta Deportivo play the *Clásico del Oriente Colombiano* against their historic rivals Atlético Bucaramanga.

AMÉRICA CALI
The People's Passion

Founded: **1927** • Stadium: **Pascual Guerrero (Cali)**

With thirteen league titles and four runners-up places in the Copa Libertadores, the club are giants of Colombian football. They were relegated in 2011, following a major internal crisis. Since then, their fans, mostly working-class, have mobilized support across the Americas to help get them promoted.

INDEPENDIENTE SANTA FE
The Cardinals

Founded: **1941** • Stadium: **El Campin (Bogotá)**

Santa Fe were founded by students and are one of only three clubs in the country to have always played in the first division, and indeed they won the first league championship of the professional era. Over the past twenty years, the club have enjoyed the support of new generations of supporters.

DEPORTIVO PEREIRA
The Matecaña Wrath

Founded: **1944** • Stadium: **Hernán Ramírez Villegas (Pereira)**

The club's heyday was in the 1950s, a golden era of Colombian football. It was originally made up of workers and artisans. Deportivo Pereira have never been league champions, despite signing many great Paraguayan players. They contest the *clásico cafetero* with Once Caldas.

LOS MILLONARIOS
The Ambassadors

Founded: **1946** • Stadium: **El Campín (Bogotá)**

Considered to be the greatest club in the world in the 1940s–1950s, Los Millonarios still hold the record for league championship victories (fourteen). The club has twice reached the semi-finals of the Copa Sudamericana, in 2007 and 2012.

ONCE CALDAS
The White

Founded: **1947** • Stadium: **Palogrande (Manizales)**

Having long remained in the shadow of the bigger Colombian clubs, Once Caldas hit it big in the 2000s, even winning the 2004 Copa Libertadores against Boca Juniors. Their supporters proudly claim to be the greatest in Colombia.

DEPORTIVO PASTO
The Volcanic Team

Founded: **1949** • Stadium: **Departamental Libertad (Pasto)**

The club had to wait nearly fifty years before reaching the first division, eventually winning the national title in 2006. Attake Massivo and La Banda Tricolor are the two main supporters' groups.

DEPORTES TOLIMA
The Burgundy and Gold

Founded: **1954** • Stadium: **Manuel Murillo Toro (Ibagué)**

Deportes Tolima have played in six Copas Libertadores (reaching the semi-finals in 1982) and won the end-of-season tournament in 2003. They are one of the most dependable teams in Colombian football. Since the 1990s, they have found a worthy regional rival in the form of Atlético Huila.

REAL CARTAGENA
The Heroic Team

Founded: **1971** • Stadium: **Jaime Morón León (Cartagena)**

Ten years after their founding, the club became a subsidiary of Millonarios (Bogotá), focussing on youth training. The plan worked so well that Real Cartagena ended up playing in the first division in 1992. Since then, they have yo-yoed between the first and second divisions.

CD LA EQUIDAD
Insurers

Founded: **1982** • Stadium: **Metropolitano de Techo (Bogotá)**

Founded by an insurance company, La Equidad have played in the first division since 2006, and regularly participate in the Copa Sudamericana. Their stadium has the peculiarity of possessing two distinct stands along one touchline

ENVIGADO FC
The Forgers of Heroes

Founded: **1989** • Stadium: **Polideportivo Sur (Envigado)**

These relative newcomers to Colombian football soon carved out a place for themselves in the shadow of bigger teams, thanks to the quality of their youth development programme, of which the club are very proud. In 2012, Envigado played in the Copa Sudamericana for the first time

BOYACÁ CHICÓ
The Chequered

Founded: **2002** • Stadium: **Metropolitano de Techo (Bogotá)**

This young club, the first incorporated company in Colombian sport, has shot to glory, rising from the third division to the Copa Libertadores, by way of a league title (2008). The club was founded in Bogotà, moved to Tunja in 2005, but returned to Bogotà in 2015.

PATRIOTAS FC
The Lancers

Founded: **2003** • Stadium: **La Independencia (Tunja)**

Patriotas grew out of one city's desire to have a top-flight team. In 2011, they entered the first division. Since then, Tunja has had two high-level clubs—the other being Boyacá Chico—who contest a local *clásico*.

CLUB GUARANÍ
The Aboriginal

Founded: **1903** • Stadium: **Rogelio Livieres (Asunción)**

Founded by Olimpia supporters, Guaraní were the first winners of the league, and have remained in the top flight since 1906. Ten-time league champions, they are also known for their goal-keeper, Pablo Aurrecochea, who wore shirts adorned with cartoon characters.

CLUB NACIONAL
El Tricolor

Founded: **1904** • Stadium: **Arsenio Erico (Asunción)**

Founded by students, the club won nine titles between 1909 and 2013. They were also runners-up in the 2014 Copa Libertadores. Known for being Paraguay's "most loved club," they contest the *Clásico de Barrio Obrero* against their neighbour, Cerro Porteño.

CLUB LIBERTAD
El Gumarelo

Founded: **1905** • Stadium: **Dr. Nicolás Leoz (Asunción)**

Club Libertad were founded during a period when the country was finding its freedom again after a revolution, but it was not until the twenty-first century that they experienced their finest period—winning ten of their eighteen titles in the years since 2002. Although they play the *Clásico Blanco y Negro* against Olimpia, their greatest rivals are Guaraní.

CLUB SOL DE AMÉRICA
The Dancers

Founded: **1909** • Stadium: **Luis Alfonso Giagni (Asunción)**

Club Sol de América have contested nearly one hundred first division league seasons, and have been runners-up so many times that they were given the nickname, "the champion without a crown." They finally won the league title in 1986, and again in 1991, and have contested the Copa Libertadores six times.

CERRO PORTENO
The Cyclone

Founded: **1912** • Stadium: **General Pablo Rojas (Asuncion)**

Present in the first division since 1913, Paraguay's most popular club Cerro Porteño bring the whole country together with their blue and red colours evoking the two major political parties. They have won the league thirty-one times, and have reached the semi-finals of the Copa Libertadores on six occasions.

CLUB RUBIO NU
Nuenses

Founded: **1913** • Stadium: **La Arboleda (Ascunsion)**

Named in memory of children killed in the battle of Acosta Ñu, in 1869, the club put their activities on hold during the Chaco War (1932 to 1935), and their players and management headed off to the front. Rubio Ñu have contested twenty-four seasons in the first division since 1927.

12 DE OCTUBRE FC
The Globe

Founded: **1914** • Stadium: **Juan Canuto Pettengill (Itaugua)**

In 2002, the club became the first league champions from outside the capital. Their name commemorates Columbus' arrival in America. The international Salvador Cabañas, a former player of the club, returned to play for the team after being shot in the head in 2010.

CS LUQUEÑO
The Pig

Founded: **1921** • Stadium: **Feliciano Càceres (Luque)**

Twice league champions in the 1950s, Luqueño were runners-up in 2001 and 2007. On match days, their supporters like to dress up a pig in the club's colours—the town where they are based (in the outskirts of Asunción) is known for its pig farms.

"Advance, colossus / Express dean / Towards the goal / The final triumph." **Olimpia anthem.**

CLUB OLIMPIA

The Dean

Founded: **1902** • Stadium: **Manuel Ferreira (Asuncion)**

Founded by a Dutch gymnastics teacher who introduced football to Paraguay, Olimpia are the oldest and the most successful club in the country. They have been champions thirty-nine times—winning six of those titles in a row from 1978 to 1983. On the international scene, they have performed consistently at the highest level, reaching the final of the Copa Libertadores seven times, starting with the first competition in 1960, and most recently in 2013. Three-time continental champions, they rank fifth for the number of these titles won. The "King of Cups"—one of the club's nicknames—enjoys great popularity, even if they originally represented the European upper classes. When Olimpia triumphed in the 1979 Copa Libertadores in Buenos Aires, more than 10,000 supporters crowded into the Boca Juniors stadium. Their duel with Cerro Porteño in the Superclásico has enthralled Paraguayan football fans since 1913.

39 League Titles

3 Copa Libertadores

1 Intercontinental Cup

December 19, 2011
Olimpia are crowned champions for the thirty-ninth time in their history.

Star players: Raul Vicente Amarilla, Gustavo Benitez, Luis Monzon, Hugo Talavera, Hugo Almeida, Gabriel González, Adriano Samaniego, Cristóbal Cubilla, Aurelio González, Ricardo Tavarelli, Jorge Guasch, Rogelio Delgado, Denis Caniza, Roque Santa Cruz, Carlos Paredes, Julio César Caceres.

Honours: League: 1912, 1914, 1916, 1925, 1927, 1928, 1929, 1931, 1936, 1937, 1938, 1947, 1948, 1956, 1957, 1958, 1959, 1960, 1962, 1965, 1968, 1971, 1975, 1978, 1979, 1980, 1981, 1982, 1983, 1985, 1988, 1989, 1993, 1995, 1997, 1998, 1999, 2000, 2011; Copa Libertadores: 1979, 1990, 2002; Intercontinental Cup: 1979.

"That's not volcanic ash, it's the Peñarol supporters."
Fox Sports, final of the 2011 Copa Libertadores between Peñarol and Santos.

CA PEÑAROL

Manyas

Founded: **1891**
Stadium: **Centenario (Montevideo)**

Peñarol, who get their name from a neighbourhood of Montevideo, are the oldest club in Uruguayan football. Founded within a railroad company, they took their colours from a locomotive. A real football legend, they hold numerous records, such as forty-nine league titles, and their performance in 1905, when they became champions without conceding a single goal. Most of the 1950 Uruguayan World Cup winning team came from within their ranks. At an international level, they have the most successful Copa Libertadores record after the Argentinian clubs Independiente and Boca Juniors, and have been runners-up five times.

49 League Titles

5 Copa Libertadores

3 Intercontinental Cups

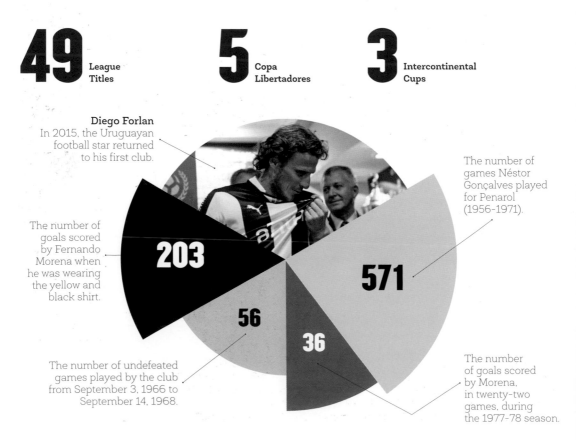

Diego Forlan
In 2015, the Uruguayan football star returned to his first club.

The number of goals scored by Fernando Morena when he was wearing the yellow and black shirt.

203

The number of games Néstor Gonçalves played for Penarol (1956-1971).

571

The number of undefeated games played by the club from September 3, 1966 to September 14, 1968.

56

36

The number of goals scored by Morena, in twenty-two games, during the 1977-78 season.

PEÑAROL–NACIONAL, A SUPER CLASICO THAT'S ONE OF A KIND

In a town like Montevideo, more than a dozen teams play in the first division, but there is only one rivalry that grabs everyone's attention, and that is the one between Peñarol and Nacional—ninety-two titles between them—dating from 1900, making it the oldest in world football outside of the British Isles. The two clubs have already played more than 500 matches, with Peñarol leading Nacional when it comes to the number of victories. History records that Peñarol achieved the highest score (5-0) in 2014, as well as a victory—in 1987—with eight men against eleven, after three of their players were sent off. Peñarol also leads its historic rival in terms of popularity in Uruguay.

URUGUAY

October 31, 1987
Penarol's supporters are thrilled: the players having just won the fifth Copa Libertadores in the club's history.

Star players: José Piendibene, Roque Máspoli, Obdulio Varela, Raúl Antonio Schiaffino, Oscar Míguez, Juan Eduardo Hohberg, Julio Cesar Abbadie, Néstor Gonçalves, Ladislao Mazurkiewicz, Alberto Spencer, Pedro Rocha, Gustavo Matosas, Fernando Morena, Pedro Bengoechea.

Honours: League: 1900, 1901, 1905, 1907, 1911, 1918, 1921, 1924, 1926, 1928, 1929, 1932, 1935, 1936, 1937, 1938, 1944, 1945, 1949, 1951, 1953, 1954, 1958, 1959, 1960, 1961, 1962, 1964, 1965, 1967, 1968, 1973, 1974, 1975, 1978, 1979, 1981, 1982, 1985, 1986, 1993, 1994, 1995, 1996, 1997, 1999, 2003, 2010, 2013; Copa Libertadores: 1960, 1961, 1966, 1982, 1987; Intercontinental Cup: 1961, 1966, 1982.

CLUB NACIONAL DE FOOTBALL
The Bag

Founded: **1899** • Stadium: **Gran Parque Central (Montevideo)**

Club Nacional de Football, who are rivals of Peñarol, are dominant at both domestic and international level, with forty-five league titles and three Copas Libertadores. The irrepressible enthusiasm of one of their fans from the early twentieth century, Prudencio Reyes, is considered to have influenced the way fans support teams all over the world.

MONTEVIDEO WANDERERS FC
The Bohemians

Founded: **1902** • Stadium: **Parque Alfredo Victor Viera (Montevideo)**

Named after Wolverhampton Wanderers, the club won the league title three times during the amateur era, but have had to tolerate podium places in the professional era. They were Enzo Francescoli's first professional club, and they play River Plate in the *Clásico del Prado*.

CENTRAL ESPANOL
Palermitanos

Founded: **1905** • Stadium: **Parque Palermo (Montevideo)**

Central Español, who get their name from Montevideo's central cemetery, had three players in Uruguay's 1950 World Cup winning squad (contested in Brazil). Crowned league champions in 1984, they are one of that select group of Uruguayan league title holders.

DEFENSOR SC
El Violetta

Founded: **1913** • Stadium: **Luis Franzini (Montevideo)**

Founded by workers from a glass factory, the club caused a sensation in 1976 by winning the league title, putting an end to forty-four years of domination by Nacional and Peñarol. They are the country's third most popular club, and hold four league titles.

LIVERPOOL FC
The Knife

Founded: **1915** • Stadium: **Belvedere (Montevideo)**

Named in homage to the famous English club; in 1938 they became the first second-division club to beat a first-division team in the playoffs, and enter the top flight, where they remained for seventy-four years. It was in their stadium that the squad wore their "celestial" strip for the first time.

CA BELLA VISTA
The Popes

Founded: **1920** • Stadium: **Parque José Nasazzi (Montevideo)**

This club's colours are those of the Vatican. Four of their players were in Uruguay's 1930 World Cup winning squad. Present in the first division for fifty-two seasons, they became champions in 1990, the seventh Uruguayan club to win the league title.

DANUBIO FC
The Stripe

Founded: **1932** • Stadium: **Jardines del Hipòdromo (Montevideo)**

Named by the mother of one of the club's founders, who was of Bulgarian origin, Danubio have been the fourth biggest club in Uruguay since 1988—when they won the first of their four titles. They contest the *Clásico de los medianos* with Defenso, their rivals. Edinson Cavani started his career here.

TACUAREMBÓ FC
Tacua

Founded: **1998** • Stadium: **Raúl Goyenola (Tacuarembó)**

Tacuarembó were created from the merger of all of the town's teams, in response to a call from the federation to create football centres outside of the capital. They have played in the first division for thirteen seasons, and contest the *Clásico del Norte* against Cerro Largo.

QUILMES AC
The Brewers

Founded: **1887** • Stadium: **Estadio Centenario (Buenos Aires)**

An elitist club that accepted only British players when they were founded, Quilmes cultivate paradox. Their most famous supporters club is called "The Kilmes Indians," in homage to the last Amerindian tribe to resist the Spanish colonists.

ROSARIO CENTRAL
The Scoundrel

Founded: **1889** • Stadium: **Gigante de Arroyito (Rosario)**

Founded by railway workers, Rosario Central were one of the first clubs to have players from indigenous groups. In 1971, they caused a stir by becoming the first club outside Buenos Aires to win the national title. Ernesto "Che" Guevara was a fan of the club.

CA BANFIELD
The Drill

Founded: **1896** • Stadium: **Florencio Solá (Buenos Aires)**

Banfield have been in the first division for forty-six years, but only won their first early-season league title in 2009, with an eighteen-year-old James Rodriguez in their ranks. The club is located in the southern suburbs of Buenos Aires and counted the writer Julio Cortázar among its fans.

CA ARGENTINO DE QUILMES
El Mate

Founded: **1899** • Stadium: **Argentino de Quilmes (Buenos Aires)**

Argentino de Quilmes are proud of having been the first club to be founded by Argentinians. Their one and only season in the first division (1939) may have been a failure, but the club can be proud that in 2013 they beat San Lorenzo's record for the biggest number of consecutive victories.

GIMNASIA LA PLATA
The Wolf
Founded: **1901** • Stadium: **Juan Carmelo Zerillo (Buenos Aires)**

Gimnasia La Plata is the oldest multi-sports club in Argentina. They were founded among the abattoirs of La Plata, and are still proud of their working-class origins. A great rival of Estudiantes, they have not won the Argentine championship since 1929, but remain the city's most popular club.

CA TIGRE
The Killers
Founded: **1902** • Stadium: **José Dellegiovanna (Buenos Aires)**

More used to winning second place (early-season championships 2007 and 2008, late-season championship 2012, Copa Sudamericana 2012), Tigre have a very loyal following. Even when they were in the third division, their stadium drew larger crowds than some first division sides.

ATLÉTICO TUCUMÁN
The Doyen
Founded: **1902** • Stadium: **Monumental (San Miguel de Tucumán)**

The oldest club in Tucumán, Atlético were the first to sport a shirt with sky-blue and white vertical stripes—widely copied throughout Argentine football. Their mainly middle-class fans sometimes mock their rivals, San Martin, as "paupers."

NEWELL'S OLD BOYS
The Leprosy
Founded: **1903** • Stadium: **Marcelo Bielsa (Rosario)**

Although Newell's Old Boys have several national titles, nothing makes their fans happier than defeating Rosario Central, against whom the club plays the oldest derby in Argentina. Before this *clasico*, Newell's train in front of tens of thousands of fans.

RACING CLUB DE AVELLANEDA
The Academy
Founded: **1903** • Stadium: **Juan Domingo Perón (Buenos Aires)**

Racing Club de Avellaneda won the Intercontinental Cup in 1967, and also hold seventeen national league titles. They are known for the fervour of their fans, particularly the "Guardia Imperial" group. Indeed the club was taken over by its *socios* in 2009.

ARGENTINOS JUNIORS
Red Bugs
Founded: **1904** • Stadium: **Diego Armando Maradona (Buenos Aires)**

Argentinos Juniors, which will always be remembered as the club where Diego Maradona made his debut, have a predilection for attacking football. In 1985, they achieved one of the most beautiful moments in their history by beating Michel Platini's Juventus to win the Intercontinental Cup.

CA ATLANTA
The Bohemians

Founded: **1904** • Stadium: **Estadio Don León Kolbowsky (Buenos Aires)**

Atlanta, who are closely associated with the Jewish community of Buenos Aires, have racked up a total of forty-four seasons in the first division. They share a historic rivalry with Chacarita Juniors, although All Boys have become a recent opponent of choice.

FERRO CARRIL OESTE
Ferro

Founded: **1904** • Stadium: **Ricardo Etcheverri (Buenos Aires)**

Founded by railway workers, Ferro Carril Oeste (the name means "west railway") dominated Argentinian football in the early 1980s, and were recognized by UNESCO in 1988 for their social, cultural, and sports work. The club more recently underwent some difficulties before being bought by its *socios* in 2014.

CLUB ATLÉTICO SAN TELMO
The Drummers

Founded: **1904** • Stadium: **Dr. Osvaldo Baletto (Buenos Aires)**

Dock Sud's rival in one of the great clasicos of Argentina's lower divisions, San Telmo's nickname—"The Drummers"— says much about the atmosphere that reigns in their stadium in the Buenos Aires suburb of Isla Maciel, where visiting teams are often reluctant to play.

CA COLÓN DE SANTA FE
The Oven Grille

Founded: **1905** • Stadium: **Estasnislao López (Santa Fe)**

Although they have never won a national title, Cólon Santa Fe often shine when playing major teams. In 1964, when in the third division, they even beat the great Pelé's Santos, earning its stadium the nickname "the elephants' graveyard."

CA CHACARITA JUNIORS
The Undertakers

Founded: **1906** • Stadium: **Chacarita Juniors (Buenos Aires)**

Founded by workers, the colours of Chacarita Juniors evoke their origins: red for socialism, white for purity, and black for the local cemetery—the reason for their nickname—enough to scare Atlanta, their historic rival in the *Clasico de Villa Crespo*.

CA SAN MARTIN DE SAN JUAN
The Saint

Founded: **1907** • Stadium: **Hilario Sánchez (Mendoza)**

Since the 1990s, San Martin de San Juan have faced off against Godoy Cruz in the *Clasico de Cuyo*, and the last few years they have played in the first division. The "Green and Black" (their alternative nickname) can count on the support of the "Banda del Pueblo Viejo," (The Old Town Band) the largest group of fans in the province.

CA UNION
El Tatengue
Founded: **1907** • Stadium: **15 de Abril (Santa Fe)**

Unión's best sporting performance was finishing runner-up in the 1979 championship of Argentina, but Unión are still incredibly proud of having beaten Chelsea 5–0 in 1929, at a time when the English club was invincible.

CLUB ATLÉTICO HURACÁN
The Balloon
Founded: **1908** • Stadium: **Tomás Adolfo Ducó (Buenos Aires)**

In the years 2000 to 2010, the club was known for a certain kind of idealized version of football, playing an inventive game. The coach, Angel Cappa, even declared: "Whatever the results, football is above all an emotional affair."

SAN MARTÍN DE TUCUMÁN
The Tramps
Founded: **1909** • Stadium: **Ciudadela (San Miguel de Tucumán)**

San Martín, who represent the impoverished population of Miguel de Tucumán, have had their moments of glory, such as when they defeated Boca Juniors 6–1 at La Bombonera in 1988. Their supporters are sometimes portrayed as being the most fervent in Argentina.

VÉLEZ SARSFIELD
The Fort
Founded: **1910** • Stadium: **José Amalfitani (Buenos Aires)**

The club achieved global glory when they won the Intercontinental Cup in 1994 against AC Milan. At the time, Vélez were managed by a former supporter, who brought financial independence to the club.

NUEVA CHICAGO
The Bull-Calf
Founded: **1911** • Stadium: **Nueva Chicago (Buenos Aires)**

Nueva Chicago, from the western suburb of Buenos Aires, were finally able to enter the first division following the reformation of the league in 2015. Previously, their supporters had made a name for themselves by singing songs from the shanty towns of the northern suburbs.

ALL BOYS
The Whites
Founded: **1913** • Stadium: **Islas Malvinas (Buenos Aires)**

After hearing their fans repeatedly singing a popular song called "Imposible," the players of this team from the Floresta neighbourhood say they have routinely achieved the impossible. Since 2010, the club where Carlos Tevez made his debut as a footballer has played in the first division.

CA LANÚS
The Garnets

Founded: **1915** • Stadium: **Néstor Diaz Pérez (Buenos Aires)**

Lanús were a second-rate club for many years, until the tide began to turn in the 1990s. In 1996, they won the Copa Conmebol, and ten years later the opening championship of the 2007 season, followed by the Copa Sudamericana in 2013.

CLUB SPORTIVO DOCK SUD
The Flooded

Founded: **1916** • Stadium: **Estadio De los Inmigrantes (Buenos Aires)**

Dock Sud have never known the joys of the first division, but their highly enthusiastic supporters have made their reputation. This makes sense when you consider that one of its old slogans was "Follow me if you can", and that the club was named in honour of the dockworkers.

GODOY CRUZ
The Wine Producers

Founded: **1921** • Stadium: **Feliciano Gambarte (Mendoza)**

Godoy Cruz gets their nickname from a merger with a team founded by winery workers. They are the largest club in Mendoza. The club's main rivals are San Martin de San Juan, but they have recently played international competitors in the Copa Libertadores.

CA ALMIRANTE BROWN
The Frigate

Founded: **1922** • Stadium: **Fragata Presidente Sarmiento (Isidro Casanova)**

The club, named after an Argentine naval officer, has never been in the first division. This has not stopped the team from proclaiming themselves "Pride of the People" and going all out in the *Clasico del Oeste* against Deportivo Moron.

DEPORTIVO MORON
The Rooster

Founded: **1947** • Stadium: **El Stadio Nuevo (Buenos Aires)**

Although Deportivo Moron have only had one season in the first division (1969), local rivalries give their fans—including the famous "Borrachos" (Drunks)— many exciting moments to savour in their 19,000-capacity stadium.

ARSENAL FC
The Viaduct Men

Founded: **1957** • Stadium: **Julio Grondona (Buenos Aires)**

Arsenal de Sarandí were founded by the all-powerful Julio Grondona, who was president of the Argentina Football Federation from 1979 to 2014. One of the club's star players was Jorge Burruchaga, who scored the winning goal in the final of the 1986 FIFA World Cup. Arsenal won their first league title in 2012.

"I played in a Barcelona–Real Madrid (fixture), which is a very important match because it involves two huge cities, but Boca–River is something else. It's like sleeping with Julia Roberts." **Diego Maradona.**

BOCA JUNIORS
Half plus one

Founded: **1905**
Stadium: **La Bombonera (Buenos Aires)**

Boca Juniors were founded in the Boca neighbourhood of Buenos Aires by Italian immigrants—from where they get one of their nicknames: Xeneizes (Genoese). They are considered to be the club of the working classes, as opposed to their great rival, River Plate, but they are also the most popular club in Argentina—which explains another of their nicknames: "Half plus one." So intense is the passion this club arouses, they have even opened a cemetery for their deceased fans.

31 League Titles

3 National Cups

6 Copa Libertadores

3 Intercontinental Cups

Diego Maradona
In 1981, *el Pibe de Oro* was crowned Argentinian league champion with Boca.

The number of titles won by Sebastian Battaglia while he was playing for Boca.

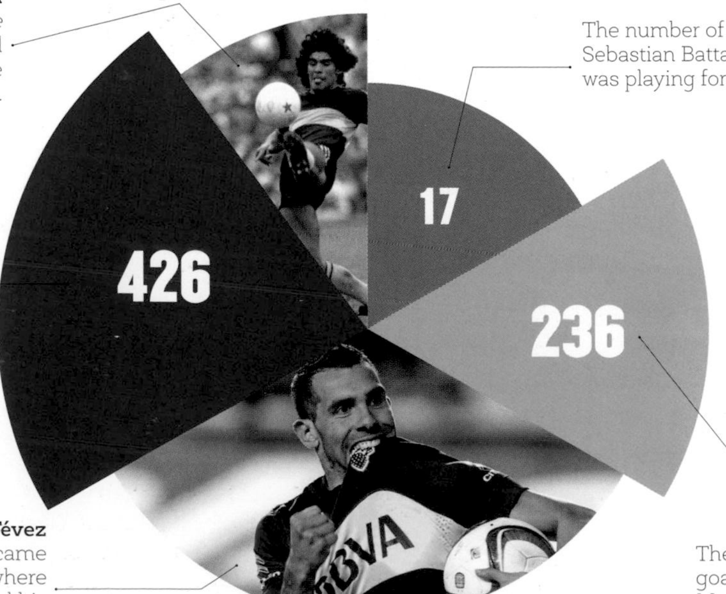

The number of games played by Roberto Mouzo while he was wearing the yellow and blue shirt.

426

17

236

Carlos Tévez
In 2015, Tévez came back to Boca, where he had started his professional career.

The number of goals scored by Martin Palermo for Boca Juniors.

December 18, 2005
Boca becomes the first club to win the Copa América twice.

KING OF INTERNATIONAL COMPETITIONS

Although Boca have won many national and metropolitan championships (thirty-one), they don't hold the record. However, their success in the Recopa Sudamericana in 2008 made them the world's joint top club for international titles (eighteen), along with AC Milan. Their victories include six Copas Libertadores (1977, 1978, 2000, 2001, 2003, 2007) and three Intercontinental Cups (1977, 2000, 2003).

ARGENTINA

RIQUELME, THE ILLUMINATOR

Although Diego Maradona had a brief but much remarked upon stint with Boca in 1981, followed by a less impressive one from 1995 to 1997, the fans' number one player is Juan Roman Riquelme. A true aesthete of football, Riquelme enchanted La Bombonera from 1996 to 2002 and from 2007 to 2014. His highly subtle style of play, sidesteps, and feints perfectly embodied the Argentinian *enganche*, an offensive midfielder capable of destabilising an entire defence with a clever move. In 2012, a journalist supporter of River Plate paid him homage in these terms: "How could someone like me appreciate a Boca idol? But I couldn't ignore you either. You are too great to go unnoticed by anyone who loves football."

LA BOMBONERA, THE HEART OF BOCA

La Bombonera stadium is the beating heart of the "Blue and Gold"—literally, for it is said that when the fans all jump as one during matches, "the stadium doesn't shake, it beats." This "beating" has even become the club's hallmark, for which the Boca fans are world famous. Ever since the 1920s, supporters have called themselves "The 12," in memory of a fan (the "twelfth" player) from a rich family who helped fund part of their European tour. In homage to their fans, the club have made December 12 'supporters' day.'

Star players: Hugo Gatti, Martin Palermo, Guillermo Barros Schelotto, Juan Roman Riquelme, Diego Maradona, Roberto Mouzo.

Honours: League: 1919, 1920, 1923, 1924, 1926, 1930, 1931, 1934, 1935, 1940, 1943, 1944, 1954, 1962, 1964, 1965, 1969, 1970, 1976, 1976-II, 1981-I, 1992-I, 1998-I, 1999-II, 2000-I, 2003-I, 2005-I, 2006-II, 2008-I, 2011-I, 2015; Copa Libertadores: 1977, 1978, 2000, 2001, 2003, 2007; Intercontinental Cup: 1977, 2000, 2003.

"The Superclasico between Boca and River sets half the country against almost the entire other half. The whole of Argentina is invested in the match." **Carlos Bianchi.**

CA RIVER PLATE

The Chickens

Founded: **1901** • Stadium: **Monumental (Buenos Aires)**

River Plate boast the most national honours in Argentina. Like their great rivals, Boca Juniors, they were founded in the working-class neighbourhood of La Boca. After moving further north in 1923, River became a professional club, spending prodigiously to build up a competitive team, which earned them the nickname "Los Millonarios" (The Millionaires). In the 1940s, their fearsome front line was dubbed "La Máquina" (The Machine). Fifty years later, the team led by Enzo Francescoli made history by winning the Copa Libertadores.

34 League Titles

3 Copa Libertadores

1 Intercontinental Cup

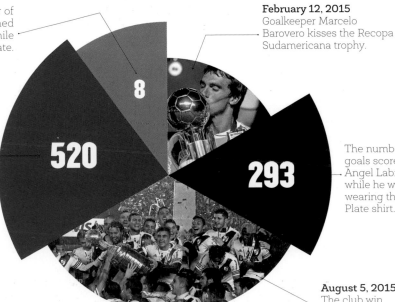

The number of Argentinians crowned world champions while playing for River Plate.

8

February 12, 2015
Goalkeeper Marcelo Barovero kisses the Recopa Sudamericana trophy.

The number of games played by Amadeo Carrizo for River Plate (1945-1968).

520

293

The number of goals scored by Angel Labruna while he was wearing the River Plate shirt.

August 5, 2015
The club win their third Copa Libertadores.

RIVER FANS SET A WORLD RECORD

On October 8, 2012, thousands of River Plate supporters filled the streets of Buenos Aires to beat the record for the longest banner in the world. Measuring 15 feet wide by 8,530 yards long (just under five miles), the banner in the club's colours of red and white was carried by over 50,000 fans to the Monumental stadium in the course of a day—a real show of force for Los Millonarios.

ENZO, PRINCE OF RIVER PLATE

When he left the club he'd set on the path to triumph in the Copa Libertadores, Enzo Francescoli promised: "One day I'll return to play with River Plate at the Monumental, that's for sure." Eight years later, the man called 'The Prince' by his supporters kept his promise. He had lost nothing of his elegance, nor his effectiveness. As fate would have it, River Plate lost the Intercontinental Cup to Juventus, a side that included Zinedine Zidane, for whom Francescoli was an idol.

Star players: Alfredo Di Stefano, José Manuel Moreno, Angèl Labruna, Oscar Màs, Ubaldo Fillol, Daniel Passarella, Enzo Francescoli, Hernàn Crespo.

Honours: League: 1920, 1932, 1936-I, 1936-II, 1937, 1941, 1942, 1945, 1947, 1952, 1953, 1955, 1956, 1957, 1975-I, 1975-II, 1977-II, 1979-I, 1979-II, 1980-II, 1981-I, 1986, 1990, 1991-I, 1993-I, 1994-I, 1996-I, 1997-I, 1997-II, 1999-I, 2000-II, 2002-II, 2003-II, 2004-II, 2008-II, 2014-I; Copa Sudamericana 2014; Copa Libertadores 1986, 1996, 2015; Intercontinental Cup 1986.

"Nine players who came through our youth academy now represent the national team. Can Estudiantes say the same?"

Independiente spokesperson before a match versus Estudiantes, February 2015.

INDEPENDIENTE

The King of Cups

Founded: **1904**

Stadium: **Libertadores de América (Buenos Aires)**

Independiente's list of honours would make any club green with envy, for it includes seven Copas Libertadores and two Intercontinental Cups. Theirs is a massive fan base—in 2014, it exceeded 100,000 *socios*—but their supporters are known for being nonchalant, so much so that at one time they contented themselves with light applause whenever a penalty was scored. The *Clasico d'Avellaneda* sees them play their fierce rivals, Racing Club, whose stadium lies just 300 yards away from Independiente's.

14
League Titles

7
Copa Libertadores

2
Intercontinental Cups

Francisco Sa
He won the Copa Libertadores four times in a row with Independiente (1972-1975).

The cost, in millions of euros, of Sergio Agüero's transfer from Independiente to Atlético Madrid.

The number of games played by Ricardo Bochini with the club (1972-1991).

22

740

293

The number of goals scored by Arsenio Erico while he was wearing the Independiente shirt (1933-1946).

November 28, 1973
The club win their first Intercontinental Cup.

A LUNAR CLUB

In 1969, when Apollo XI lifted off to take Neil Armstrong, Michael Collins and Edwin Aldrin to the moon, the astronauts took Independiente club pennants with them. The idea came from the club's general secretary. Several months before the mission's launch, he sent each of the three space adventurers a *socio* card, a complete strip for their children, and pennants in the colours of Independiente.

SERGIO AGÜERO, A PRECOCIOUS HERO

Although Sergio Agüero left Independiente when he was just eighteen years old, he will forever be remembered as one of the club's idols. He joined the Independiente youth team at the age of nine, and played his first game for the adult side when he was fifteen, making him the youngest-ever professional player in Argentine football. He made his mark during the 2005–2006 season, scoring eighteen goals and humiliating Racing Club's defence in one particularly memorable encounter that Independiente won 4–0. His departure for Atlético Madrid in mid-2006 earned Independiente enough to pay for most of the new stadium.

Star players: Arsenio Erico, Daniel Bertoni, Enzo Trossero, Jorge Burruchaga, Diego Forlan, Gabriel Milito, Sergio Agüero.

Honours: League: 1938, 1939, 1948, 1960, 1963, 1967, 1970, 1971, 1977, 1978, 1983, 1989, 1994–II, 2002–I; Copa Sudamericana: 2010; Copa Libertadores: 1964, 1965, 1972, 1973, 1974, 1975, 1984; Intercontinental Cup: 1973, 1984.

"He who wishes to see a show need only go to the theatre. This is a football match, a World Cup Final."
Juan Sebastiàn Veròn, before the final of the 2009 FIFA Club World Cup.

ESTUDIANTES DE LA PLATA

The Rat Stabbers

Founded: **1905**
Stadium: **Estadio Jorge Luis Hirschi (La Plata)**

Founded by medical students, hence their nickname "The Rat Stabbers," Estudiantes de La Plata have remained at the top of Argentine, and even world, football for nearly fifty years. The club won the Intercontinental Cup in 1968, and were close to lifting the FIFA Club World Cup in 2009, but were beaten in the final by FC Barcelona in extra time (1–2). This pride in their historical legacy continues, and former club star Juan Sebastiàn Veròn, son of Juan Ramon, was elected chairman by the *socios* in 2014, as soon as he retired from the game.

5 League Titles

4 Copa Libertadores

December 12, 2010
Juan Sebastian Veron celebrates the fifth league title in the history of the club.

Star players: Juan Ramon Veròn, Carlos Bilardo, José Luis Brown, Juan Sebastiàn Veròn.

Honours: League: 1967, 1982, 1983, 2006, 2010; Intercontinental Cup: 1968; Copa Libertadores: 1968, 1969, 1970, 2009.

"In my view, the San Lorenzo fans are the most exciting in Argentina. They sing the cleverest songs, they entertain you. I love them, I love them very much. I would have liked to play in this strip."
Diego Maradona.

SAN LORENZO

The Crow

Founded: **1908** • Stadium: **Pedro Bidegain (Buenos Aires)**

San Lorenzo are one of the "big five" clubs in the Argentine league. The favourite club of Pope Francis, it was the last of them to win the Copa Libertadores, in 2014. There remains an aura around the club, mainly due to their charismatic and inventive fans, who also fought a long campaign against a supermarket giant to reclaim the land where the club's original stadium once stood.

12 League Titles

1 Copa Libertadores

August 14, 2014
San Lorenzo win their first Copa Libertadores.

Star players: Oscar Ortiz, Jorge Olguin, José-Luis Chilavert, Oscar Ruggeri, Ezequiel Lavezzi.

Honours: League: 1933, 1936, 1946, 1959, 1968, 1972, 1972, 1974, 1995, 2001, 2007, 2013; Copa Libertadores: 2014; Copa Sudamericana: 2002.

AFRICA

"There are very few clubs in the world who don't have the right to lose a single match. Al Ahly is one of them."
Manuel José, head coach of Al Ahly (2001–02, 2003–09, 2010–11).

AL AHLY
The Red Devils

Founded: **1907**
Stadium: **Cairo International (Cairo)**

The club's first chairman may have been English, but Al Ahly (Arabic for 'The National') was historically an emancipative project for young Egyptian men, at a time when the country was still under British occupation. Considered to be "the people's club," Al Ahly were closed to foreign players from 1925. It was around this time that the club began to collect what is now a record number of national and international trophies—currently 130—making Al Ahly Africa's leading club and, with some fifty million supporters, Egypt's most popular club.

37
League Titles

35
National Cups

December 7, 2014
Al Ahly win the CAF Confederation Cup, beating the Ivorians of Séwé Sport.

Star players: Mokhtar El Tetsh, Refaat El Fanagily, Mamoud El Khatib, Mohamed Aboutrika, Essam El Hadary, Wael Gomaa, Mohamed Barakat, Gilberto, Flavio Amado, Hossam Hassan.

Honours: League: 1949, 1950, 1951, 1953, 1954, 1956, 1957, 1958, 1959, 1961, 1962, 1975, 1976, 1977, 1979, 1980, 1981, 1982, 1985, 1986, 1987, 1989, 1994, 1995, 1996, 1997, 1998, 1999, 2000, 2005, 2006, 2007, 2008, 2009, 2010, 2011, 2014; National Cup: 1924, 1925, 1927, 1928, 1930, 1931, 1937, 1940, 1942, 1943, 1945, 1946, 1947, 1949, 1950, 1951, 1953, 1956, 1958, 1961, 1966, 1978, 1981, 1983, 1984, 1985, 1989, 1991, 1992, 1993, 1996, 2001, 2003, 2006, 2007; CAF Champions League: 1982, 1987, 2001, 2005, 2006, 2008, 2012, 2013; African Cup Winners' Cup: 1984, 1985, 1986, 1993; CAF Confederation Cup: 2014.

ZAMALEK SC
The White Knight
Founded: **1911** • Stadium: **Cairo International (Cairo)**

Having won the Egyptian Premier League twelve times, and the CAF Champions League on five occasions, Zamalek could claim to be the top club in the country if it weren't for Al Ahly. In 1948, the club played their first derby against their great Cairo rivals with whom they now share their stadium.

AL-ITTIHAD ALEXANDRIA
Kings of the Town
Founded: **1914** • Stadium: **Alexandria (Alexandria)**

A founding member of the Egyptian Football Association, Al-Ittihad are one of the most popular clubs in the country, and have won the Egypt Cup six times. They play in the oldest stadium in the country, as do their local rivals, Smouha SC.

AL-MASRY CLUB
The Green Eagles
Founded: **1920** • Stadium: **Port Said (Port-Said)**

The club was founded by Egyptians to play against the teams created by foreign communities in Port Said during the British occupation. Many years later, Al-Masry would be managed by the Hungarian star Ferenc Puskas. In 1983, the club also became the first in Egypt to turn professional. They won the Egypt Cup in 1998, and enjoy continued popularity.

ISMAILY SC
Mango Boys
Founded: **1924** • Stadium: **Ismailia (Ismailia)**

With their three league titles (1967, 1991, 2002), Ismaily are one of the few clubs to have edged out Al Ahly and Zamalek. Their victory in the 1969 CAF Champions League— a first for an Arab team— made them even more popular throughout Egypt.

EL MOKAWLOON SC
Mountain Wolves
Founded: **1972** • Stadium: **Arab Contractors (Cairo)**

Founded by a powerful Egyptian entrepreneur, El Mokawloon are one of very few clubs to have snatched a league championship victory—in 1983—from the duo of Al Ahly and Zamalek. They have also shone on the continental scene, taking three CAF Cup Winners' Cups (1982, 1983, 1996).

PETROJET FC
Blaugrana
Founded: **1980** • Stadium: **Suez (Suez)**

Founded in Cairo by an Egyptian oil company, the club moved to Suez after their promotion to the first division in 2006. Far from the competitiveness of the capital, they have made a name for themselves, finishing towards the top of the league several times over the past eight seasons.

AL-ITTIHAD CLUB
Tehaa

Founded: **1944** • Stadium: **11 juin (Tripoli)**

The most successful club in Libyan football, with sixteen league titles, they have reached the semi-finals of three CAF competitions (Champions League, Cup Winners' Cup, and Confederation Cup). Their supporters are among the most devoted in Libya.

AL-AHLI SC
Alzaeem

Founded: **1950** • Stadium: **11 juin (Tripoli)**

Al-Ahli have won the league eleven times and the cup six times, and qualified for the final of the 1984 CAF Cup Winners' Cup, before withdrawing for political reasons. Linked to the country's struggle for independence, they are Libya's most popular club.

CLUB AFRICAIN
Zanatir

Founded: **1920** • Stadium: **Olympique de Radès (Tunis)**

With thirteen league victories, and eleven cups, the club are the most successful in Tunisian football after their rivals, Espérance. Winner of the 1991 CAF Champions League, they have been runners-up in the Cup Winners' Cup and the Confederation Cup.

ETOILE SPORTIVE DU SAHEL
The Star

Founded: **1925** • Stadium: **Olympique de Sousse (Sousse)**

Nine-time league champions, they have the best African record of all Tunisian clubs, having won one CAF Champions League, two African Cup Winners' Cups, two CAF Cups, and one Confederation Cup. They are known for having a very strong midfield.

CA BIZERTIN
The Sharks of the North

Founded: **1928** • Stadium: **15 octobre (Bizerte)**

The club enjoying a successful period in the 1940s, and returned to form in the 1980s, thanks to a squad composed of players from their youth teams. Four-time league champions, they were the first Tunisian club to win an African trophy, lifting the 1988 Cup Winners' Cup.

CS SFAXIEN
The Arab Juventus

Founded: **1928** • Stadium: **Taïeb Mehiri (Sfax)**

Sfaxien have played in the first division since 1946, without ever being relegated. Eight-time champions, they hold an impressive list of continental achievements: runners-up in the 2006 Champions League, winner of the CAF Cup, and three Confederation Cups.

"In Tunis, they ask your name, and then they ask you whether you support Tunis Espérance or Club Africain." **Hocine Ragued.**

ESPÉRANCE

Blood and Gold

Founded: **1919**

Stadium: **Olympique de Radès (Tunis)**

Named after the café in the Tunisian capital where the club was founded, Espérance Tunis was the first Arab-speaking club in the country. Present in the first division since 1936, they have never been relegated. In addition to being the most successful club in the country, they are also a force in Africa, having won four continental titles, including two CAF Champions Leagues: the first in 1994—against the Egyptians of Zamalek—and the second in 2011—against Wydad Casablanca. For nearly a century, they have maintained a strong rivalry with Club Africain—the other big Tunis team—who were founded one year after Espérance. Despite being viewed as having benefited from the favour of the authorities following the country's independence, Espérance have nevertheless affirmed their supremacy on the pitch.

26 League Titles

14 National Cups

2 CAF Champions League Titles

December 14, 2011
ES Tunis prepare to play Monterrey in the Club World Cup.

Star players: Hicham Aboucheraouane, Michael Eneramo, Khaled Badra, Tarek Dhiab, Radhi Jaidi, Nabil Maaloul, Tarek Thabet, Ali Zitouni, Oussama Darragi, Issam Jemâa, Yannick N'Djeng, Youssef Msakni, Harrison Afful, Hocine Ragued.

Honours: League: 1942, 1959, 1960, 1970, 1975, 1976, 1982, 1985, 1988, 1989, 1991, 1993, 1994, 1998, 1999, 2000, 2001, 2002, 2003, 2004, 2006, 2009, 2010, 2011, 2012, 2014; National Cup: 1939, 1957, 1964, 1979, 1980, 1986, 1989, 1991, 1997, 1999, 2006, 2007, 2008, 2011; CAF Champions League: 1994, 2011; African Cup Winners' Cup 1998; CAF Cup: 1997.

"JSK are a club that cannot be stopped when they want something."
Essaid Belkalem, former player.

JS KABYLIE
The Canaries

Founded: **1946** • Stadium: **Stade du 1er Novembre 1954 (Tizi Ouzou)**

The club were promoted to the first division in 1969, with a semi-professional status, and have stayed there ever since, winning more titles than any other club in the country. They dominated Algerian football in the 1970s and 1980s, under the name JE Tizi-Ouzou, much to the dismay of the clubs in the capital. JS Kabylie are considered to be a true emblem of Kabyle identity, and their fans often flock to Algiers for matches, such as in 2001, when 100,000 supporters travelled to the city for an inter-continental final against the Tunisian team Etoile du Sahel.

14 League Titles

5 National Cups

2 CAF Champions League Titles

October 17, 2010
JS Kabylie celebrate after scoring against Mazembe during the CAF Champions League semi-finals.

Star players: Ali Fergani, Mouloud Iboud, Nacer Bouiche, Sadmi Hamid, Farid Ghazi, Fawzi Chaouchi, Moussa Saib, Tarek Adlane.

Honours: League: 1973, 1974, 1977, 1980, 1982, 1983, 1985, 1986, 1989, 1990, 1995, 2004, 2006, 2008; National Cup: 1977, 1986, 1992, 1994, 2011; CAF Champions League: 1981, 1990; African Cup Winners' Cup: 1995; CAF Cup: 2000, 2001, 2002.

MOULOUDIA CLUB ALGER
The People's Club
Founded: **1921** • Stadium: **Stade du 5 Juillet 1962 (Algiers)**

Officially the oldest club in Algerian football, Mouloudia Club Alger won five league championships and one CAF Champions League in the 1970s, but did not taste such success again until the 2000s. The club is particularly proud of its working-class roots, and one of its nicknames is "Noble Sons of the Kasbah."

CS CONSTANTINOIS
The Smurfs
Founded: **1926** • Stadium: **Mohamed Hamlaoui (Constantine)**

Constantinois consider themselves the doyens of Algerian football, having played a role in the country's independence by attempting to form a regional league for native teams. The club won the league championship once, in 1997, and draw on a strong, working-class fan base.

ES SÉTIF
The Black Eagles
Founded: **1958** • Stadium: **Stade du 8 Mai 1945 (Sétif)**

The second most successful club in Algeria, with six league titles and eight cups, ES Sétif also won the CAF Champions League twice (1988, 2014). Their home turf, nicknamed "Stadium of Fire and Victory," is brought to life by several bands of supporters, such as "Ouled El Garita."

CR BÉLOUIZDAD
The Reds
Founded: **1962** • Stadium: **Stade du 20 Août 1955 (Algiers)**

With six league titles and as many Algerian Cups, CR Bélouizdad have one of the best records in the country. Islam Slimani, one of the star players of "The Foxes," (the nickname of the national team) played for the club. Most CR Bélouizdad fans come from the working-class districts of Algiers.

ACS KSAR
The Greens
Founded: **1978** • Stadium: **Stade Olympique (Nouakchott)**

Five-time league champions and four-time cup winners, ASC Ksar have edged out the historic AS Garde Nationale and ASC Police to become the number one team in the capital, Nouakchott. They currently supply the largest contingent of players to the national team.

FC NOUADHIBOU
The Orange Club
Founded: **1999** • Stadium: **Municipal (Nouadhibou)**

The most successful club in the country since the start of the twenty-first century—the local press has even nick-named them "the locomotive of Mauritanian football." They have won the league championship four times, and the cup twice.

"I really put them through it. But when I left Raja, they came round to my house, crying like kids; it was the most emotional moment of my career."

Vahid Halilhodžić, Raja coach 1997–1998.

RAJA CLUB ATHLETIC

The Green Eagles

Founded: **1949**

Stadium: **Mohammed V (Casablanca)**

Founded by a theatre company, Raja are one of the most successful clubs in Africa, thanks to three victories in the CAF Champions League. Moroccan Champions for the eleventh time in 2013, the club automatically qualified for the FIFA Club World Cup, which took place in the country that same year. After having eliminated the New Zealanders of Auckland (2-1) in the playoffs, Raja knocked out the Mexicans of Monterrey (2-1) in the quarter-finals. They faced off against Ronaldinho's Atletico Mineiro in the semis, and caused a sensation by beating them 3-1, before losing the final to Bayern Munich. Raja had just equalled the performance of TP Mazembe, the first African club to be runner-up in the FIFA Club World Cup.

11 League Titles

7 National Cups

3 CAF Champions League Titles

December 18, 2013
Raja qualify for the Club World Cup final after beating Atlético Meneiro.

Star players: Hicham Aboucherouane, Sofiane Alloudi, Salaheddine Bassir, Mustapha Chadli, Amine Erbati, Abdelmajid Dolmi, Abdelilah Fahmi, Talal El Karkouri.

Honours: League: 1988, 1996, 1997, 1998, 1999, 2000, 2001, 2004, 2009, 2011, 2013; National Cup: 1974, 1977, 1982, 1996, 2002, 2005, 2013; CAF Champions League: 1989, 1997, 1999; CAF Cup 2003.

WYDAD ATHLETIC CLUB
The Red and Whites
Founded: **1937** • Stadium: **Mohammed V (Casablanca)**

Thanks to a series of top-notch coaches—Benito Floro, Lucien Leduc, and John Toshack—Wydad have won thirteen league titles (a Moroccan record), the 1992 CAF Champions League, and the 2002 CAF Cup Winners' Cup. They enjoy middle-class support, and are Raja's great rivals.

MAGHREB AS FÈS
Yellow Tigers
Founded: **1946** • Stadium: **Complexe Sportif de Fès (Fès)**

Founded by nationalists, MAS Fès were the first Moroccan club to play a French Cup match—in Paris, in 1954. Very popular, they have won the league four times, as well as the 2011 CAF Confederation Cup. They contest the Atlas derby against Meknès.

KAWKAB MARRAKECH
The Planet
Founded: **1947** • Stadium: **Marrakech (Marrakech)**

Twice league champions, in 1958 and 1992, Kawkab have also won six Moroccan Cups. In 1996, they were the first Moroccan club to win the CAF Cup. Since 2010, they have played in a new 45,000 capacity stadium, backed by the Ultra Crazy Boys.

FAR RABAT
Black Army
Founded: **1958** • Stadium: **Prince Moulay Abdellah (Rabat)**

Founded by the future King Hassan II within the Royal Moroccan Armed Forces, the club has won twelve league titles, the 1985 CAF Champions League, and the 2005 Confederation Cup. In 2007, six thousand of its supporters travelled to Fès, a record in Africa.

DJOLIBA AC
DAC
Founded: **1960** • Stadium: **26 Mars (Bamako)**

Founded in the year of independence, they are the most successful club in the country, winners of twenty-two league titles and nineteen cups. Chaired by one of its former players, they have one of the most modern youth academies in Africa.

STADE MALIEN
The Stadiens
Founded: **1960** • Stadium: **26 Mars (Bamako)**

This historic rival of Djoliba has racked up nineteen league titles and eighteen cups. Stade Malien lost the final of the 1964 CAF Champions League, but won the 2009 Confederation Cup, the only continental trophy held by a Malian club.

AS REAL BAMAKO
The Scorpions
Founded: **1960** • Stadium: **Modibo Keita (Bamako)**

Real Bamako is the third biggest club in Malian football. Just like Djoliba and Stade Malien, they have won the league championship six times. Runner-up in the 1966 CAF Champions League, the club launched the career of Salif Keita, the first African Footballer of the Year (1970).

OFFICE DU NIGER SPORTS
The Rice Growers
Founded: **2011** • Stadium: **Amary Daou (Ségou)**

Founded by employees of the Office du Niger, a government agency that administers a major irrigation scheme, the club started out in the regional division, before entering the first division just nine months later. They are one of the few clubs not to be based in the capital, Bamako.

ASC JEANNE D'ARC
Sporting
Founded: **1921** • Stadium: **Léopold Senghor (Dakar)**

Founded by a French priest, ASC Jeanne d'Arc have won ten league titles and six cups. They are the only Senegalese club to have been runners-up in the CAF Cup (1998). In 2004, they reached the semi-finals of the CAF Champions League. They contest the big derby of the capital, Dakar, against Diaraf.

ASC DIARAF
The Noblemen
Founded: **1933** • Stadium: **Stade de Diaraf (Dakar)**

Founded as France Foyer Sénégal, they changed their name the year of Senegal's independence, and became the most successful club in the country, winning eleven league titles and thirteen cups. Their training academy produced the former Manchester United and current Stoke City player Mame Biram Diouf.

AS DOUANES
The Gabelous
Founded: **1980** • Stadium: **Demba Diop (Dakar)**

Their five league titles and six cup victories have made them the third greatest club in the history of Senegalese football. Relegated to the second division in 2013, they immediately won promotion back to the top flight. The Newcastle striker Papiss Cissé began his career here.

DIAMBARS FC
The Warriors
Founded: **2003** • Stadium: **Fodé Wade (Saly)**

Established as part of the Diambars training academy—mainly by Patrick Vieira and Bernard Lama—the club became professional in 2009, and moved up to the first division in 2012. League runners-up in their first season in the top flight, they won the title in 2013.

REAL DE BANJUL
City Boys
Founded: **1966** • Stadium: **Banjul Mini (Banjul)**

Formed by students on their way home from an international tournament in Senegal, the club very quickly became one of the best in the country, supplying nine players to the national team. Their twelve league titles make them the number one rivals of Wallidan.

WALLIDAN FC
The Blue Stripes
Founded: **1969** • Stadium: **Independence (Banjul)**

With fifteen league titles and fifteen cups, Wallidan are the most successful club in the country. They were the last club of Biri Biri, the first African footballer to play professionally in Denmark. In 2015, the club was relegated to the second division for the first time in forty-five years.

CLUBE SPORTIVO MINDELENSE
Red Devils
Founded: **1919** • Stadium: **Estádio Municipal Adelito Sena (Mindelo)**

This club from the island of São Vicente dominates Cape Verdean football and has twenty league titles as well as one appearance in the Portuguese Cup (1971). Mindelense's great rivals are Académica, whom they play with the backing of their main group of supporters, the Orange Army.

SPORTING CLUBE DA PRAIA
The Lions
Founded: **1929** • Stadium: **Estádio da Várzea (Praia)**

This club, from the island's capital, are descended from Sporting Clube du Portugal. They have won twelve league championships. Their supporters' group—Torcida Verde Santiago—create a stirring atmosphere, especially at matches against local rivals Boavista and Travadores.

MIGHTY BLACKPOOL FC
The Tis-Tas Boys
Founded: **1923** • Stadium: **National (Freetown)**

The oldest club in the country, in 1954, they took the name of the club led at the time by the legendary Stanley Matthews. Eleven-time champions, they hold the most titles in Sierra Leone, and are also the only Sierra Leonan club to have reached the quarter-finals of the CAF Champions League.

EAST END LIONS FC
The Killers
Founded: **1928** • Stadium: **National (Freetown)**

Eleven-time league champions, the club holds the joint record for league victories with their great rival from the capital, Mighty Blackpool, against whom they play a hotly contested derby. The club were also runners-up in the UFOA Cup (West Africa) in 1996.

GAMBIA

CAPE VERDE

SIERRA LEONE

SPORTING CLUBE DE BISSAU
The Green and Whites

Founded: **1936** • Stadium: **Estádio Nacional 24 de Setembro (Bissau)**

Named after Portugal's Sporting Clube, the club played in the Portuguese Cup four times during the 1960s–1970s. Since Guinea-Bissau's independence, Sporting de Bissau have become the most successful club in the country, with fourteen league titles between 1983 and 2010, and six national cups.

CF OS BALANTAS
The First Champion

Founded: **1974** • Stadium: **Corca Sow (Mansõa)**

Founded just after independence, the club, who are based in a small provincial town, won the first national league championship after the Portuguese era, in 1975. Four-time champions, most recently in 2013, the club are the most successful outside the capital, Bissau.

AS KALOUM STAR
The Yellow Submarine

Founded: **1958** • Stadium: **Stade du 28 Septembre (Conakry)**

With their thirteen national titles, the last of which was won in 2014, AS Kaloum Star are close to the record of their great historic rival Hafia (fifteen-time champions). Twice a semi-finalist in the CAF Champions League, they were also runners-up in the 1995 CAF Cup.

HOROYA AC
H.A.C.

Founded: **1975** • Stadium: **Stade du 28 Septembre (Conakry)**

The youngest of the three great clubs in Conakry—the Guinean capital—Horoya have racked up thirteen national titles, including three in a row (2011, 2012, 2013), as well as a CAF Cup Winners' Cup (1978). Their greatest rival over the last few seasons has been AS Kaloum.

FELLO STAR DE LABÉ
The Blue and Blacks

Founded: **1988** • Stadium: **Saïfoulaye Diallo (Labé)**

This club from the Fouta-Djallon province, whose name means "star over the mountain," is the only club from outside the capital to have won the league championship—four times in fact, between 2006 and 2010. They have also won two national cups.

SATELLITE FC
The Satellites

Founded: **2000** • Stadium: **Stade du 28 Septembre (Conakry)**

Founded just fifteen years ago, Satellite enjoyed very early successes, with their first league title coming in 2002, followed by a second in 2005. They draw on a reservoir of talent—a youth academy that seeks to train its young players both athletically and intellectually.

"I know that the whole of Africa, the whole world even, has their eyes on the club today."
Kerfalla Camara, President of Hafia FC.

HAFIA FC

Tri Campeao

Founded: **1951** • Stadium: **28 Septembre (Conakry)**

Originally named Conakry II, after the neighbourhood of the Guinean capital where they were founded, the club dominated African football in the 1970s. Led by Souleymane Cherif—the only African Footballer of the Year to come from Guinea—the club won the 1972 CAF Champions Cup, then contested four more consecutive finals between 1975 and 1978, winning two of them. After lifting a fifteenth league trophy in 1985, Hafia fell back a little and they were even relegated to the second division. In 2014, they returned to the top flight, signing several Brazilian players at some considerable cost. The club is a unique case in Africa. They command vast financial resources since being taken over by one of the richest entrepreneurs in West Africa—he has set the goal of making Hafia African champions again.

15 League Titles

3 National Cups

3 CAF Champions Cups

2015–16 season
Hafia chase their glorious past.

Star players: Souleymane Cherif, Petit Sory, Papa Camara, Maxime Camara, Mamadou Aliou Kéïta, Morciré Sylla, Edenté, Smith Samuel, Mory Kone, Ousmane Tolo Thiam, Abdoulaye Emerson, Ousmane Fernandez, Mohamed Sylla, Abdoul Salam Sow.

Honours: League: 1966, 1967, 1968, 1971, 1972, 1973, 1974, 1975, 1976, 1977, 1978, 1979, 1982, 1983, 1985; National Cup: 1992, 1993, 2002; CAF Champions Cup: 1972, 1975, 1977.

UNION OF INVINCIBLE ELEVEN
The Yellow Boys
Founded: **1943** • Stadium: **Antoinette Tubman (Monrovia)**

Founded by students, Invincible Eleven are the most successful club in the country—along with Mighty Barolle—having won thirteen league titles. Some of the biggest stars of Liberian football have played for the team, such as George Weah and Christopher Wreh—who played for Monaco and Arsenal.

MIGHTY BAROLLE
The Rollers
Founded: **1964** • Stadium: **Doris Williams (Buchanan)**

Thirteen-time champions of Liberia, the club shares the honour with Invincible Eleven of being the most successful team in the country. They share another stat with their great rival: one of their former players is George Weah, who was European Footballer of the Year 1996 and one of the best African players in history.

AFRICA SPORTS NATIONAL
The Eaglets
Founded: **1947** • Stadium: **Robert Champroux (Abidjan)**

Africa Sports National were originally founded by the Bété people, but subsequently opened up to all ethnicities. A great rival of Asec Mimosas, the club have won seventeen league titles and two African Cup Winners' Cups.

ASEC MIMOSAS
The Mimosas
Founded: **1948** • Stadium: **Houphouët-Boigny (Abidjan)**

Founded by a group of businessmen, the club's youth academy have trained such great players as Yaya Touré, Gervinho, and Salomon Kalou. The "Black and Yellows" hold the record for league championships, with twenty-four trophies. They also won the 1998 CAF Champions League.

STELLA D'ADJAMÉ
The Magnans
Founded: **1953** • Stadium: **Robert Champroux (Abidjan)**

Although Stella are somewhat overshadowed by the giants Africa Sport and Asec, the club have won the league title on three occasions, and done well at continental level, taking the CAF Cup in 1993 and finishing runners-up in the 1975 African Cup Winners' Cup.

SÉWÉ SPORT
Séwéké
Founded: **1977** • Stadium: **Auguste Denise (San Pédro)**

Séwé are a rising Ivorian club, having won three consecutive league titles (2012, 2013, 2014) and finishing runners-up in the 2014 CAF Confederation Cup. The club are looking to build on their rapid rise, despite their limited resources.

GHANA

"The old order changed, giving way to the new. You have taken the footsteps of your ancestors but in a different way. They with guns, bows and arrows, you with your hands and legs, and with your play."
C. Amoah, *The Pride of Ashanti Kotoko, 1940.*

ASANTE KOTOKO
Porcupine Warriors
Founded: **1935** • Stadium: **Baba Yara Stadium (Kumasi)**

This club has existed under various names since 1924 when it was founded by a driver working for the British Army. When the national league was established, Asante Kotoko carved out a place for themselves as one of the best, alongside their rivals, Hearts of Oak—against whom they play the "Super Clash." They are the most successful club in the country, and have also performed well on the continental scene. From 1967 to 1993, they contested seven CAF Champions League finals, winning two. More recently, they were runners-up in the 2002 Cup Winners' Cup and the 2004 Confederation Cup. Asante Kotoko's owner is the wealthy king of Ashanti, Asantehene Nana Osei Tutu II. They are based in the country's second city and enjoy huge popularity, with some eleven million supporters.

24 League Titles

10 National Cups

2 CAF Champions League Titles

June 4, 2014
Asante Kotoko win their twenty-fourth Ghanaian league title.

Star players: C.K. Gyamfi, Mohammed Salisu, Baba Yara, Osei Kofi, Robert Mensah, Ibrahim Sunday, Malik Jabir, Opoku Afriyie, Albert Asase, Kwesi Appiah, Samuel Opoku Nti, Addae Kyenkyehene, Papa Arko, Frimpong Manso, Karim Abdul Razak, Frank Amankwah, Alex Nyarko.

Honours: League: 1959, 1964, 1965, 1967, 1968, 1969, 1972, 1975, 1980, 1981, 1982, 1983, 1986, 1987, 1989, 1991, 1992, 1993, 2003, 2005, 2008, 2012, 2013, 2014; National Cup: 1958, 1960, 1976, 1978, 1984, 1990, 1991, 1998, 2001, 2014; CAF Champions League: 1970, 1983.

ACCRA HEARTS OF OAK SC
The Soccer Paradise
Founded: **1911** • Stadium: **Ohene Djan (Accra)**

With twenty league titles, this club is the most successful in the country behind Asante Kotoko, their national rivals. Winner of the 2000 CAF Champions League, and twice runner-up, they were ranked eighth in the world by CNN/World Soccer in 2001.

ASHANTI GOLD SC
The Miners
Founded: **1978** • Stadium: **Len Clay (Obuasi)**

Ashanti Gold SC were founded by workers from gold mines in the Ashanti region. They enjoyed their heyday between 1994 and 1997, when the mining company, AGC, gave them a cash injection, enabling the club to win the league three times in a row, as well as reach the final of the 1997 CAF Champions League.

ADUANA STARS FC
Aduana Ogya
Founded: **1985** • Stadium: **Agyeman Badu (Dormaa Ahenkro)**

This club, from a small town in the south of the country, caused a stir in 2010 when they became league champions in their first season in the top flight—something that had never previously happened in Ghana.

BEREKUM CHELSEA FC
Blues
Founded: **2000** • Stadium: **Golden City Park (Berekum)**

Established to provide an opportunity for local players, the club entered the first division in 2008, and won the league title in 2011. During the 2010 World Cup, the Berekum defender, Lee Addy, played for the national side. The club's local rivals are Berekum Arsenal.

AS FASO-YENNENGA
The Old Lady
Founded: **1947** • Stadium: **Stade du 4 Août (Ouagadougou)**

UNION - DISCIPLINE - VICTOIRE

ASFA are the most successful club in Burkina Faso, having won thirteen league titles. Their best continental performance was in the quarter-finals of the 2001 CAF Cup Winners' Cup. This continued success has earned the club their nickname "The Old Lady," which is a local term of respect.

ETOILE FILANTE OUAGADOUGOU
Queen of the Stadiums
Founded: **1955** • Stadium: **Stade du 4 Août (Ouagadougou)**

These great local and national rivals of AS Faso-Yennenga were founded by foreign players from countries such as Togo and Benin. In 2014, the club won their twelfth league title. They also hold twenty national cups, a record in the country.

ETOILE FILANTE DE LOMÉ
The Blue and Whites
Founded: **1932** • Stadium: **Oscar Anthony (Lomé)**

Holder of seven league titles won between 1961 and 1992, and a place in the final of the 1968 CAF Champions League, the club has long dominated Togolese football. In 2006, they were the only club in the country to have a player in the squad that had played in the World Cup.

DYNAMIC TOGOLAIS
Dyto
Founded: **1961** • Stadium: **Agoè-Nyivé (Lomé)**

Six-time league champions between 1970 and 2012, the club, who have also won the cup three times, are a dependable force in Togolese football. Their best perform-ance in a CAF competition was a place in the quarter-finals of the 1971 Champions League.

OLYMPIQUE CLUB AGAZA
The Black Scorpions of Tokoin
Founded: **1978** • Stadium: **Agoè-Nyivé (Lomé)**

The club dominated in the 1980s, winning two league titles, as well as a place in the final of the 1983 CAF Cup Winners' Cup. They are also famous for having fielded Emmanuel Adebayor before his departure for Europe.

AC SEMASSI FC
Tchaoudjo Warriors
Founded: **1978** • Stadium: **Municipal (Sokodé)**

Based in the country's second city, the club hold the record for national championship victories with ten titles. In 1984, they reached the semi-finals of the CAF Champions League, their best continental performance. Their local rivals are Tchaoudjo AC.

AS DRAGONS FC DE L'OUÉMÉ
Dragons
Founded: **1977** • Stadium: **Charles-de-Gaulle (Porto-Novo)**

Dragons hold the most titles in Beninese football, with twelve league championships and six cups. Their best continental performance was as finalists in the 1987 African Cup Winners' Cup. The star Ghanaian player Abédi Pelé played for Dragons in 1984.

MOGAS 90 FC
The Oilmen
Founded: **1990** • Stadium: **Charles-de-Gaulle (Porto-Novo)**

The club, who have links to the petroleum and gas supplier SONACOP, are the great rivals of AS Dragons FC. Mogas have won ten Benin Cups and hold three Benin Premier League titles.

SAHEL SPORTING CLUB
The Sahelians

Founded: **1974** • Stadium: **Général Seyni Kountché (Niamey)**

Based in the capital, Sahel are the most successful club in the country. They won their first league title in 1973, under the name "Secteur 7," and have since won twelve more league championships. The most popular club in Niger, they have a highly-regarded youth academy.

OLYMPIC FC DE NIAMEY
The Lions of Lakouroussou

Founded: **1974** • Stadium: **Général Seyni Kountché (Niamey)**

Heir to "Secteur 6,"—who won the league five times—the club have added another seven titles since 1976. They also hold five cups. Great rivals of Sahel SC, against whom they play the Niamey Derby, they have returned to prominence after a rather less illustrious period.

SHOOTING STARS SC
Oluyole Warriors

Founded: **vers 1950** • Stadium: **Lekan Salami (Ibadan)**

Five-time league champions, Shooting Stars were the first club in the country to win an African trophy—the 1976 CAF Cup Winners' Cup—and were twice runners-up in the Champions League. They are very popular in Ibadan, a town of over three million inhabitants.

ENUGU RANGERS
Flying Antelopes

Founded: **1970** • Stadium: **Nnamdi Azikiwe (Enugu)**

Founded after the Biafran War, and linked to the Igbo people, the club won the league six times between 1974 and 1984, and have never been relegated. The first club in the country to be listed on the stock market, it was where Jay-Jay Okocha, star of Paris Saint-Germain and Bolton, started his career.

BRIDGE FC
The Bridge Boys

Founded: **1976** • Stadium: **Agege (Lagos)**

Bridge FC were founded by the Julius Berger construction firm—whose name they carried until 2010—and have won two league titles and played in two finals of the CAF Cup Winners' Cup. They have fielded such players as Taribo West, Sunday Oliseh, and Emmanuel Amuneke.

ENYIMBA INTERNATIONAL FC
Peoples' Elephant

Founded: **1976** • Stadium: **Enyimba International (Aba)**

Founded by the regional government, Enyimba have benefited from the financial largesse of the governor since 1999, enabling them to become the country's top club, winning six titles between 2001 and 2010, as well as two CAF Champions Leagues. The club has some ninety million supporters.

HEARTLAND FC
Spartans
Founded: **1976** • Stadium: **Dan Anyiam (Owerri)**

Six-time champion in the 1980s–1990s, this club, where Nwankwo Kanu made his debut, saw success in the years after 2006, when they were bought by the regional government. Runners-up in the 2008 league championship, in 2009 they reached their second CAF Champions League final since 1988.

KANO PILLARS
Masu Gida
Founded: **1990** • Stadium: **Sani Abacha (Kano)**

Established at the same time as the creation of the professional league, Kano Pillars have won four titles since 2008, making them the most successful Nigerian club of the last decade. In March 2015, a bus carrying the team was attacked by terrorists, wounding five people.

RENAISSANCE FC
Mayaye
Founded: **1954** • Stadium: **Omnisports Idriss Mahamat Ouya (N'Djamena)**

Winner of five league titles, including four in a row between 2004 and 2007, RFC have legendary status in Chadian football. Oppressed under the presidency of François Tombalbaye (1960–1975), Renaissance have remained popular across all levels of society.

FOULLAH EDIFICE FC
The Sky Blues
Founded: **2007** • Stadium: **Omnisports Idriss Mahamat Ouya (N'Djamena)**

The youngest of the major clubs of the capital, N'Djamena, Foullah Edifice entered the first division in 2008. They won the league championship in 2011, 2013, and 2014, as well as the cup in 2014, making them the biggest local rivals of Renaissance FC.

AS TEMPÊTE MOCAF
The Red and Blacks
Founded: **1940** • Stadium: **Barthélémy Boganda (Bangui)**

This club from Bangui is the country's most successful, with eleven league titles and six national cups. The derbies they contest against Olympic Real, Stade Centrafricaine Tocages, and the other teams from Bangui draw the attention of the entire country.

OLYMPIC REAL DE BANGUI
The Yellows
Founded: **1945** • Stadium: **Barthélémy Boganda (Bangui)**

Ten-time winner of the national league championship, and twice winner of the cup, this club from the capital—that was originally called Réal Olympique Castel—is one of the country's most successful. In 1974, the club played in the first round of the CAF Champions League.

NIGERIA

CHAD

CENTRAL AFRICAN REPUBLIC

"It was seeing Thomas N'Kono play that made me want to become a goalkeeper." **Gianluigi Buffon**

CANON YAOUNDÉ
Kpa-Kum

Founded: **1930**
Stadium: **Ahmadou Ahidjo (Yaoundé)**

The legendary Canon Yaoundé were ranked fourth in the list of top African clubs of the twentieth century. They were formed to play against Etoile Indigène in a gala match on November 11, 1930. The club began to dominate national and continental football in the 1970s. Their successes have made them the most popular club in the country. ⚽ The golden age of "the Brazilians of Africa": Through their playing style and their many victories, the Canon Yaoundé players of the 1970s-1980s were nicknamed "the Brazilians of Africa," forming the backbone of the national team that remained unbeaten in three matches during the 1982 World Cup in Spain. Two players in this era were even awarded the African Footballer of the Year award: Thomas N'Kono (1979) and Jean Manga Onguéné (1980).

10 League Titles

11 National Cups

3 CAF Champions League Titles

A golden generation
At the end of the 1970s and the beginning of the 1980s, Canon Yaoundé reigned over the national and continental arena.

Star players: Jean Manga-Onguene, Théophile Abega, Grégoire Mbida, Thomas N'Kono, Jacques Songo'o, François Oman Biyik, Mac-Vivien Foé.

Honours: League: 1970, 1974, 1977, 1979, 1980, 1982, 1985, 1986, 1991, 2002; National Cup: 1967, 1973, 1975, 1976, 1977, 1978, 1983, 1986, 1993, 1995, 1999; CAF Champions League: 1971, 1978, 1980; CAF Cup Winners' Cup: 1979.

CAMEROON

DRAGON CLUB DE YAOUNDÉ
The Red Dragons
Founded: **1928** • Stadium: **Ahmadou Ahidjo (Yaoundé)**

Originally called Allico Maritime, the oldest club in the Cameroonian capital was Canon's first rival. Winner of the national cup in 1982, it won the second division championship in 2014, returning to the top flight after a break of twenty-eight years.

ORYX CLUB DE DOUALA
The Black and Yellows
Founded: **1907** • Stadium: **Stade de la Réunification (Douala)**

This legendary Cameroonian club won five of the first seven seasons of the league championship, as well as the first CAF Champions League, in 1965. Oryx Club de Douala currently play in the second division

TONNERRE KALARA CLUB DE YAOUNDÉ The Book
Founded: **1934** • Stadium: **Ahmadou Ahidjo (Yaoundé)**

The team's honours are limited to five league titles won between 1981 and 1988, and one CAF Cup Winners' Cup, in 1975. Tonnerre Yaoundé are idolized, though, for having nurtured the talents of such legendary players as Roger Milla and the Liberian George Weah.

UNION SPORTIVE DE DOUALA
The Foreigners
Founded: **1958** • Stadium: **Stade de la Réunification (Douala)**

Union de Douala entered the first division in 1958, and have remained there ever since. They have won five league titles, and have lifted the 1979 CAF Champions League trophy with the legendary Joseph-Antoine Belle in goal.

COTON SPORT FC DE GAROUA
The Cotton Workers
Founded: **1986** • Stadium: **Roumdé-Adjia (Garoua)**

The youngest of the great Cameroonian clubs, Coton Sport have the biggest budget of all the country's teams, thanks to the support of the cotton industry. Since being promoted to the first division in 1992, they have won thirteen league titles and been runners-up five times.

KADJI SPORT ACADEMY
The Academics
Founded: **1995** • Stadium: **Akwa (Douala)**

This modest second-division club is famous for having the foremost training academy in Cameroon, producing players who have gone on to world renown, such as Samuel Eto'o, Stéphane M'Bia, Carlos Kameni, and Jean II Makoun.

SONY ELÁ NGUEMA
The Meringues
Founded: **1976** • Stadium: **Malabo (Malabo)**

Fifteen-time national champions, including eight times in succession between 1984 and 1991, and seven-time winners of the national cup, Sony Elá Nguema are by far the country's most successful club. Their major rivals are local team Atlético Malabo, and Akonangui FC of the town of Ebebiyin.

LEONES VEGETARIANOS FC
The Vegetarians
Founded: **2000** • Stadium: **Malabo (Malabo)**

This first-division club was founded as Vegetarianos CF by a militant Spanish vegetarian, who later staged a hunger strike in India in support of a local team who lacked a pitch to play on. His example was followed in Cameroon, where a club chose the same name.

SPORTING CLUBE DO PRÍNCIPE
Sporting
Founded: **1915** • Stadium: **Campo de Futebol de Santo António (Santo António)**

Situated on the island of Principe, the club was established as a subsidiary of Sporting Clube Portugal. Twice winners of the league title, in 2011 and 2012, they also won the cup in 2012, and played in their first CAF Champions League, in 2013.

SPORTING PRAIA CRUZ
The Lions
Founded: **1939** • Stadium: **Nacional 12 de Julho (São Tomé)**

The most successful club in the country, with six league titles to their credit, Sporting Praia Cruz maintain strong links with Sporting Clube Portugal. In 2000, after the Lisbon team's victory in the Portuguese league championship, the supporters of Praia Cruz paraded through the streets of São Tomé.

AS MANGASPORT
Manga
Founded: **1962** • Stadium: **Henri Sylvoz (Moanda)**

Founded at a time when manganese was beginning to be extracted in the Moanda region, the club is today linked to major industrial companies such as Total. They have dominated Gabonese football over the last twenty years, winning the national league championship seven times.

FOOTBALL CANON 105 LIBREVILLE   The Bandits
Founded: **1975** • Stadium: **Omar-Bongo (Libreville)**

The club's motto is "efficiency, availability, skill," and they have certainly put these precepts into practice by winning thirteen league titles and five cups, making them one of the most successful clubs in Gabon. FC 105 Libreville also won the 2004 Central African Cup (Uniffac).

"No matter how hard I shouted instructions, the players didn't hear me. The music drowned out my voice. But how could I resent them for giving us such fantastic support?" **Lamine Ndiaye, coach of TP Mazembe, talking about the "One Hundred Per Cent" group of supporters during the 2010 FIFA Club World Cup.**

TP MAZEMBE

The Ravens

Founded: **1939**
Stadium: **TP Mazembe (Lubumbashi)**

Founded by Benedictine missionaries, under the name FC Saint-Georges, the club was bought by Englebert, a tyre manufacturer. To celebrate winning their first title in 1966, the club took the name Tout Puissant (All Powerful) Englebert. They are now called Tout Puissant Mazembe. Four-time champions of Africa, the club surprised the whole world in 2010 by reaching the final of the FIFA Club World Cup, after having eliminated Internacional Porto Alegre. It was a first for an African club. Their goalkeeper, Robert Kidiaba, is a unique figure, an almost impassable barrier who celebrates whenever his side scores a goal by doing his "little dog" dance (Kidiboikié), which has since become famous.

9 League Titles

5 National Cups

5 CAF Champions League Titles

December 18, 2010
TP Mazembe's fans put on a show at the Club World Cup final.

Star players: Raymond Tshimenu Bwanga, Pierre Kalala, André Kalonzo, Pierre Katumba, Robert Kazadi, Léonard Saïdi, Martin Tshinabu, Benoît Nyembo, Trésor Mputu, Alain Kaluyituka Dioko, Given Singuluma, Robert Kidiaba, Stopila Sunzu, Patou Kabangu, Dieumerci Mbokani.

Honours: League: 1966, 1967, 1969, 1976, 1987, 2000, 2001, 2006, 2007; National Cup: 1966, 1967, 1976, 1979, 2000; CAF Champions League: 1967, 1968, 2009, 2010, 2015.

AS VITA CLUB
The Black Dolphins

Founded: **1935** • Stadium: **Stade Tata Raphaël (Kinshasa)**

The biggest club in the capital, Kinshasa, they have been league champions thirteen times, and won the 1973 CAF Champions League. In 2014, they contested their third final in that competition, while their national rivals, TP Mazembe, were eliminated in the semi-final.

DARING CLUB MOTEMA PEMBE
The Immaculate

Founded: **1936** • Stadium: **Stade Tata Raphaël (Kinshasa)**

Founded as Daring Faucon, they were renamed Imana (from 1949 to 1985), the name under which they won the first of their twelve national titles. They also won the 1994 CAF Cup Winners' Cup. Their traditional local rivals are AS Vita and AS Dragons.

ÉTOILE DU CONGO
The Stars

Founded: **1951** • Stadium: **Alphonse Massemba-Débat (Brazzaville)**

Founded following a split within the club Renaissance, Étoile du Congo are today among the most successful teams in Congolese football, with thirteen league titles. The derbies they play against Cara—also an offshoot of Renaissance—and Diables Noirs are a major event in the capital city.

AC LÉOPARDS
The Beasts from Niari

Founded: **1953** • Stadium: **Denis Sassous N'Guesso (Dolisie)**

Since the arrival of a chairman/sponsor—Colonel Ikounga—in 2009, AC Léopards have become the new darlings of Congolese football. Champions in 2012, 2013, and 2014, and four-time winners of the Congolese Cup, they also won the 2012 CAF Confederation Cup.

AL-MERRIKH SC
The Red Devils

Founded: **1927** • Stadium: **Al-Merrikh Stadium (Omdurman)**

Heir to a club that had existed since 1908, Al-Merrikh are the oldest club in the country. Nineteen-time league champions, and winners of the 1989 CAF Cup Winners' Cup, they fill their 45,000-capacity stadium, nicknamed the "Red Castle," for the derbies they contest with Al-Hilal.

AL-HILAL EDUCATIONAL CLUB
The Blue Wave

Founded: **1930** • Stadium: **Al-Hilal (Omdourman)**

Founded by students, this club was the first to bear the name Al-Hilal ("crescent"), which is now very common among clubs in the Arab world. Their twenty-seven league titles (a record) and their two CAF Champions League finals have earned them the nickname "leader of the country."

AL-MALAKIA FC
The Red and Whites
Founded: **ca. 1930** • Stadium: **Juba (Juba)**

The oldest club in South Sudan, they won the cup in 2013 before achieving the cup/league double in 2014. Al-Malakia are known for the warm welcome they extend to their adversaries, such as recently in the 2015 CAF Champions League against Kano Pillars.

WAU SALAAM FC
The Greens
Founded: **2012** • Stadium: **Wau (Wau)**

Founded after independence, the club won the first season of the national league in 2012. In July 2012, their players travelled to Tanzania by car for the first participation in an international competition (The Kagame Interclub Cup) by a South Sudanese team.

RED SEA FC
Elpa
Founded: **1945** • Stadium: **Cicero (Asmara)**

Red Sea are the most popular club in the country, and dominate Eritrean football, having won twelve titles since the creation of the league in 1994. They also play regularly in CAF competitions, and reached the semi-finals of the 2011 CECAFA Cup (East and Central Africa).

ADULIS SPORT CLUB
Sporting
Founded: **1946** • Stadium: **Cicero (Asmara)**

The club, which was founded when the country was under Italian occupation, has won three titles since the establishment of the new league (1996, 2004, 2006). In 1995, some Eritreans then living in south London renamed their club Adulis FC.

AS PORT
The Doyens
Founded: **1978** • Stadium: **El Hadj Hassan Gouled Aptidon (Djibouti City)**

With nine cups and seven league titles, including three in a row (2010, 2011, 2012), the country's oldest club currently dominate football in the capital. Over the last few years, its duel with Djibouti Télécom has become the *clasico* of Djiboutian football.

DJIBOUTI TÉLÉCOM
The Sons of Arrey
Founded: **1988** • Stadium: **Stade du Ville (Djibouti City)**

The club initially played local tournaments, only entering the first division in 1998. The sponsorship provided by Djibouti Télécom since 2005 has given them fresh impetus, making the club the most successful in Djiboutian football, with three league championships to their name (2009, 2013, 2014).

SAINT GEORGE SC
Kidus Giorgis
Founded: **1935** • Stadium: **Addis Ababa (Addis Ababa)**

Founded by a Greek immigrant, the club quickly became a symbol of the struggle against Italian occupation. Saint George have won twenty-six league titles since the start of the league in 1947, making them the most successful club in the country. Their supporters have been financially carrying the club since 1999.

ETHIOPIAN COFFEE FC
Coff Coff
Founded: **1976** • Stadium: **Addis Ababa (Addis Ababa)**

Founded by the workers of a coffee factory, the club has won two league titles (1997, 2011) and five Ethiopian Cups. Known for their attractive, technical football, Ethiopian Coffee are one of the most popular clubs in the country. They contest "the great Ethiopian derby" against Saint George.

AFC LEOPARDS
The Leopards
Founded: **1964** • Stadium: **Nyayo National (Nairobi)**

Leopards have won thirteen league titles and nine cups, making them one of the most successful clubs in the country, even if their last title dates back to 1998. Supported by the Luhya people, their great local and national rival is Gor Mahia, against whom they play the Ingo-Dala derby.

GOR MAHIA FC
Son of Ogalo
Founded: **1968** • Stadium: **Nairobi City (Nairobi)**

With fourteen league titles, ten national cups, and the 1987 CAF Cup Winners' Cup—the only one ever won by a Kenyan club—Gor Mahia are the most successful Kenyan team. Very popular among the Luo people, they regularly fill their 15,000-seat stadium.

TUSKER FC
The Elephants
Founded: **1969** • Stadium: **Kinoru (Nairobi)**

Sponsored by a local brewery, Tusker have notched up ten league championships and three national cups. They were runners-up in the 1994 CAF Cup Winners' Cup. In 2015, a former presidential election candidate declared that Tusker's players were the finest.

ULINZI STARS FC
Kenya Army
Founded: **1995** • Stadium: **Afraha (Nakuru)**

Ulinzi Stars were formed when several military teams were merged—hence their motto, "Soldiers first." They won four league titles between 2003 and 2010, making them the most successful team in Kenyan football outside of the capital, Nairobi.

SOMALIA

ELMAN FC
Xamar Star
Founded: **1993** • Stadium: **Mogadishu (Mogadishu)**

Despite their age, this club from the capital have quickly risen to become the most successful in the country, winning ten titles since 1998. They regularly draw the largest crowds to its Banadir stadium, where all league matches are played.

BANADIR SC
Minishiibiyo
Founded: **1993** • Stadium: **Mogadishu (Mogadishu)**

With six league titles won since 1999—the last in 2014 when they remained unbeaten (something that hadn't happened since 1956 in Somalia), Banadir are now the main rivals of Elman FC, against whom they play the Mogadishu Derby.

UGANDA

KAMPALA CAPITAL CITY AUTHORITY FC Garbage Collectors
Founded: **1963** • Stadium: **Lugogo Stadium (Kampala)**

Founded by the head of the Ugandan capital's sewage works, their first players were sewage workers. KCC were dominant in the 1970s–1980s, and returned to prominence in 2008, winning the league championship, then repeating the feat in 2012 and 2013, taking their title tally to ten.

SC VILLA
Big Cockerel
Founded: **1975** • Stadium: **Sazza Grounds (Mityana Town)**

A permanent fixture in the top flight of Ugandan football since 1979, SC Villa have won sixteen league titles, and have also shone on the continental scene, reaching the final of the first season of the CAF Cup, in 1992.

RWANDA

RAYON SPORTS FC
Gikundiro
Founded: **1968** • Stadium: **Amahoro (Kigali)**

Rayon Sports are now based in the Nyanza province, after having spent over fifteen years in the capital, Kigali. They won the first Rwandan championship, in 1975, and have racked up seven titles to date. In 1998, they were the first club in the country to win the CECAFA Cup.

ARMÉE PATRIOTIQUE RWANDAISE FC A.P.R.
Founded: **1993** • Stadium: **Amahoro (Kigali)**

Established within President Kagame's Rwandan Patriotic Front, A.P.R. have become the stronghold of football in Rwanda, having won thirteen of the last twenty seasons of the league championship. They have also shone at an East and Central African level, winning the CECAFA Cup in 2004, 2007, and 2010.

VITAL'O FC
The Mauves
Founded: **1957** • Stadium: **Prince Louis Rwagasore (Bujumbura)**

Burundi's number one club have won eighteen league titles, and were finalists in the 1992 CAF Cup Winners' Cup. Vital'O draw on heavy support from all the neighbourhoods of Bujumbura, the nation's capital. The club's mauve strip is an homage to the Belgian team Anderlecht.

AS INTER STAR
The Black and Whites
Founded: **1973** • Stadium: **Prince Louis Rwagasore (Bujumbura)**

AS Inter Star were formed from the merger of Etoile du Nil and Inter FC—then the oldest club in the country. Inter Star are the great local rivals of Vital'O in Bujumbura. The club have won four league championships (1991, 1992, 2005, 2008) and one Burundian Cup (1990).

CRD DO LIBOLO
Orange and Blue
Founded: **1942** • Stadium: **Patrice Lumumba (Libolo)**

Clube Recreativo Desportivo do Libolo are a rising club in Angola, having been promoted to the first division in 2008, as well as being cup finalist in 2008, and winning three league titles in 2011, 2012 and 2014. Key to their development has been the renovation of their stadium.

GD INTERCLUBE
Inter
Founded: **1953** • Stadium: **Estádio 22 de Junho (Luanda)**

Grupo Desportivo Interclube are attached to the Angolan police force. In 1986, they won the National Cup, but had to wait until 2007 to triumph in the league, a victory they repeated three years later. In 2011, the club reached the semi-finals of the CAF Confederation Cup, the best result achieved by an Angolan club.

CD PRIMEIRO DE AGOSTO
The Soldiers
Founded: **1977** • Stadium: **Estádio 11 de Novembro (Luanda)**

Clube Desportivo Primeiro de Agosto are attached to the armed forces, and were one of the first clubs founded after independence. Their victories in the first league championships (1979, 1980, 1981) earned them the nickname "The Glorious." Their biggest local and national rival is Petro Atlético.

ATLÉTICO PETRÓLEOS DE LUANDA Petro Atlético
Founded: **1980** • Stadium: **Estádio 11 de Novembro (Luanda)**

With fifteen league titles in a little over thirty years, Atlético Petróleos de Luanda are by far the most successful Angolan football club. The continental title is all that's missing to satisfy their 8,000 *socios* (club members), who each have a stake in the most popular club in the country.

NKANA FC
The Red Devils

Founded: **1935** • Stadium: **Nkana (Kitwe)**

Based in the country's second city, Nkana are the most successful club in Zambia, having won twelve league titles between 1982 and 2013, and been runners-up in the CAF Champions League final (1990). They are also the most popular club in the country, and contest a derby with Power Dynamos.

ZESCO UNITED
Team Ya Ziko

Founded: **1974** • Stadium: **Levy Mwanawasa (Ndola)**

Owned by the national electricity company, Zesco United currently dominate Zambian football, having won four league titles since 2007. They also draw the biggest crowds in the league, thanks to their 50,000-capacity stadium, opened in 2012.

MIGHTY WANDERERS FC
The Nomads

Founded: **1962** • Stadium: **Kamuzu (Blantyre)**

Five-time champions, Mighty Wanderers are one of the most successful clubs in Malawi. They are hugely popular and maintain a strong rivalry with Big Bullets. Their derbies excite the capital, Blantyre, and fill the 50,000-capacity Kamuzu stadium.

BIG BULLETS FC
The People's Team

Founded: **1967** • Stadium: **Kamuzu (Blantyre)**

Big Bullets are both Malawi's most popular and most successful club. They have played in the first division since its founding in 1967, and have won the title eleven times under various names. In 2004, they played in the group stage of the CAF Champions League.

YOUNG AFRICANS SC
Yanga

Founded: **1935** • Stadium: **National (Dar es Salaam)**

Young Africans are the most successful club in Tanzanian football, having won twenty league titles. They were also runners-up in the CAF Champions League and Cup Winners' Cup. Very popular, they boast twenty million supporters around the world.

SIMBA SC
The Lions

Founded: **1936** • Stadium: **National (Dar es Salaam)**

With eighteen league titles, Simba are the great rivals of Young Africans. They have often performed well in continental competitions, reaching the semi-finals of the Champions League in 1974, and the final in 1993.

MOZAMBIQUE

COMOROS

CD MAXAQUENE
Maxaca
Founded: **1920** • Stadium: **Maxaquene (Maputo)**

A subsidiary of Sporting Lisbon, when the country was a Portuguese colony, the club became famous for having nurtured the talents of Eusebio, one of the greatest Portuguese footballers in history, alongside Cristiano Ronaldo. Five-time league champions, they have won the cup on nine occasions.

DESPORTIVO MAPUTO
The Black Eagles
Founded: **1921** • Stadium: **Desportivo (Maputo)**

The club was Benfica's oldest subsidiary in Mozambique, winning two league titles during the colonial period, and six since independence. Under Portuguese rule, the club had strong support among Mozambican natives, and have remained very popular in the capital.

CLUBE FERROVIÁRIO DE MAPUTO The Locomotives
Founded: **1924** • Stadium: **Machava (Maputo)**

Founded within Mozambique's railroad company, Ferroviário are the most successful club in the country, with eight league titles won during the colonial period, and nine since independence. Very popular, they have opened subsidiary clubs in every region of the country.

CD DA COSTA DO SOL
The Canaries
Founded: **1955** • Stadium: **Costa do Sol (Maputo)**

This former subsidiary of Benfica (Lisbon) are joint holders of the record for league championships, with nine titles. They have also won the cup ten times, and twice reached the quarter-finals of the CAF Cup Winners' Cup (1996, 1998).

COIN NORD DE MITSAMIOULI
The Red House
Founded: **1960** • Stadium: **Coin Nord (Mitsamiouli)**

With seven league titles and five national cups, Coin Nord from the island of Grande Comore are the most successful club in the country. They were also the first to participate in the CAF Champions League, in 2006. Coin Nord play the Mitsamihuli derby against Apache Club.

FOMBONI FC
The Blues
Founded: **1985** • Stadium: **El Hadj Mattoire (Fomboni)**

Fomboni FC are the club of the capital of the island of Mohéli. They were formed from a merger between Molaïli and Kaza Sport, and have dominated their local league for the past twenty-five years. Twice national champions (2001, 2014), they have also played in the Indian Ocean Champions Cup.

AS PORT-LOUIS 2000
The Musketeers
Founded: **2000** • Stadium: **Saint François-Xavier (Port-Louis)**

This recently-created club based in the Mauritian capital—and owned by the worldwide pharmaceutical giant Sanofi-Aventis—has become the most successful on the island, winning the league championship five times between 2002 and 2011, as well as lifting two cups.

CUREPIPE STARLIGHT SC
CSSC
Founded: **2001** • Stadium: **George V (Curepipe)**

Based in Mauritius's second city, Curepipe Starlight are now among the most successful teams on the island, having won the league championship four times, and won two cups. In 2008, they qualified for the opening round of their first CAF Champions League.

AS ADEMA
Sporting
Founded: **1955** • Stadium: **Mahamasima (Antananarivo)**

Famous throughout the world for having won a match in 2002 with the record score of 149-0 against the defending league champions—who were protesting against the refereeing, Adema have won the league three times, and in 2002 reached the quarter-finals of the CAF Cup.

CNAPS SPORT
The Psychics
Founded: **2009** • Stadium: **Toamasina (Miarinarivo)**

Established within the national social security department, CNaPS Sport are currently the island's best club, with three titles won since 2010. They play in CAF competitions, and have won the CAF Champions League (founded in 2011) twice.

SAINT MICHEL UNITED FC
SMU
Founded: **1996** • Stadium: **Linité (Victoria)**

Based in Anse-aux-Pins, Saint Michel have dominated football in the Seychelles ever since they were founded. Champions in their first season, they have racked up twelve league titles and ten cups. In 2015, they got the better of Mamelodi Sundowns in the first round of the CAF Champions League (1–1, 3–0).

SAINT LOUIS SUNS UNITED
The Suns
Founded: **2007** • Stadium: **Linité (Victoria)**

Based in the capital, they are the fruit of a merger between Sunshine SC (former league champions) and FC Saint-Louis (thirteen-time champions, including nine consecutive titles from 1985 to 1994). In 2010, the club won the Seychelles Cup, following two defeats by Saint Michel in the final.

MAURITIUS

MADAGASCAR

SEYCHELLES

BLUE WATERS FC
Beautiful Birds

Founded: **1936** • Stadium: **Kuisebmund (Walvis Bay)**

UP THE BIRDS

Blue Waters are not only one of Namibia's oldest football clubs, they are also one of the few outside the capital, Windhoek, to have won the league championship. Linked to the country's mining industry, they have taken four titles and one cup.

ORLANDO PIRATES SC
Buccaneers

Founded: **1963** • Stadium: **Sam Nujoma (Windhoek)**

Twice winners of the league, and holder of three cups, Orlando are one of the most popular clubs in the country. Their supporters are recognizable from their rallying gesture: closed fists, and arms raised and crossed, in imitation of the pirate flag.

CIVICS FC
Bethlehem Boys

Founded: **1983** • Stadium: **Sam Nujoma (Windhoek)**

Founded by students, the club brought together players from an impoverished neighbourhood of the capital. Civics worked their way up to the first division, and won three league titles in the 2000s. Very popular, they are one of the few Namibian clubs to have played in Europe.

BLACK AFRICA SC
Lively Lions

Founded: **1986** • Stadium: **Sam Nujoma (Windhoek)**

With ten league titles and three cup victories, Black Africa are the most successful club in Namibian football by quite a sizeable margin. Based in the country's capital, they have several local rivals, including Orlando Pirates and Civics FC.

TOWNSHIP ROLLERS FC
The Happy People

Founded: **1961** • Stadium: **Botswana National Stadium (Gaborone)**

With twelve league titles making them the most successful club in the country, Township Rollers, who were founded by workers in Botswana's capital, certainly deserve their nickname "The Happy People." This very popular team maintain a strong local rivalry with Gaborone United.

MOCHUDI CENTRE CHIEFS
The Graduates

Founded: **1972** • Stadium: **Botswana National Stadium (Gaborone)**

Winner of the domestic cup competition in 1991, the club won their first league title in 2008, before taking the title again in 2012 and 2013. Thanks to these successes, their rivalry with Township Rollers has become the fiercest in Botswanan football.

HIGHLANDERS FC
Siyinqaba

Founded: **1926** • Stadium: **Barbourfields (Bulawayo)**

Founded by the grandson of a king of the Ndebele people, this club initially comprised players from a township. Seven-time league winners since independence, they are the second most successful club in the country behind the Dynamos. Their local rivals are Chicken Inn and How Mine.

DYNAMOS FC
The Glamour Boys

Founded: **1963** • Stadium: **Rufaro (Harare)**

The Dynamos from the capital dominate football in Zimbabwe. Champions from their first season, they have racked up twenty-two league titles, and were runners-up in the final of the 1998 CAF Champions League. Their attacking style of play has helped make them the most popular club in the country.

MBABANE SWALLOWS FC
Umkhonto Kashaka

Founded: **1948** • Stadium: **Somhlolo National (Mbabane)**

The club spent many years in the shadow of their local rivals, Highlanders, with whom they contest the Mbabane derby. Recently, the club has significantly improved, winning five league titles, starting in 1993. Four of these titles were won over the last ten seasons thanks to a more offensive game.

MBABANE HIGHLANDERS FC
Ezimnyama Ngenkanie

Founded: **1952** • Stadium: **Somhlolo National (Mbabane)**

With twelve league titles and seven cups, Highlanders, who are based in the capital, are the most successful club in Swaziland. They are supported by an army of fans, who set the stadium abuzz with their vuvuzelas. Their relegation in 2013 caused shockwaves throughout the country.

MATLAMA FC
Locomotive

Founded: **1932** • Stadium: **Setsoto (Maseru)**

Established to play against the police team, Matlama have won nine league titles, making them the most successful club in the country. Based in the capital, Maseru, like most teams in the national league, their main rival is Defence Forces FC.

LIOLI FC
Tse Nala

Founded: **1934** • Stadium: **Lioli Ground (Teyateyaneng)**

Based in Teyateyaneng, Lioli FC are the country's most successful club outside the capital. They won their first league championship in 1985, but didn't return to the big time until 2007, when the support of an insurance firm enabled them to win three titles (2009, 2013, 2015).

AMAZULU FC
Heroes

Founded: **1932** • Stadium: **Moses Mabhida (Durban)**

Founded by Zulu workers, the Heroes are one of the most popular clubs in KwaZulu-Natal province. As they say themselves, "it was created for the people and belongs to the people." In 1972, AmaZulu won the league championship reserved for black teams.

ORLANDO PIRATES FC
The Buccaneers

Founded: **1937** • Stadium: **Orlando (Johannesburg)**

Founded in the township of Soweto, the Orlando Pirates are the oldest club in the country. Nine-time league champions, and winners of the 1995 CAF Champions League, they dominate South African football along with their rival, Kaizer Chiefs. They are very popular, with over twelve million supporters.

MOROKA SWALLOWS FC
The Beautiful Birds

Founded: **1947** • Stadium: **Volkswagen Dobsonville (Johannesburg)**

Founded by a Soweto taxi driver with his own money, the Moroka Swallows were league champions in 1965. In 1971, they became the first ever football team in the country to register as a private company. Since the end of apartheid, the club has won a number of national cups.

BLOEMFONTEIN CELTIC FC
Phunya Sele Sele

Founded: **1969** • Stadium: **Free State (Bloemfontein)**

Bloemfontein Celtic are named in honour of Celtic from Glasgow, whose colours they wear. In 2009, they set up the Academia Sporting Africa training academy in collaboration with Sporting Portugal—who also share these same colours.

KAIZER CHIEFS FC
Chiefs

Founded: **1969** • Stadium: **FNB (Johannesburg)**

Kaizer Chiefs were founded by Kaizer Motaung, formerly of the Orlando Pirates, who brought three teammates with him in 1969. They are the most successful club in the country, with twelve league titles and one African Cup Winners' Cup (2001). They are also the most popular, with fifteen million supporters throughout Africa.

MAMELODI SUNDOWNS FC
The Brazilians

Founded: **1970** • Stadium: **Loftus Versfeld (Pretoria)**

Mamelodi Sundowns from the country's administrative capital are owned by an industrialist in the mining sector. They hold nine league titles, six of which were won since the start of the current league in 1996. They were also a finalist in the 2001 CAF Champions League.

FREE STATE STARS FC
Ea Lla Koto
Founded: **1977** • Stadium: **Goble Park (Bethlehem)**

Originally from the village of Makwane, the club moved to the small town of Phuthaditjhaba—where they reached the first division in 1986—and then to the larger town of Bethlehem. They have grown in popularity throughout the province of Free State, where their rivals are Bloemfontein Celtic.

SANTOS FC
The People's Team
Founded: **1982** • Stadium: **Athlone (Cape Town)**

While playing in a league that accepted players of all origins, the club won the title six times between 1982 and 1990, earning their nickname "The People's Team." They were also champions of the Premier Soccer League in 2002.

JOMO COSMOS FC
King of Soccer
Founded: **1983** • Stadium: **Makhulong (Johannesburg)**

The club was founded upon the remnants of Highlands Park FC—established in 1959, and eight-times league champions—who were bought in 1983 by Jomo Sono (a former teammate of Pelé at the New York Cosmos) and renamed. Jomo Cosmos were National Soccer League champions in 1987.

SUPERSPORT UNITED FC
The Swanky Boys
Founded: **1994** • Stadium: **Lucas Moripe (Pretoria)**

The club were initially called Pretoria City, but were bought by a major television network, owner of the SuperSport channel. The club won the league championship three seasons consecutively (2008, 2009, 2010). They are the major rivals of Mamelodi Sundowns in the capital.

PLATINUM STARS FC
Crocodiles
Founded: **1998** • Stadium: **Royal Bafokeng (Rustenburg)**

Platinum Stars are owned by the Royal Bafokeng Nation, who govern a territory rich in platinum. The club finished runners-up in the 2007 league championship. The following season, they gave the Egyptian giant Al Ahly a fright, beating them 2-1 in the CAF Champions League, before being knocked out.

AJAX CAPE TOWN FC
Urban Warriors
Founded: **1999** • Stadium: **Cape Town (Cape Town)**

A subsidiary of Ajax Amsterdam, who are the majority shareholders, the club's development is centred on a youth academy—just like their parent team. It seems to work: Steven Pienaar and Eyong Enoh played in the first team before leaving to join Amsterdam.

ASIA AND
OCEANIA

AL-AIN FC
The Boss

Founded: **1968** • Stadium: **Hazza bin Zayed (Abu Dhabi)**

With twelve league titles, as well as one victory and one runners-up place in the AFC Champions League, the club is the most successful in the Emirates, forging this tally of honours with such players as Boubacar Sanogo, Asamoah Gyan, and Ryan Babel.

AL-AHLI DUBAI FC
Knights

Founded: **1970** • Stadium: **Rashed (Dubai)**

With six league titles and eight cups, the club is currently the greatest rival of Al-Ain. Very popular since it was founded, Al-Ahli contests the Dubai derby against Al-Wasl. The Italian centre-back Fabio Cannavaro finished his career with the club.

AL-ITTIHAD CLUB
The Tiger of Asia

Founded: **1927** • Stadium: **King Abdullah (Jeddah)**

Based on the shores of the Red Sea, and pioneers of football in Saudi Arabia, the club remained in the shadow of Al-Hilal for a long time, before overtaking their national rival. Al-Ittihad have dominated the league since the mid-1990s, and have also won two Asian Champions League titles.

AL-SHABAB FC
The White Lions

Founded: **1947** • Stadium: **King Fahd (Riyadh)**

This historic Riyadh club have won six league titles, including three in succession (1991 to 1993). Like Al-Hilal, they have employed numerous Brazilian coaches, including Felipe Scolari in 1984-1985. They were also the first Saudi club to invest in real estate.

AL-NASSR
The Knight of Najd

Founded: **1955** • Stadium: **Prince Faisal bin Fahd (Riyadh)**

The height of the club's success came during the 1980s, when Al-Nassr won three league titles, though they have been champions seven times. In 2000, the club represented Asia in the first FIFA Club World Cup. Their great rivals are Al-Hilal, against whom they play a derby at King Fahd Stadium.

AL-FATEH SPORTS CLUB
The Role Model

Founded: **1958** • Stadium: **Prince Abdullah bin Jalawi (Al-Hassa)**

Having spent many years alternating between the first and second divisions, the club placed second in the league in 2008, before winning the league/cup double in 2013. Their success has earned them international support.

"Have you heard about the fans of Al-Hilal? We play in front of sixty-five thousand people, and they create an incredible atmosphere."
Laurentiu Reghecampf, Al-Hilal FC manager.

AL-HILAL FC

The Boss

Founded: **1957** · Stadium: **King Fahd (Riyadh)**

Originally called El-Olympy, the club was renamed one year after its founding, by royal decree. Al-Hilal have won more than forty national and international trophies in over fifty years, including the first Saudi league championship in 1977. Al-Hilal are the most popular team in the kingdom, and have had a number of star players, such as goalkeeper Mohamed Al Deayea, the second-most capped player in world football, with 178 appearances for the national side. ⊕ A club with a Brazilian flavour: In 1978, Al-Hilal caused a stir when they signed the Brazilian legend Rivelino. Famed for his skilled left foot, he stayed with the club for three years, winning two league titles with them, in 1980 and 1981. In 1979, Al-Hilal also recruited, as a coach, another great Brazilian name: Mario Zagallo, manager of the 1970 World Cup winning team. Al-Hilal have hired around twenty Brazilian coaching staff in total.

13 League Titles

12 National Cups

2 Asian Cup Winners' Cups

October 25, 2014
Al-Hilal's fans cheer on their team during the AFC Champions League final.

Star players: Nawaf Al Temyat, Sami Al Jaber, Mohamed Al Deayea.

Honours: League: 1977, 1979, 1985, 1986, 1988, 1990, 1996, 1998, 2002, 2005, 2008, 2010, 2011; National Cup: 1964, 1995, 2000, 2003, 2005, 2006, 2008, 2009, 2010, 2011, 2012, 2013; Asian Champions League: 1991, 2000; Asian Cup Winners' Cup: 1997, 2002.

HILAL AL-QUDS CLUB
The Blues

Founded: **1972** • Stadium: **Faisal Al-Husseini International (Al Ram)**

Champions in 2012, and winners of the cup in 2011 and 2014, this club, based in a suburb of Jerusalem, was the main supplier of players to the Palestine team during the country's first participation in the Asian Cup, in 2015.

SHABAB AL-DHAHIRIYA SC
The Deers of the South

Founded: **1974** • Stadium: **Dura International (Hebron)**

Holders of two league titles (2013, 2015) and two cups, the club rely mainly on players who have come through their youth academy. The most popular club in the country, they are fervently supported by the Ultras Ghozlani 74.

HOMENETMEN BEIRUT FC
Orange Devils

Founded: **1924** • Stadium: **Bourj Hammoud (Beirut)**

Founded by Beirut's Armenian community, the club has had success in both the cup and the league championship since the 1940s. Seven-time champions, they finished third in the 1970 AFC Champions League, the best result for a Lebanese club.

AL-ANSAR SC
The Greens

Founded: **1951** • Stadium: **Beirut Municipal (Beirut)**

Al-Ansar are very popular across all religions and communities in Lebanese society. They hold the record for league championships, having won the league thirteen times—including eleven in a row between 1988 and 1999—as well as thirteen Lebanese Cups.

AL-KARAMAH SC
The Blue Eagles

Founded: **1928** • Stadium: **Khalid ibn al-Walid (Homs)**

Eight-time league champions of Syria, the club caused a splash when they reached the final of the 2006 AFC Champions League—their first time participating—after having eliminated the Saudis of Al-Ittihad who are two-time winners of the competition. In 2007 and 2008, Al-Karamah reached the quarter-finals.

AL-JAISH SC
The Red and Black

Founded: **1947** • Stadium: **Abbasiyyin (Damascus)**

Twelve-time league champions, eight-time winners of the cup, and winners of the 2004 AFC Cup, Al-Jaish are the most successful club in Syrian football. Based in the capital, Damascus, they play a derby against their historic rivals, Al-Wahda, with whom they also share a stadium.

AL-FAISALY SPORTS CLUB
The Blue Eagles
Founded: **1932** • Stadium: **Prince Mohammed (Amman)**

This club from Amman has racked up the greatest list of titles in the history of Jordanian football, having won the national league championship thirty-two times, and the national cup on eighteen occasions. They have also won the AFC Cup twice, in 2005 and 2006.

AL-WEHDAT SPORTS CLUB
The Green Giant
Founded: **1956** • Stadium: **Stade du Roi Abdullah (Amman)**

Established in a Palestinian refugee camp, the club is the main rival of Al-Faisaly. They have won fourteen league titles and ten cup competitions. Very popular, their team have included the Nigerian international Emmanuel Amuneke, who has played for FC Barcelona.

AL-MUHARRAQ SC
The Red Wolf
Founded: **1928** • Stadium: **Bahrain National Stadium (Riffa)**

Based in Bahrain's former capital, Al-Muharraq are the kings of Bahraini football, having won the league thirty-three times since 1957. They draw many players from their youth academy, but also from abroad, such as the Brazilian "Rico" (Leandson Dias da Silva), who helped them to victory in the 2008 AFC Cup.

RIFFA SC
Their Excellencies
Founded: **1953** • Stadium: **Bahrain National Stadium (Riffa)**

Founded by a former prime minister of the kingdom—hence the nickname—Riffa have won eleven national titles and have been firm rivals of all-powerful Al-Muharraq since the early 1990s. They have an advantage in that all league matches are hosted in their stadium.

AL-ARABI SC
The Boss
Founded: **1953** • Stadium: **Sabah Al-Salem (Kuwait City)**

The club won the first three seasons of the national league, and have won a total of sixteen, which means they share the top spot for most successful team with Qadsia SC, against whom they play the Kuwaiti Classico. Al-Arabi is twinned with Celtic from Glasgow—the two clubs run a joint youth academy in Kuwait.

QADSIA SC
The Kings
Founded: **1953** • Stadium: **Mohammed Al-Hamad (Kuwait City)**

Qadsia from the Hawalli region were the first club to be established in the country, along with Al-Arabi, and they are one of the most popular. Qadsia have won the national league championship sixteen times. In 2014, they achieved international success by winning the AFC Cup.

"We are really looking forward to the challenge that Kuwait Sporting Club will give us, and also, importantly, to meet with the passionate Kuwaiti fans." **Karl-Heinz Rummenigge, FC Bayern Munich manager, December 2013.**

KUWAIT SC
The Brigadiers

نادي الكويت الرياضي

Founded: **1947**
Stadium: **Al Kuwait (Kuwait City)**

As Kuwait's first football club, Kuwait SC is a national legend. In 2015, they won their twelfth league title, after an undefeated season, bringing them closer to the achievements of Qadsia and Al-Arabi—sixteen-time champions. The club have also caused a stir on the Asian scene, having won three AFC Cups since 2009—something a Kuwaiti club had never done before. The icing on the cake was a decisive victory over Qadsia in 2013. This success can be explained by the judicious choice of foreign players, such as the Angolan midfielder André Macanga, the Brazilian attacking midfielder Rogerio Silva, and the Tunisian striker Issam Jemaa.

12 League Titles

11 National Cups

3 AFC Cups

Star players: Abdul-Aziz Al-Anbari, Saad Al-Houti, Waleed Al-Jasem, Ahmad Al-Tarabulsi, Skander Sophan, André Macanga, Jason Mbokang, Dalil Annariah, Axelak Touroujouvic, Kader Omeyade, Frank De Tall, Jarah Al Ateeqi, Issam Jemaa, Rogerio Silva.

November 2, 2013
Kuwait SC win the third AFC Cup in their history by defeating their compatriots, Qadsia, in the final.

Honours: League: 1965, 1968, 1972, 1974, 1977, 1979, 2001, 2006, 2007, 2008, 2013, 2015; National Cup: 1976, 1977, 1978, 1980, 1985, 1987, 1988, 2005, 2011, 2012, 2014; AFC Cup: 2009, 2012, 2013.

AL SADD SC
The Boss

Founded: **1969** • Stadium: **Jassim Bin Hamad (Doha)**

Founded by high-school students, the club won their first national title three years later. They have relied on foreign stars such as Raùl to help them to thirteen league titles—a record in Qatar—and to win two AFC Champions Leagues. They are known as the club of the upper classes.

LEKHWIYA SC
The Red Nights

Founded: **2009** • Stadium: **Abdullah Bin Khalifa (Doha)**

Winners of the title on their first participation in 2011, Lekhwiya have won four of the last five seasons of the league. To do this, they have wielded the largest budget in the league, and hired renowned coaches, such as Eric Gerets and Michael Laudrup.

DHOFAR SCSC
The Boss

Founded: **1968** • Stadium: **Al-Saada (Salalah)**

Founded as Al-Shaab, they changed their name in 1970. Dhofar have been league champions nine times, and have won the cup on eight occasions, making them the most successful club in Oman. Unlike their great local rivals, Al-Nasr, they have not been relegated to the second division since 1976.

FANJA SC
The Desert Bees

Founded: **1970** • Stadium: **Al-Seeb (Seeb)**

The first winners of the professional league (1976), Fanja can boast a total of eight titles, and are the only team in the country to have won an international trophy: the 1989 Gulf Cup for Clubs. They are owned by the government and are popular throughout the Arab world.

AL-TILAL SC
The Hills

Founded: **1905** • Stadium: **Al-Tilal (Aden)**

Heir to Muhammadan's Union, the oldest club in the country, they are the most successful club in South Yemen. Since reunification in 1990, Al-Tilal have been league champions twice, and have finished in the top three places on ten occasions. They play the "Aden Summit" derby against Al-Wahda Aden.

AL-AHLI CLUB SANA'A
The National

Founded: **1937** • Stadium: **Ali Mohsen Al-Muraisi (Sana'a)**

Founded as Red Star, Al-Ahli who are the oldest club in the capital, have been league champions ten times. Very popular, they are the only club in the country who properly organize for their fans to travel to games around Yemen.

AL-QUWA AL-JAWIYA
The Falcons

Founded: **1931** • Stadium: **Al-Quwa Al-Jawiya (Baghdad)**

Founded by air force personnel, this was Iraq's first football club. Five-time league champions and seven-time winners of the national cup, they are one of the most popular teams in the country. Their most fervent fans belong to a group called Ultras Blue Hawks.

AL-ZAWRA'A SPORT CLUB
The Gulls

Founded: **1969** • Stadium: **Al-Zawra'a (Baghdad)**

Twelve-time league champions, fourteen-time winners of the national cup, and finalists in the 2000 Asian Cup Winners' Cup, Al-Zawra'a, who are attached to the Ministry of Transport, are the most successful club in the country. A major rival of Al-Quwa Al-Jawiya, the team boasts eight million fans.

ESTEGHLAL TEHRAN FC
Crown of Asia

Founded: **1945** • Stadium: **Azadi (Teheran)**

The most popular club in the country—along with Persepolis, with whom they share a stadium—Esteghlal hit the big time in 1970 when they won the AFC Champions League, beating Hapoel Tel Aviv. In 1991, they repeated this exploit against the Chinese team, Liaoning FC.

PERSEPOLIS TEHRAN FC
The Red Army

Founded: **1963** • Stadium: **Azadi (Teheran)**

After absorbing almost all of Shahin FC when they were founded, the club soon became the most successful club in Iran—with nine league titles and one Asian Cup Winners' Cup—thanks largely to Ali Parvin, the biggest name in Iranian football.

BALKAN FK
Oil Workers

Founded: **1960** • Stadium: **Balkanabat (Balkanabat)**

Four-time league champions since 2004, Balkan were the first club in the country to win an international competition, the 2013 AFC President's Cup. Nearly 600 fans travelled to Malaysia for the final against the Pakistanis of KRL.

FC INTERNATIONAL TURKMEN-TURKISH UNIVERSITY Students

Founded: **2003** • Stadium: **HTTU (Ashgabat)**

ITTU are a rising force in Turkmenistani football, and have been on the podium of the championship nearly every year since 2005. Four-time league champions, and winners of the 2014 AFC President's Cup, they currently form the backbone of the national team.

PAKHTAKOR TASHKENT FK
The Lions
Founded: **1956** • Stadium: **Pakhtakor Stadium (Tashkent)**

The club spent twenty-two seasons in the Soviet first division, and were runners-up in the 1967 USSR Cup, making them the greatest club in Uzbek football history. Since independence, they have won a record ten league titles, and play the "Uzbek El Clasico" against Neftchi Farg'ona.

FC BUNYODKOR
The Swallows
Founded: **2006** • Stadium: **Bunyodkor (Tachkent)**

This recently established club imposed themselves straightaway as the main rivals of the capital's other big club, Pakhtakor. Five times champion since 2008, they fielded the Brazilian midfielder Rivaldo, and hired as coaches his compatriots, Zico, and Felipe Scolari.

REGAR-TADAZ TURSUNZODA
The Metalworkers
Founded: **1975** • Stadium: **Metallurg (Tursunzoda)**

Founded in a metal plant during the Soviet era, Regar-TadAZ established themselves as the new stronghold of Tajik football, winning seven league titles between 2001 and 2008. They also won the AFC President's Cup in 2005, 2008, and 2009.

FC ISTIKLOL
The Reds
Founded: **2007** • Stadium: **Central Republican (Dushanbe)**

This club from the capital relied on young Tajik internationals to reach the top flight two years after their founding, winning four titles from 2010 to 2014. In 2012, they won the AFC President's Cup. In 2015, they played in the quarter-finals of the AFC Cup.

FC ALGA BISHKEK
The Blue-Whites
Founded: **1947** • Stadium: **Dynamo (Bishkek)**

The oldest club in Bishkek, the capital, Alga played in the old Soviet second division, before dominating the decade following independence, winning five national titles between 1992 and 2002. They were dissolved in 2005, and were relaunched in 2010, becoming one of the main rivals of FC Dordoi.

FC DORDOI BISHKEK
The Yellow-Blues
Founded: **1997** • Stadium: **Spartak (Bichkek)**

Founded relatively recently—by a wealthy businessman—the club soon reached the heights of Kyrgyz football, winning nine of the last eleven league championships. At an international level, they have contested six finals of the AFC President's Cup in six years, taking two titles.

SHAHEEN ASMAYEE FC
Falcon of Asmayee
Founded: **2012** • Stadium: **Ghazi (Kaboul)**

This Kabul-based club was founded at the same time as the creation of the Afghan league. They finished third in 2012, before winning the league championship in 2013 and 2014. All of their players were recruited through a reality TV show.

DE MAIWAND ATALAN FC
Maiwand Champions
Founded: **2012** • Stadium: **Ghazi (Kaboul)**

De Maiwand Atalan FC represent the Kandahar region but have played their matches in Kabul since the league was launched in 2012. The club's fans willingly brave a whole day's bus journey to support their team.

WAPDA FC
The Watermen
Founded: **1983** • Stadium: **Punjab (Lahore)**

Established by the national water and power company, the club won four titles in the old league championship, and four in the new one, including the first season in 2004. They were also semi-finalists in the 2009 AFC President's Cup.

KRL FC
Khans
Founded: **1995** • Stadium: **KRL (Rawalpindi)**

Established within the state research laboratory, KRL are one of the most successful clubs in the country, with four league championship victories, three of which were consecutive (2012, 2013, 2014). Runners-up in the 2013 AFC President's Cup, they are one of the most popular teams in the country.

THREE STAR CLUB
The Patanes
Founded: **1954** • Stadium: **Dasarath Rangasala (Kathmandu)**

Four-time league champions, Three Star have also won eleven cup competitions over the last fifteen years, beating some of Nepal's best teams. Based in Patan, and popular throughout the country, they have their own youth academy. Their biggest rivals are Manang Marshyangdi Club.

MANANG MARSHYANGDI CLUB
Manange
Founded: **1982** • Stadium: **Dasarath Rangasala (Kathmandu)**

Seven-time league champions, Kathmandu-based Manang are the most successful club in Nepalese football. In 2014, they qualified for the final round of the AFC President's Cup. Manang are very socially engaged, and since 1997 have even organised blood donations.

DRUK UNITED FOOTBALL CLUB
The Dragons

Founded: **2002** • Stadium: **Changlimithang (Thimpu)**

Based in Bhutan's capital, the club played only one season in the first division before joining the new league in 2014 and winning the national title. This meant that they became the first Bhutanese team to play in the AFC Cup.

UGYEN ACADEMY FC
The Academics

Founded: **2012** • Stadium: **Lekeythang (Punakha)**

With links to the university in the town of Lekeythang, the club joined the professional league in 2012, finishing their first season in third place. In 2013, Ugyen became the first Bhutanese club from outside the capital to win the national league. In 2014, they finished in second place.

ABAHANI LIMITED
The Sky Blue Brigades

Founded: **1972** • Stadium: **Bangabandhu National Stadium (Dhaka)**

After winning the Dhaka League eleven times, the club went on to win the Bangladesh Premier League on four occasions. They have their own training centre, and employ a number of coaches from abroad.

SHEIKH JAMAL DHANMONDI CLUB Bengal Yellows

Founded: **2010** • Stadium: **Bangabandhu National Stadium (Dhaka)**

The club won the Bangladesh Premier League the first season they played in it (2010–2011), a performance they repeated again in 2013–2014, thanks to their Haitian striker Wedson Anselme. The "Bengal Yellows" are great local and national rivals of Abahani Limited.

SAUNDERS SC
The Giants

Founded: **1918** • Stadium: **Price Park (Colombo)**

Founded by four brothers who were all internationals, Saunders have dominated Sri Lankan football for nearly a century. Winners of their first trophy in 1949, the club have amassed sixteen cups and twelve league titles since the establishment of the league in 1985.

RATNAM SC
The Blues

Founded: **1950** • Stadium: **Sugathadasa (Colombo)**

Five-time league champions, six-time winners of the cup, and semi-finalists of the AFC President's Cup (2007), they are one of the most successful clubs in the country. Very popular since their establishment, Ratnam have supplied many players to the national team.

"For us, life has always been football. The Churchill brothers and football remain inseparable." **Churchill Alemao, Churchill Brothers' president.**

CHURCHILL BROTHERS SC

The Red Machine

Founded: **1988**
Stadium: **Fatorda (Margao)**

Initially called Varca Club, the club took the name of their new owner, the Member of the Indian Parliament for Goa, Churchill Alemao, one year after their founding. In 1996, the club first played in the National Football League, where they were runners-up three times. A founding member of the I-League (2007), they have twice won the title, and twice been runners-up. Over the last ten years, the club have relied on the Nigerian strikers Ogba Kalu Nnanna, Felix Chimaokwu, and Odafe Onyeka Okolie—three times the top scorer in the league, having racked up one hundred goals for the club. Owing to financial problems, the club have been forbidden from playing in the league championship since 2014, but in 2015 they began playing in regional tournaments against their local rivals, Dempo, Salagaocar FC, and Sporting Goa, with whom they share their stadium.

2 League Titles

1 National Cup

May 7, 2013
Churchill Brothers win their second Indian league title.

Star players: Igor Shkvyrin, Mboyo Iyomi, Kayne Vincent, Felix Chimaokwu, Ogba Kalu Nnanna, Roberto Mendes da Silva "Beto", Akram Moghrabi, Bineesh Thottunkal Balan, Lalrindika Ralte, Nbusiyu David Opara, Daniell Zelený, Odafe Onyeka Okolie, Henry Antchouet, Lenny Rodrigues, Balwant Singh.

Honours: League: 2009, 2013; National Cup: 2014.

INDIA

MOHUN BAGAN AC
Mariners
Founded: **1889** • Stadium: **Salt Lake (Kolkata)**

Founded by independence militants during the colonial period, the club made history in 1911 by beating East Yorkshire Regiment 2–1 to take the IFA Shield. Even more startling, they won that victory playing barefoot. They are extremely popular, and they have won the Federation Cup thirteen times, and the I-League once, in 2015.

KINGFISHER EAST BENGAL
Red and Gold Brigade
Founded: **1920** • Stadium: **East Bengal (Kolkata)**

East Bengal are one of the most successful clubs in the Indian professional era, having won six titles since 2001, and one AFC Cup semi-final (2013). They play at East Bengal and also share Salt Lake, the largest stadium in India (120,000 capacity) with their great local rivals, Mohun Bagan FC.

DEMPO SC
Golden Eagles
Founded: **1968** • Stadium: **Fatorda (Margao)**

Founded by a mining company, Dempo have been playing in the professional league ever since it was founded in 1996. They have won five national titles, and reached the semi-finals of the 2008 AFC Cup. Their fans are among the most fervent in the country.

MUMBAI CITY FOOTBALL CLUB
Blue Devils
Founded: **2014** • Stadium: **DY Patil (Mumbai)**

Created from the outset to be a major player in the new Indian Super League, the club, owned by the famous Bollywood actor, Ranbir Kapoor, immediately signed up stars such as the Swedish winger, Fredrik Ljungberg, and the French forward, Nicolas Anelka.

FC GOA
The Gaurs
Founded: **2014** • Stadium: **Fatorda (Margao)**

FC Goa, which counts famous cricketers and the boss of Dempo SC among their owners, were established to play in the Indian Super League. Managed by the Brazilian legend, Zico, their first squad included the French World Champion, Robert Pirès.

DELHI DYNAMOS FC
The Lions
Founded: **2014** • Stadium: **Jawaharlal Nehru (Delhi)**

The Lions are one of the eight franchises chosen to play in the Indian Super League. Established in collaboration with Feyenoord Rotterdam, they made a name for themselves in their first season by fielding the Italian star, Alessandro Del Piero.

FINANCE AND REVENUE FC
Customs

Founded: **1924** • Stadium: **Aung San (Yangon)**

Based in the country's former capital, this club, operated by the Ministry of Finance and Revenue, has dominated Burmese football, winning twenty-eight national titles. In 2009, when the game turned professional, the club sold its seventeen players for 100,000 dollars.

YADANARBON FC
The Red Devils

Founded: **2009** • Stadium: **Bahtoo (Mandalay)**

Established to play in the country's first professional league, the club soon rose to the top, winning the first two seasons (2009, 2010), and then again in 2014. The club also won the 2010 AFC President's Cup, a first for a Burmese team.

YOTHATIKAN FC
Tigers

Founded: **1997** • Stadium: **New Laos National (Vientiane)**

Founded within the Ministry of Transport and Public Works, Yotha have won three national titles, making them the most successful club in the country behind Lao Army FC.

LAO ARMY FC
The Reds

Founded: **1998** • Stadium: **New Laos National (Vientiane)**

Club of the year in Laos, they are the country's most successful, having won eight league championship titles since the establishment of the national league in 1990. One of their current rivals in the league is the club of the Ministry of the Interior: Lao Police FC.

NATIONAL DEFENSE MINISTRY FC Army FC

Founded: **1982** • Stadium: **Lambert (Phnom Penh)**

Founded before the professional era, the club initially played against the Ministry of Trade and Ministry of Transport, winning three national titles. Since joining the professional league in 2005, they have performed well in the national cup, lifting the trophy in 2010 and coming second in 2013.

PHNOM PENH CROWN FC
Crown

Founded: **2001** • Stadium: **RSN (Phnom Penh)**

Playing under different names, the club has won five league titles since the renaissance of the Cambodian league in 2000, which is a record. Finalists of the 2011 AFC President's Cup, the club opened their training academy that same year.

AIR FORCE CENTRAL FC
The Blue Eagles

Founded: **1937** • Stadium: **Thupatemi (Rangsit)**

This historic club was founded by the air force, and is based in a suburb of Bangkok. Air Force Central won eleven league titles before the creation of the professional league in 1996, and have won two more titles since then. Their great rivals are Police United, who are based in the same town.

BURIRAM UNITED FC
The Thunder Castles

Founded: **1970** • Stadium: **I-Mobile (Buriram)**

Initially based in Ayutthaya, and linked to an electricity company, the club was promoted to the first division in 2004, and won the title in 2008. They were bought by a former minister of agriculture in 2010, moved to Buriram, and became the most successful club in the country, winning three more league titles.

MUANGTHONG UNITED FC
Twin Qilin

Founded: **1989** • Stadium: **SCG (Nonthaburi)**

Promoted to the first division in 2009, the club immediately won the first of their three titles. In 2010, they reached the semi-finals of the AFC Cup and in 2011, the club signed Robbie Fowler as player-manager. Muangthong United are very popular, and regularly have a sold-out stadium.

CHONBURI FC
The Sharks

Founded: **1997** • Stadium: **Chonburi (Chonburi)**

Chonburi have been one of the most successful clubs in the country since reaching the first division in 2006. Champions in 2007, they have been runners-up five times since 2008. Now the third most popular club in Thailand, Chonburi also played in the semi-finals of the 2012 AFC Cup.

HO CHI MINH CITY FC
Ho Chí Minh City

Founded: **1975** • Stadium: **Thong Nhat (Ho Chi Minh Ville)**

This club from the country's largest city, the former Saigon, won four league titles under their old name, Cang Sài Gòn, in 1986, 1994, 1997, and 2002, as well as two cups, in 1992 and 2000. Such success has made them one of the greatest names in Vietnamese football.

BECAMEX BÌNH DUONG FC
Chelsea of Vietnam

Founded: **1976** • Stadium: **Go Dau (Thu Dau Mot)**

Winner of the cup in 1994, Bình Duong took on a new dimension in 2002, when they were bought by a powerful industrial firm that gave them their current name. Having moved up to the first division in 2003, they have won the league three times, in 2007, 2008, and 2014.

INDERA SC
The Red and Blacks

Founded: **1972** • Stadium: **Padang dan Balapan (Bandar Seri Begawan)**

This prominent club won the first two seasons of the Brunei Super League—a new version of the national league—in 2013 and 2014, as well as the national cup in 2012. Half the team play for the national side.

DULI PENGIRAN MUDA MAHKOTA FC   The Wasps

Founded: **2000** • Stadium: **Hassanal Bolkiah National Stadium (Bandar Seri Begawan)**

Owned by the crown prince of Brunei, DPMM FC have the peculiarity of having participated in the leagues of three different countries. After starting out in Brunei, the club entered the Malaysian league, and then the Singaporean championship, where they won the League Cup twice.

SELANGOR FA
The Red Giants

Founded: **1936** • Stadium: **Shah Alam (Shah Alam)**

Selangor is Malaysia's king of cups, having won no less than thirty-two of them, as well as seven league titles—a Malaysian record. In 1967, the club reached the final of the first season of the AFC Champions League.

KELANTAN FA
The Red Warriors

Founded: **1946** • Stadium: **Sultan Muhammad IV (Kota Bahru)**

Promoted to the first division in 2009, the club won their first league title in 2011, before achieving the cup/league double in 2012. They regularly fill their 22,000-capacity stadium, and contest the East Coast Derby against Terrengganu.

PAHANG FA
The Elephants

Founded: **1959** • Stadium: **Darul Makmur (Kuantan)**

Founded by the authorities of the state of Pahang, the club have won five national titles in twenty-years of playing in the first division, making them one of the most consistent at this level. Their rivals are Selangor, against whom they won the first of their four cups in 1983.

JOHOR DARUL TA'ZIM FC
Southern Tigers

Founded: **1972** • Stadium: **Larkin (Johor Bahru)**

Managed by the state of Johor, the club has been professional since 1972, but had to wait until 2014 before winning their first Malaysian league championship. They rely on the contribution of several Argentine players, including the international Pablo Aimar.

TAMPINES ROVERS FC
The Stags
Founded: **1945** • Stadium: **Jurong West (Singapore)**

Tampines were league champions three times during the amateur era, and have won the title five times since the establishment of the S-League in 1996. They also won the 2005 ASEAN Champions League. One of the most popular clubs in the country, their main local rivals are Geylang International.

WARRIORS FC
The Warriors
Founded: **1975** • Stadium: **Choa Chu Kang (Singapore)**

Warriors FC were founded to allow career soldiers and conscripts of the Singaporean armed forces to play at a high level. They turned professional in 1996, and are the most successful club in the country since the start of the league, with nine victories and four second places.

PERSEBAYA SURABAYA
The Green Crocodile
Founded: **1927** • Stadium: **Gelora Bung Tomo (Surabaya)**

Persebaya Surabaya are based in the capital of East Java, the most enthusiastic part of the country regarding football, and are composed of local players. They were a founding member of the Football Association of Indonesia. Supported by boisterous fans, the club have won nine titles, three of which have been as professionals.

PERSIJA JAKARTA
The Kemayoran Tigers
Founded: **1928** • Stadium: **Gelora Bung Karno (Jakarta)**

Persija Jakarta have won the league championship ten times—once since the start of the professional era. They are the biggest club in the Indonesian capital, Jakarta, and were a founding member of the Football Association of Indonesia in 1930. They play in an 88,000-seater stadium, and their major rivals are Persib Bandung.

PERSIB BANDUNG
The Blue Prince
Founded: **1933** • Stadium: **Jalak Harupat Soreang (Bandung)**

Based in the capital of East Java, the club belonged to the municipality before being privatized. Today, their main shareholder also owns Inter Milan and DC United. They have won seven amateur league championships and two professional titles.

PERSIPURA JAYAPURA
Black Pearl
Founded: **1963** • Stadium: **Mandala (Jayapura)**

Persipura Jayapura from the Papuan capital were twice crowned semi-professional league champions before 1994. Since the start of the professional league, they have won the title four times, making them the country's most successful club. They played in the semi-finals of the 2014 AFC Cup.

TATUNG FC
The Blues
Founded: **1969** • Stadium: **Taipei Municipal (Taipei City)**

Founded by the workers of Tatung electronics company, Tatung are the oldest club in Taiwan and they are still semi-professional. They have been league champions four times, and runners-up on twelve occasions behind Taipower. In 2006, they were semi-finalists in the AFC President's Cup.

TAIPOWER FC
Southern Overlord
Founded: **1979** • Stadium: **Kaohsiung National (Kaohsiung)**

Founded within the national electric company, Taipower have dominated Taiwanese football for the past thirty years. Winner of fifteen titles in the Enterprise Football League, including ten in a row, they have already won five titles in the Intercity League—set up in 2007.

SOUTH CHINA AA
Shaolin Temple
Founded: **1904** • Stadium: **Hong Kong (Hong Kong)**

Founded by a group of Chinese students, South China are by far and away the most successful club in the history of Hong Kong football, with forty-one league titles. They are also the most popular club in Hong Kong, and they fielded an entirely Chinese team until the early 1980s.

KITCHEE SC
Hong Kong Barça
Founded: **1931** • Stadium: **Mong Kok (Hong Kong)**

With six league titles, Kitchee are one of the top clubs in Hong Kong. They are also known for their good results against major European teams in friendly matches, beating AC Milan, and drawing against Juventus and Arsenal.

CD MONTE CARLO
The Canaries
Founded: **1984** • Stadium: **Macau (Macau)**

Monte Carlo are one of the most successful clubs in Macau's semi-professional league, having won five league titles since 2002. Such success has been achieved by the signing of Brazilian players, and a strip that evokes the Seleçaō.

GD LAM PAK
The Blue and Whites
Founded: **1988** • Stadium: **Campo Desportivo (Macao)**

Champions in 1992, just four years after their founding, Lam Pak have won the title eight more times to date, becoming the most successful club in the Macau league championship, established in 1973. Coached by Chan Man Kin for over twenty years, they suspended activity in 2014.

"The tiger is the king of animals, at the top of the food chain." **gzevergrandefc.com**

GUANGZHOU EVERGRANDE

Southern China Tigers

Founded: **1954**
Stadium: **Tianhe (Guangzhou)**

The club enjoyed major success even before the start of professional football in China. During the last few years, they have confirmed their status as giants of Chinese football by winning five consecutive league championships—immediately after being promoted from the second division—and two AFC Champions League titles. Guangzhou have extraordinary support, with average crowds of over 40,000. The spectators are in part drawn by foreign stars, such as the Italian international Alberto Gilardino or Luiz Felipe Scolari—who replaced Fabio Cannavaro as head coach in June 2015. The club have a keen interest in youth training, and have opened academies in Spain and the Netherlands.

5 League Titles

2 AFC Champions League Titles

Star players: Feng Junyan, Luis Ramirez, Lucas Barrios, Zheng Zhi, Muriqui, Alessandro Diamanti, Alberto Gilardino.

Honours: League: 2011, 2012, 2013, 2014, 2015; National Cup: 2012; AFC Champions League: 2013, 2015.

Alberto Gilardino
The 2006 world champion played at Guangzhou during the 2014-15 season.

BEIJING GUOAN
The Imperial Guards
Founded: **1951** • Stadium: **Workers (Beijing)**

For a long time, Beijing Guoan were a semi-professional club called Beijing FC, before becoming a founder member of the professional league in 1992. The club is mainly owned by a state-owned investment company, but one of their minor shareholders is Real Madrid. Beijing Guoan won the league title in 2009.

LIAONING WHOWIN FC
Northeast Tigers
Founded: **1953** • Stadium: **Panjin Jinxiu (Panjin)**

These pioneers of Chinese football have modern facilities and an effective youth academy training programme. In 1990, Liaoning Whowin FC became the first-ever Chinese football team to win the Asian Club Championship.

JIANGSU GUOXIN-SAINTY FC
Bloody Jasmine
Founded: **1958** • Stadium: **Nanjing Olympic Sports Center (Nankin)**

Jiangsu were one of the founding members of the first professional league in China, although they were soon relegated to the second division. In 2009, they won promotion back into the first division. In 2012, the club recorded their best result, finishing second at the end of the season, before winning the 2013 Chinese FA Super Cup.

DALIAN SHIDE FC
Eight Star
Founded: **1983** • Stadium: **Jinzhou (Dalian)**

Finalists of the Asian Club Championship (1998) and the Asian Cup Winners' Cup (2001), Dalian Shide became the most popular club in the country, thanks to seven titles in their first ten seasons. Foreign players have included the Czech midfielder Václav Němeček and the French striker Nicolas Ouédec. In 2012, the club merged with local rivals Dalian Aerbin F.C.

GUANGZHOU R & F
Blue Lions
Founded: **1986** • Stadium: **Yuexiushan (Guangzhou)**

Originally founded in Shenyang, the club moved a number of times before settling in Guangzhou in 2011. Since then, their popularity has grown, along with improved results. The club finished the 2014 season ranked third in the league, their best result for twenty years.

SHANDONG LUNENG FC
Orange Fighters
Founded: **1993** • Stadium: **Jinan Olympic Sports Center (Shandong)**

The club was founded during the launch of the professional league and boast an ambition of wanting to be "the club of the century." The long road towards this dream title started with four league titles. Their supporters already call the club the "Chinese Real Madrid."

SHANGHAI GREENLAND SHENHUA The Blue Devils

Founded: **1993** • Stadium: **Hongkou (Shanghai)**

These long-time rivals of Dalian Shine were the first privately owned Chinese club, operating independently of the government. Shenhua are known for their offensive style, which they have cultivated thanks to the signing of great foreign players, such as Junior Baiano, Nicolas Anelka, and Didier Drogba.

GUIZHOU RENHE FC

Inter Xi'an

Founded: **1995** • Stadium: **Guiyang Olympic Center (Guizhou)**

Guizhou Renhe FC were initially based in Shanghai, but their fortunes soared after they moved to Guizhou. In 2013, the club won their first title, the Chinese FA Cup, beating Guangzhou Evergrande in the final. Guizhou Renhe have a very high proportion of Chinese players.

CHANGCHUN YATAI FC

The Tigers of the Northwest

Founded: **1996** • Stadium: **Development Area (Changchun)**

The club was founded by an industrial conglomerate, and arrived in the Chinese Super League in 2006, becoming league champions the following year, thanks to the efforts of several Honduran players. Today, most of the team are Chinese, as are the coaching staff.

HANGZHOU GREENTOWN

Greentown

Founded: **1998** • Stadium: **Huanglong (Hangzhou)**

The club started out in the third division, before entering the Chinese Super League in 2006. In 2010, they signed several Chinese internationals and finished the season in fourth place. Greentown cultivated their popularity by inviting major English teams to play them.

ERCHIM FC

The Electricians

Founded: **1994** • Stadium: **National Sports (Ulaanbaatar)**

Supported by an electricity generating plant in the Mongolian capital, Erchim are the most successful club in the country over the last twenty years, with eight league titles and seven cups. They field Japanese, Korean, and Brazilian players.

KHOROMKHON FC

International

Founded: **1999** • Stadium: **MFF Football Centre (Ulaanbaatar)**

Khoromkhon are a rising team in Mongolia, having won two league titles, in 2005 and 2014. In order to further progress, they decided in 2012 to sign players from Slovenia, Singapore, Nigeria, Japan, Trinidad, and Canada.

"At the Seoul stadium, an average of 30,000 fans could be seen every match, and it served as a terrific morale booster for Seoul, and a terrible morale buster for the other side. Even in away games, Seoul outstripped the opponent by the number of visiting fans." **fcseoul.com**

FC SEOUL

Seoul

Founded: **1983** • Stadium: **Seoul World Cup (Seoul)**

This Seoul club proudly claims to be the best football club in Asia. Although FC Seoul can perhaps lay claim to this title in their own country—as demonstrated by the record attendance of 60,747 spectators in their stadium for a match against Seongnam in 2010—they have yet to conquer the AFC Champions League, in which they have finished runners-up on two occasions (2002, 2013). Their position at the summit of Korean football sees them play the Super Match against Suwon Samsung Bluewings, a rivalry that stretches back to the days when FC Seoul played in the city of Anyang, not far from Suwon.

5 League Titles

2 National Cups

February 27, 2008
Lee Eul-Yong and David Beckham swap shirts during an LA Galaxy tour in South Korea.

Star players: Cho Young-Jeung, Piyapong Pue-On, Choi Yong-Soo, Adilson dos Santos, Park Chu-Young, Dejan Damjanovic, Choi Tae-Uk.

Honours: League: 1985, 1990, 2000, 2010, 2012; National Cup: 1998, 2015; League Cup: 2006, 2010.

SOUTH KOREA

"Everyone here loves football, and the fans create an extraordinary atmosphere in the stadium. It's unbelievable. I am happy to be here and I think you can see it on the pitch." **Lee Dong-Gook.**

JEONBUK HYUNDAI MOTORS
Mad Green Boys

Founded: **1994**
Stadium: **"Fort Jeonju" (Jeonju)**

After some initial difficulties, the club attained consistency in the 2000s. In 2006, they won the AFC Champions League against the Syrian team Al-Karama, and followed this with three league championship titles in the K League. Although they have benefited from several South American players, Jeonbuk have also enjoyed contributions made by local footballers, such as Lee Dong-Gook, the top scorer in the 2009 league championship. This new era has consolidated the support of their fans for major matches, like the Hyundai derby against Ulsan Hyundai FC, or the regional derby against Jeonnam Dragons FC.

4 League Titles

3 National Cups

1 AFC Champions League Title

May 26, 2015
Jeonbuk qualify for the AFC Champions League quarter-finals.

Star players: Dong-Hyuk Park, Choi Jin-Cheul, Seo Hyuk-Su, Milton Rodriguez, Edmilson Dias de Lucena, Magno Alves, Zé Carlo, Eninho, Lee Dong-Gook.

Honours: League: 2009, 2011, 2014, 2015; National Cup: 2000, 2003, 2005; AFC Champions League: 2006.

POHANG STEELERS FC
Steelers

Founded: **1973** • Stadium: **Pohang Steel Yard (Pohang)**

The club, who play in the first custom-made football stadium in the country, have an enthusiastic following. This strong support has helped them win five national league championships, as well as three Asian Champions Leagues (1997, 1998, 2009)—a record.

BUSAN IPARK FC
IPark

Founded: **1979** • Stadium: **Busan Asiad (Busan)**

A pioneer of the Super League, the club is one of the most successful in the country, having won four league titles in the 1980s and 1990s, as well as one AFC Champions League (1986), under the name Daewoo, its first owner. Busan IPark has spent thirty-three seasons in the upper echelons of the league.

SEONGNAM FC
Magpie

Founded: **1989** • Stadium: **Tancheon Sports Complex (Seoul)**

Seongnam are the most successful club in South Korea, with seven league titles. They are also one of the most popular in Seoul, thanks to their successes in the 1995 and 2010 AFC Champions Leagues. In 2013, it looked like the club might be sold to the city of Ansan, but they were eventually bought by Seongnam municipality.

SUWON SAMSUNG BLUEWINGS FC   Blue Wing

Founded: **1995** • Stadium: **Suwon World Cup (Suwon)**

The club experienced considerable success between 1998 and 2002, with two national titles (1998, 1999) and two Asian Super Cups (2001, 2002). Their supporters group, The Big Blue—named after the French film—is the largest in South Korea.

APRIL 25 SPORTS CLUB
4.25

Founded: **1949** • Stadium: **Yanggakdo (Pyongyang)**

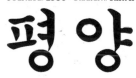

April 25 are named after the date of the founding of the Korean People's Army (in 1932), to which they belong. They hold the record for league championships, with fourteen titles. In 1991, the club were semi-finalists in the AFC Champions League.

PYONGYANG CITY SPORTS CLUB   Chollima City

Founded: **1956** • Stadium: **Kim Il-sung (Pyongyang)**

평 양

Founded by Kim Il-sung, the then future president of North Korea, Pyongyang City have won the league title five times. The great rivals of 4.25, they play in a stadium where, during matches, spectators can also watch athletics competitions accompanied by a live orchestra.

"Kashima Antlers were all set to become a company club. But Zico helped it to mature, by giving it a history and a tradition." **Oswaldo de Oliveira Filho, Kashima Antlers manager, 2007–2011.**

KASHIMA ANTLERS
The Deers

Founded: **1947**

Stadium: **Kashima Soccer (Kashima)**

Like many Japanese clubs, Kashima Antlers—founded by Sumitomo Metal Industries in Osaka and based in Kashima since 1975—have relied heavily on Brazilian players. Unlike other clubs, it has brought in some major stars. Zico ended his career here between 1992 and 1994. Next to play for the club was a fighting-fit Leonardo, before he headed off to Europe, then there was Bebeto, who played briefly here in 2000, the year the club achieved a historic triple: the league championship, Emperor's Cup, and J. League Cup. Kashima Antlers have won the league a record seven times, and have never been relegated.

7 League Titles

4 National Cups

Star players: Zico, Hisashi Kurosaki, Yoshiyuki Hasegawa, Yasuto Honda, Alcindo, Yutaka Akita, Leonardo, Naoki Soma, Jorginho, Takayuki Suzuki, Atsushi Yanagisawa, Akira Narahashi, Mitsuo Ogasawara.

Honours: League: 1996, 1998, 2000, 2001, 2007, 2008, 2009; Emperor's Cup: 1997, 2000, 2007, 2010; J. League Cup: 1997, 2000, 2002, 2011, 2012.

Yuya Osako
The Japanese international scored sixty-two goals while wearing the Antlers' shirt (2009-2014), before playing in the German league.

"We never change based on the identity of our opponents. We go there to play good football, beautiful football." **Dragan Stojković, manager of Nagoya Grampus, 2008–2013.**

NAGOYA GRAMPUS
The Red Whales

Founded: **1939**
Stadium: **Toyota (Nagoya)**

Originally founded by car manufacturer Toyota, Nagoya Grampus have long played in the top flight—they were last promoted from the second division in 1990. In 1995, the club hired a new manager, Arsène Wenger, who led the team to victory in the Emperor's Cup, ably assisted by Gary Lineker and Dragan Stojkovic on the pitch. Fifteen years later, Stojkovic was back, but this time on the manager's bench, coaching the same kind of attacking football enforced by Wenger. In 2010, the club won their first J. League title. In honour of Wenger, who had brought the club out of the shadows, the supporters regularly sing the French national anthem, La Marseillaise, in the stands.

3 League Titles

2 National Cups

Arsène Wenger
The Frenchman is a Nagoya legend, having managed the club from 1994 to 1996.

Star players: Dragan Stojkovic, Gary Lineker, Franck Durix, Marcus Tulio Tanaka, Seigo Narazaki, Yoshizumi Ogawa, Keiji Tamada, Mu Kanazaki, Joshua Kennedy.

Honours: League: 1958, 1970, 2010; Emperor's Cup: 1995, 1999.

FC TOKYO
The Blue and Reds

Founded: **1935** • Stadium: **Ajinomoto (Tokyo)**

Originally named Tokyo Gas, the club was promoted to the J. League in 1999. In 2011, while playing in the second division, they won the Emperor's Cup. FC Tokyo play an attacking type of football, and are more popular in the capital than their rivals, Tokyo Verdy.

SANFRECCE HIROSHIMA
Sanfre

Founded: **1938** • Stadium: **Hiroshima Big Arch (Hiroshima)**

Sanfrecce were the first winners of the Japan Soccer League in 1965, going on to win four more titles by 1970. Owned by Mazda since 1981, the club joined the J. League when it was established, winning the title twice (2012, 2013). Interestingly, their mascot, Sanccе, has a partner.

KASHIWA REYSOL
Sun Kings

Founded: **1940** • Stadium: **Hitachi Kashiwa (Kashiwa)**

Founded by the Hitachi company, Kashiwa were playing among the elite from 1965 onward, becoming league champions in 1972. Relegated to the second division, they signed the Brazilian Careca in 1993, and went back up to the first division in 1995. Crowned league champions once more in 2011, Kashiwa have also won three Emperor's Cups.

JEF UNITED ICHIHARA CHIBA
The Dogs

Founded: **1946** • Stadium: **Fukuda Denshi Arena (Chiba)**

Jointly owned by a rail company and an electric company, JEF United were twice champions of the Japan Soccer League before the establishment of the J. League. They have won the Emperor's Cup four times, and the 1987 AFC Champions League.

URAWA RED DIAMONDS
Reds

Founded: **1950** • Stadium: **Saitama Stadium 2002 (Saitama)**

Present at the highest level of Japanese football since 1965, the club—established by industrial giant Mitsubishi—won the J. League in 2006 and the AFC Champions League in 2007. For the last ten years, Urawa Red Diamonds have drawn an average attendance of nearly 40,000 spectators.

CEREZO OSAKA
Cherry Blossom

Founded: **1957** • Stadium: **Yanmar (Osaka)**

Founded by an engine manufacturer, Cerezo Osaka are a historic club of the Japan Soccer League, winning four titles before 1980. Their results have been more erratic since the founding of the J. League, though the club maintains one of the fiercest rivalries in Japanese football, against Gamba Osaka.

MATSUMOTO YAMAGA FC
Ptarmigans
Founded: **1965** • Stadium: **Matsumoto (Matsumoto)**

Known initially for their exploits against major teams in the Emperor's Cup, the club became professional in 2010 and entered the J. League in 2014. Matsumoto are also famous for their "Green Army" of fans.

TOKYO VERDY
Verdy
Founded: **1969** • Stadium: **Ajinomoto (Tokyo)**

The club dominated Japanese football in the 1980s, and went on to win the first two seasons of the J. League (1993, 1994). Tokyo Verdy have won the Emperor's Cup five times, and the 1988 AFC Champions League. The club relies heavily on its youth academy to produce future stars.

JÚBILO IWATA
Júbilo
Founded: **1970** • Stadium: **Yamaha (Shizuoka)**

Originally the Yamaha company team, the club won the 1982 Emperor's Cup and entered the first division that same year. Júbilo joined the J. League in 1994, led by their Brazilian captain, Dunga. They have won three league titles and lifted the 1999 AFC Champions League trophy.

YOKOHAMA F. MARINOS
Tricolor
Founded: **1972** • Stadium: **Nissan (Yokohama)**

Yokohama were initially called Nissan Motors FC, after the name of their owner. They have played in the J. League since it was established, and have won the title three times, and the Asian Cup Winners' Cup twice. In 2014, the holding company of Manchester City bought a minority share in the club.

GAMBA OSAKA
Gamba
Founded: **1991** • Stadium: **Osaka Expo '70 (Osaka)**

Founded by an electronics company, Gamba have played in the J. League since it was established in 1993. With two league titles, victories in several national cups, and one AFC Champions League (2008), they are one of the most successful teams in Japan.

SHIMIZU S-PULSE
S-Pa
Founded: **1991** • Stadium: **IAI Stadium Nihondaira (Shizuoka)**

Founded with the backing and involvement of the people of Shizuoka, S-Pulse have played in the J. League since 1993. A cup specialist, they have won two, and been runner-up eight times, as well as winning the 2000 Asian Cup Winners' Cup. The club's supporters are very inspired by Brazilian culture.

PHILIPPINE AIR FORCE FOOTBALL CLUB The Airmen

Founded: **ca. 1980** • Stadium: **Rizal Memorial (Manila)**

Based in the capital, this club linked to the air force fields both military and civilian players. Since the establishment of the new Philippines league in 2009, they have been one of the most prominent clubs, winning two league titles (2010, 2011) and one cup (2012).

GLOBAL FC
The People's Club

Founded: **2000** • Stadium: **Emperador (Taguig)**

Established by a group of friends who played football together as a hobby, the club took part in amateur competitions before recruiting players from a company, who bought the team. After a year in the second division, they were promoted to the first division, and won two titles, in 2012 and 2014.

SPORTING CLUBE DE TIMOR
The Rising Sun

Founded: **1938** • Stadium: **Municipal (Dili)**

The oldest club in the country, they are the eighty-fifth subsidiary of Sporting Portugal. Their sporting activities were at their peak in the 1950s and 1960s, just when their rivals, Clube Sport Dili e Benfica, were also developing. They helped found the East Timor football federation in 2001.

AD DILI LESTE
The Crazy Deer

Founded: **2010** • Stadium: **Municipal (Dili)**

Based in the country's capital, the club became champions in their first year of existence (2010), and went on to win two more titles in a row (2011, 2012). This was just before the dissolution of the league and the suspension of the East Timor Football Federation by FIFA in 2013.

HEKARI UNITED FC
The Red and Whites

Founded: **2003** • Stadium: **Lloyd Robson Oval (Port Moresby)**

Winners of the first eight seasons of the semi-professional league—established in 2006—this club from the capital dominate Papuan football. In 2010, their victory in the OFC Champions League enabled them to participate in the FIFA Club World Cup.

EASTERN STARS FC
Stars

Founded: **2007** • Stadium: **Bisini Soccer Ground (Port Moresby)**

Based in a town on the eastern part of the island, the club quickly became one of the main adversaries of the powerhouse Hekari United, reaching the final on two occasions: 2011 and 2012. Several of their players were subsequently picked to play for the national team.

"When I see you Brisbane / I just go off my head /
I just can't get enough / I just can't get enough."
The Den.

BRISBANE ROAR

The Roar

Founded: **1957** • Stadium: **Suncorp (Brisbane)**

Originally founded by Dutch immigrants, Brisbane Roar are the oldest club in the current Australian A-League. They hold the national record for league victories, with three titles. Success has only boosted their popularity: the club's largest ever home crowd was for the 2014 final against Western Sydney Wanderers, with 51,153 spectators. After a short-lived derby against Gold Coast United, Brisbane Roar developed a rivalry with Central Coast Mariners. Their biggest group of fans is The Den, who have followed the team since the start of the A-League in 2005.

3 League Titles

May 4, 2014
Brisbane Roar become
Australian champions
for the third time
in their history.

Star players: Massimo Murdocca, Matt McKay, Besart Berisha, Thomas Broich.

Honours: League: 2011, 2012, 2014.

SOUTH MELBOURNE
Hellas

Founded: **1959** • Stadium: **Lakeside (Melbourne)**

South Melbourne FC were originally founded by the Greek community, and they notched up four national titles during the period of the National Soccer League (1977–2004). In 2000 they represented Oceania in the first FIFA Club World Cup. They now play in the second division.

MOOROOLBARK SOCCER CLUB
The Barkers

Founded: **1962** • Stadium: **Esther Park (Melbourne)**

The club was founded by two Dutchmen, and is based in Melbourne's eastern suburb of Mooroolbark. It began in the regional fourth division but had a meteoric rise, becoming the first club to join the new National Soccer League, in 1977. Today, Mooroolbark play in the Victorian State League.

PERTH GLORY
The Glory

Founded: **1995** • Stadium: **Perth Oval (Perth)**

Perth Glory is one of three clubs to survive from the National Soccer League, which came to an end in 2004. They are yet to recover their former glory—three NSL regular seasons and two NSL finals. But their second-place finish in 2012 was encouraging for their two groups of fans, The Shed and The Terrace.

ADELAIDE UNITED
The Reds

Founded: **2003** • Stadium: **Hindmarsh (Adelaide)**

Adelaide United were founded to fill the void created by Adelaide City's withdrawal from the National Soccer League. The club recruited local players, and played fiercely when the A-League was set up, finishing the regular season in first place. In 2014, Adelaide United won the first FFA Cup competition.

SYDNEY FC
Sky Blues

Founded: **2004** • Stadium: **Allianz (Sydney)**

The two-time winners of the national league (2006, 2010), and of the Oceania Champions League (2005), have become one of the elites of Australian football. Alessandro Del Piero's sojourn with the team from 2012 to 2014 drew an average crowd of 20,000 to the stadium for each game.

MELBOURNE VICTORY
Victory

Founded: **2004** • Stadium: **AAMI Park (Melbourne)**

The club has very quickly become the most popular in Australia, drawing an average 27,000-strong crowd to games in 2015. Victory have played a local derby against Melbourne City since 2009, but their biggest rival remains Sydney FC, whom they play in a match dubbed "The Big Blue."

CENTRAL COAST MARINERS
Mariners

Founded: **2004** · Stadium: **Central Coast (Gosford)**

The Mariners were the first professional club (of any sport) from Gosford to play at national level, winning the A-League Premiership twice. Their biggest games are the derbies against the Newcastle Jets, when their stadium is filled with nearly 20,000 fans.

WESTERN SYDNEY WANDERERS FC Wanderers

Founded: **2012** · Stadium: **Parramatta (Sydney)**

These newcomers to professional football won the league title the year after their founding (2013), followed by the Asian Champions League (2014). Their burgeoning rivalry with Sydney FC has given rise to some torrid derbies that fill the latter's 45,000-seater Allianz Stadium.

UNIVERSITY-MOUNT WELLINGTON Unimount

Founded: **ca. 2000** · Stadium: **Bill McKinley Park (Auckland)**

The club was formed from the merger of Mount Wellington—the most prestigious club in New Zealand football, with six titles and five cups—and Auckland University. They have won the cup twice since the merger, and remain an amateur, university club.

AUCKLAND CITY FC
The Navy Blues

Founded: **2004** · Stadium: **Kiwitea Street (Auckland)**

Auckland City dominate the national league and the OFC Champions League—which they have won several times. These successes have earned them slots in the FIFA Club World Cup on several occasions, with a third place finish in 2014, even though their players have jobs outside of football.

WAITAKERE UNITED
United

Founded: **2004** · Stadium: **Fred Taylor Park (Kumeu)**

A franchise involving twelve clubs from the West Auckland region, Waitakere hold five titles, making them the most successful New Zealand club behind their rivals, Auckland City. They also won the first two seasons of the OFC Champions League, in 2007 and 2008.

WELLINGTON PHOENIX FC
The Nix

Founded: **2007** · Stadium: **Westpac (Wellington)**

Founded in 2007, the club took over from Auckland's New Zealand Knights, who played in Australia's professional league. From the start, they have been able to count on their supporters, who have helped them to the final stages of the championship on three occasions, with a third place in 2010.

GUAM SHIPYARD
The Blues

Founded: **1997** • Stadium: **Guam National Football Stadium (Hagatna)**

Formed in the Guam naval shipyards, the club, who has won three national cups, holds the record for league championships, having won nine titles between 1995 and 2006. Since then Guam Shipyard have regularly finished near the top of the league table.

QUALITY DISTRIBUTORS FC
Red, White, and Blue

Founded: **2001** • Stadium: **Guam National Football Stadium (Hagatna)**

Quality Distributors FC have dominated the last decade of the national league, winning six championships between 2007 and 2013—the 2010 title having been won without losing a game—and four cups. They are the great rivals of Guam Shipyard in the local league.

KOLOALE FC
The Men in Green

Founded: **1998** • Stadium: **Lawson Tana (Honiara)**

Like most of the country's clubs, Koloale are based in Honiara, the capital of the archipelago. Koloale have been successful since the establishment of the league in 2003, with four league titles to their name. They also reached the finals of the 2009 OFC Champions League.

WESTERN UNITED FC
The Builders

Founded: **2010** • Stadium: **Lawson Tana (Honiara)**

Based in the Western Province, Western United are a subsidiary of a construction firm. After being runners-up in their second season in the elite (2012), they became the first league champions from outside the capital (2015), and made their first foray into the OFC Champions League.

GAÏTCHA FCN
The Red and Black

Founded: **1965** • Stadium: **Numa-Daly (Nouméa)**

Based in Nouméa, the capital of New Caledonia, Gaïtcha have won the league twice, in 1999 and 2013, and the cup once, in 2011. They are mainly known for having been the first club of Christian Karembeu, World Champion in 1998 with the French national team.

AS MAGENTA
Nickel

Founded: **1966** • Stadium: **Numa-Daly (Nouméa)**

AS Magenta, who have links to New Caledonia's nickel industry, hold the national record for league championships, with seven titles. In 2005, they were runners-up in the OFC Champions League against Sydney FC. They also play in the French Cup.

TAFEA FC
Tefal tave i tepsije
Founded: **ca. 1980** • Stadium: **Port Vila Municipal (Port Vila)**

The club won the first fifteen seasons of the Vanuatu league, between 1994 and 2009, setting a world record. They were also runners-up in the 2001 OFC Champions League, and maintain a local and national rivalry with Amicale.

AMICALE FC
Red Roosters
Founded: **ca. 1986** • Stadium: **Port Vila Municipal (Port Vila)**

Amicale currently dominate the national championship, which they won in 2015 for the sixth time in a row. Already runners-up in the OFC Champions League in 2011 and 2014, they are relying on Italian players to try and finally win the title.

BA FC
Men in black
Founded: **1935** • Stadium: **Govind Park (Ba)**

Formed by Ba's Indian community, Ba FC were one of the founders of the Fiji Football Association. Open to players of all ethnicities since 1962, they have won nineteen league championships and were runners-up in the 2007 OFC Champions League.

NADI FC
The Jetsetters
Founded: **1937** • Stadium: **Prince Charles Park (Nadi)**

Based in the country's third largest city, Nadi hold nine national titles and have featured prominently since the establishment of the league in 1977. In 1999, they hosted the first Oceania Club Championship, and reached the final despite their players still being amateurs.

LOTOHA'APAI UNITED FC
The White and Blues
Founded: **before 1998** • Stadium: **Loto Tonga Soka Center ('Atele)**

This Vaitongo club hold the record for league championship victories, with fourteen titles won since 1998. The club regularly play in OFC competitions, and are the only ones with youth teams, ensuring continuity as older players move on or retire.

MARIST FC
The Sky-Blue and Whites
Founded: **before 2009** • Stadium: **Loto Tonga Soka Center ('Atele)**

Marist from Ma'ufanga are the only club in the last fifteen years to break the stranglehold of Loto Ha'apai United on the national league, winning the 2009 season. They also reached the cup final in 2011 and 2012.

KIWI FC
The Kiwis
Founded: **1977** • Stadium: **National Soccer Stadium (Apia)**

Based in the capital, Apia, Kiwi have won the league six times. They are currently the largest supplier of players to the Samoan national team, and also field players from the Solomon Islands, Fiji, New Zealand, and even Japan.

LUPE O LE SOAGA
The Greens
Founded: **1998** • Stadium: **JS Blatter Football Complex (Apia)**

Based in Magiagi, the club became league champion in 2013—their first season in the first division—and succeeded in claiming the double by beating Kiwi in the cup final. The club won the league again in 2015. They have the custom of sending out their players to clean up the village in order to raise funds.

FC SAMOA KOREAN BAPTIST CHURCH The Koreans
Founded: **2011** • Stadium: **Pago Park Soccer Stadium (Pago Pago)**

FC SKBC are rising stars in American Samoan football. After winning the league/cup double in 2013, the year they were promoted into the first division, the club finished on the podium in 2014, confirming that they are here to stay.

PAGO YOUTH FC
The Eagles
Founded: **1950** • Stadium: **Pago Park Soccer Stadium (Pago Pago)**

Pago Youth are the leading club in Samoan football, having won three league titles in succession between 2010 and 2012. Pago Youth have picked up the torch from Pago Eagles, who dominated the first seasons of the Samoan league.

TITIKAVEKA FC
Bulldogs
Founded: **1950** • Stadium: **Titikaveka Field (Avarua)**

Based in the capital, Avarua, the club dominated football in the archipelago from 1950 to 1984, winning the league title fourteen times, the cup three times, and achieving three doubles (1950, 1979, 1984).

TUPAPA MARAERENGA FC
Tupapa
Founded: **ca. 1970** • Stadium: **Victoria Park (Avarua)**

In the 1990s, the club took over Titikaveka's mantle as the Cook Islands' most successful team, with eleven league championships and six cups. In 2001, Tupapa Maraerenga took part in the final round of the OFC Champions League. Their women's team is also the most successful in the archipelago.

INDEX OF CLUBS BY COUNTRY

AFGHANISTAN
Shaheen Asmayee FC 290
De Maiwand Atalan FC 290

ALBANIA
KF Tirana 121
Dinamo Tirana 121

ALGERIA
JS Kabylie 250
Mouloudia Club Alger 251
CS Constantinois 251
ES Sétif 251
CR Bélouizdad 251

AMERICAN SAMOA
FC Samoa Korean
    Baptist Church 315
Pago Youth FC 315

ANDORRA
Unio Esportiva Sant Julia 94
FC Santa Coloma 94

ANGOLA
CRD do Libolo 272
GD Interclube 272
CD Primeiro de Agosto 272
Atletico Petroleos 272

ANGUILLA
Sunset Homes
    Attackers 185
Roaring Lions FC 185

ANTIGUA AND BARBUDA
Bassa SC 186
SAP FC 186

ARGENTINA
Quilmes AC 229
Rosario Central 229
CA Banfield 229
Argentino de Quilmes 229
Gimnasia y Esgrima
    La Plata 230
CA Tigre 230
CA Tucuman 230
Newell's Old Boys 230
Racing Club de
    Avellaneda 230
CA Atlanta 231
Ferro Carril Oeste 231
CA San Telmo 231
CA Colon 231
CA Chacarita Juniors 231
CA San Martin
    (San Juan) 231
CA Union 232
CA Huracan 232
CA San Martin
    (Tucuman) 232
Vélez Sarsfield 232
Nueva Chicago 232
CA All Boys 232
CA Lanus 233
CS Dock Sud 233
CA Godoy Cruz 233
CA Almirante Brown 233
Deportivo Moron 233
Arsenal FC 233
Boca Juniors 234-237
River Plate 238-239
CA Independiente 240-241

Estudiantes de La Plata 242
San Lorenzo
    de Almagro 243

ARMENIA
FC Ararat Yerevan 138
FC Pyunik 138

ARUBA
SV Dakota 188
SV Estrella 188

AUSTRALIA
Brisbane Roar 310
South Melbourne 311
Mooroolbark SC 311
Perth Glory 311
Adelaide United 311
Sydney FC 311
Melbourne Victory 311
Central Coast Mariners 312
Western Sydney
    Wanderers FC 312

AUSTRIA
Rapid Wien 66
Grazer AK 67
Admira Wacker 67
Sturm Graz 67
Austria Wien 67
FC Wacker Innsbruck 67
FC Red Bull Salzburg 67

AZERBAIJAN
Neftchi PFK 139
Qarabag FK 139

BAHAMAS
Lyford Cay FC 181
Bears FC 181

BAHRAIN
Al-Muharraq Club 285
Riffa SC 285

BANGLADESH
Abahani Limited 291
Sheikh Jamal DC 291

BARBADOS
Weymouth Wales 187
Barbados Defence
    Force 187

BELARUS
Dinamo Minsk 136
Bate Borisov 136

BELGIUM
RSC Anderlecht 76
Club Brugge 77
Royal Antwerp 78
Union Saint-Gilloise 78
Standard Liège 78
K Beerschot VAC 78
Cercle Brugge 78
KAA Gent 78
Sporting Charleroi 79
KV Mechelen 79
Lierse SK 79
Waterschei Thor 79
KSC Lokeren 79
Racing Genk 79
KSK Beveren 80
OH Leuven 80

BELIZE
Juventus FC 188
Belmopan Bandits FSC 188

BENIN
Dragons de l'Ouémé 261
Mogas 90 FC 261

BERMUDA
Pembroke Hamilton
    Club 181
North Village Rams 181

BHUTAN
Druk United FC 291
Ugyen Academy FC 291

BOLIVIA
The Strongest 216
Club Bolivar 216
Club Blooming 217
CD Jorge Wilstermann 217

BOSNIA-HERZEGOVINA
HSK Zrinjski Mostar 120
FK Zeljeznicar 120
FK Velez Mostar 120
FK Sarajevo 120

BOTSWANA
Township Rollers FC 276
Mochudi Centre Chiefs 276

BRAZIL
Santos FC 198-201
Corinthians 202-203
Flamengo 204-205
Sao Paulo FC 206-207
Vasco da Gama 208
Cruzeiro EC 209
EC Vitoria 210
AA Ponte Preta 210
Fluminense 210
EC 14 de Julho 210
Gremio Porto Alegrense 210
America FC 210
Botafogo FR 211
SC Recife 211
Atlético Mineiro 211
Coritiba FC 211
SC Internacional 211
Guarani FC 211
Palmeiras 212
ABC Futebol Clube 212
Portuguesa
    de Desportos 212
Atlético Paranaense 212
EC Bahia 212
Goias EC 212

BRITISH VIRGIN ISLANDS
Sugar Boys 183
Islanders FC 183

BRUNEI
Indera SC 296
Duli Pengiran
    Muda Mahkota FC 296

BULGARIA
Levski Sofia 138
Lokomotiv Plovdiv 138
Ludogorets Razgrad 138
CSKA Sofia 138

BURKINA FASO
AS Faso-Yennenga 260
Étoile Filante
    Ouagadougou 260

BURMA
Finance and
    Revenue FC 294
Yadanarbon FC 294

BURUNDI
Vital'O FC 272
AS Inter Star 272

CAMBODIA
National Defense
    Ministry FC 294
Phnom Penh Crown FC 294

CAMEROON
Canon Yaoundé 264
Dragon Club
    de Yaoundé 265
Oryx Douala 265
Tonnerre Kalara Club 265
Union Sportive de Douala 265
Coton Sport de Garoua 265
Kadji Sport Academy 265

CANADA
Toronto Croatia 180
Impact Montréal 180
Toronto FC 180
Vancouver Whitecaps 180
FC Edmonton 180
Ottawa Fury 180

CAPE VERDE
CS Mindelense 255
SC da Praia 255

CAYMAN ISLANDS
Bodden Town FC 182
Scholars International SC 182

CENTRAL AFRICAN REPUBLIC
AS Tempête Mocaf 263
Olympic Real de Bangui 263

CHAD
Renaissance FC 263
Foullah Edifice FC 263

CHILE
CD Santiago Wanderers 217
Union Espanola 217
Everton Vina del Mar 217
Audax Italiano 217
CD Palestino 218
CF Universidad
    de Chile 218
CD Universidad
    Catolica 218
CD Huachipato 218
CD Cobreloa 218
CD Incas del Sur 218
Colo-Colo 219

CHINA
Guangzhou Evergrande 299
Beijing Guoan 300
Liaoning Whowin FC 300
Jiangsu Guoxin-
    Sainty FC 300
Dalian Shide FC 300
Guangzhou R&F 300

Shandong Luneng FC 300
Shanghai Greenland
    Shenhua 301
Guizhou Renhe FC 301
Changchun Yatai FC 301
Hangzhou Greentown 301

COLOMBIA
Atlético Nacional 220
Deportivo Cali 221
Deportivo Independiente
    Medellin 221
Atlético Junior 221
Cucuta Deportivo 221
América Cali 221
Independiente Santa Fe 221
Deportivo Pereira 222
Millonarios FC 222
Once Caldas 222
Deportivo Pasto 222
Deportes Tolima 222
Real Cartagena 222
CD La Equidad 223
Envigado FC 223
Boyaca Chico 223
Patriotas FC 223

COMOROS
Coin Nord
    de Mitsamiouli 274
Fomboni FC 274

COOK ISLANDS
Titikaveka FC 315
Tupapa Maraerenga FC 315

COSTA RICA
CS Cartagines 196
LD Alajuelense 196
CS Herediano 197
Deportivo Saprissa 197

CROATIA
NK Zagreb 118
NK Slaven Belupo 118
Hajduk Split 118
Dinamo Zagreb 118
HNK Rijeka 118
NK Osijek 118

CUBA
FC Villa Clara 184
FC Pinar del Rio 184

CURAÇAO
Jong Colombia 188
CS Deportivo Barber 188

CYPRUS
Anorthosis Famagusta 147
Apoel Nicosia 147
AEL Limassol 148
AC Omonia Nicosia 148

CZECH REPUBLIC
Slavia Prague 124
Sparta Prague 124
Bohemians 1905 124
Viktoria Plzen 124
Zbrojovka Brno 125
Banik Ostrava 125
Dukla Prague 125
Slovan Liberec 125

DEMOCRATIC REPUBLIC OF THE CONGO
TP Mazembe 267
AS Vita Club 268

Daring Club
    Motema Pembe 268

DENMARK
AGF Aarhus 50
Aalborg BK 50
BK Frem Copenhagen 50
Odense BK 50
AB Gladsaxe 50
Vejle BK 50
Boldklubben af 1893 51
Staevnet 51
Brondby IF 51
Christiania SC 51
FC Nordsjaelland 51
FC Copenhagen 51

DJIBOUTI
AS Port 269
Asas Djibouti Télécom 269

DOMINICA
Harlem United FC 186
Bath Estate FC 186

DOMINICAN REPUBLIC
Moca FC 182
Bauger FC 182

EAST TIMOR
SC de Timor 309
A.D. Dili Leste 309

ECUADOR
LDU Quito 214
CCD Olmedo 215
Barcelona SC 215
CS Emelec 215
3D Quito 215
CD El Nacional 215
Mushuc Runa SC 215

EGYPT
Al Ahly 246
Zamalek SC 247
Al Ittihad 247
Al Masry Club 247
Ismaily SC 247
El Mokawloon SC 247
Petrojet FC 247

EL SALVADOR
CD Aguila 194
CD FAS 194
Alianza FC 195
Isidro Metapan 195

ENGLAND
Manchester United 10-13
Liverpool FC 14-17
Arsenal FC 18-19
Chelsea FC 20-21
Manchester City 22-23
Everton FC 24
Aston Villa 25
Newcastle United 26
Tottenham Hotspur 27
Nottingham Forest 28
Sheffield FC 29
Notts County FC 29
Stoke City FC 29
Sheffield Wednesday FC 29
Reading FC 29
Bolton Wanderers FC 29
Blackburn Rovers FC 30
Middlesbrough FC 30
Port Vale FC 30

Wolverhampton
    Wanderers FC 30
Ipswich Town FC 30
West Bromwich Albion FC 30
Sunderland AFC 31
Watford FC 31
Queens Park Rangers FC 31
Coventry City FC 31
Derby County FC 31
Leicester City FC 31
Tranmere Rovers FC 32
Bury FC 32
Millwall FC 32
Shrewsbury Town FC 32
Blackpool FC 32
Bristol City FC 32
West Ham United FC 33
Scunthorpe United FC 33
Norwich City FC 33
Hull City AFC 33
Charlton Athletic 33
Crystal Palace 33
Easington Colliery AFC 34
Dick, Kerr's Ladies 34
Leeds United FC 34
London XI 34
Doncaster Rovers
    Belles Ladies 34
Arsenal Ladies FC 34
AFC Wimbledon 35
FC United of Manchester 35

EQUATORIAL GUINEA
Sony Ela Nguema 266
Leones
    Vegetarianos FC 266

ERITREA
Red Sea FC 269
Adulis Club 269

ESTONIA
Tammeka Tartu 48
FC Flora 48
Nomme Kalju 49
Levadia Tallinn 49

ETHIOPIA
Saint-George SC 270
Ethiopian Coffee FC 270

FAROE ISLANDS
Havnar Boltfelag 43
B36 Torshavn 43

FIJI
Ba FC 314
Nadi FC 314

FINLAND
HIFK Fotboll 47
HJK Helsinki 47
Turun Palloseura 48
FC Haka 48
FC Jazz 48
FC Lahti 48

FRANCE
Olympique
    de Marseille 84-85
Paris Saint-Germain 86-87
AS Saint-Étienne 88
FC Nantes 89
Olympique Lyonnais 90
AS Monaco 91
Le Havre AC 92
FC Girondins de Bordeaux 92
Racing Club de Paris 92

Red Star FC 92
AS Cannes 92
OGC Nice 92
AJ Auxerre 93
RC Lens 93
RC Strasbourg 93
En Avant de Guingamp 93
FC Metz 93
Montpellier HSC 93
FC Sochaux-Montbéliard 94
Stade de Reims 94
Lille OSC 94
Olympique Lyonnais
    Ladies 94

GABON
AS Mangasport 266
Football Canon 105 266

GAMBIA
Real de Banjul 255
Wallidan FC 255

GEORGIA
Dinamo Tbilisi 136
Torpedo Kutaïsi 136

GERMANY
Bayern Munich 52-55
Borussia Dortmund 56-57
Schalke 04 58
Hamburger SV 59
Borussia
    Mönchengladbach 60
1860 München 61
Hertha Berlin 61
FC Lokomotive Leipzig 61
VfB Stuttgart 61
Eintracht Braunschweig 61
Fortuna Düsseldorf 61
Hannover 96 62
Chemnitzer FC 62
Eintracht Frankfurt 62
TSG 1899 Hoffenheim 62
Werder Bremen 62
FC Kaiserslautern 62
1. FC Nürnberg 63
FC Carl Zeiss Jena 63
Bayer Leverkusen 63
SC Freiburg 63
1. FSV Mainz 05 63
Union Berlin 63
FC Augsburg 64
Rot-Weiss Essen 64
FC Sankt Pauli 64
VfL Wolfsburg 64
FC Köln 64
BFC Dynamo 64
Dynamo Dresden 65
1. FC Magdeburg 65
FC Hansa Rostock 65
Energie Cottbus 65
Rot-Weiss Erfurt 65
RB Leipzig 65

GHANA
Asante Kotoko 259
Hearts of Oak 260
Ashanti Gold SC 260
Aduana Stars FC 260
Berekum Chelsea FC 260

GREECE
Olympiacos FC 143
Panathinaikos 144
AEK Athens 145
Panionios GSS 146
Apollon Smyrni 146

Panachaïki GE 146
Aris Thessaloniki 146
Iraklis 1908 FC 146
Ethnikos Piraeus 146
OFI Crete 147
PAOK FC 147
AE Larissa 147
Skoda Xanthi 147

GRENADA
Carib Hurricane FC 187
Queen's Park Rangers SC 187

GUAM
Guam Shipyard 313
Quality Distributors FC 313

GUATEMALA
Xelaju MC 194
Club Social y Deportivo
    Municipal 194
Aurora FC 194
Comunicaciones
    Futbol Club SA 194

GUINEA
AS Kaloum Star 256
Horoya AC 256
Fello Star 256
Satellite FC 256
Hafia FC 257

GUINEA BISSAU
SC de Bissau 256
CF Os Balantas 256

GUYANA
Santos Georgetown 213
Alpha United FC 213

HAITI
Violette AC 182
Racing Club Haïtien 182

HONDURAS
CD Olimpia 195
CD Marathon 195
CD Motagua 195
Real Espana 195

HONG KONG
South China AA 298
Kitchee SC 298

HUNGARY
Budapest Honvéd 122
Ujpest FC 123
MTK Budapest 123
Ferencvarosi TC 123
Debreceni Vasutas 123
Gyori ETO 123
Vasas SC 123
Szombathelyi Haladas 124
Videoton FC 124

ICELAND
KR Reykjavik 43
Fram Reykjavik 43
Valur Reykjavik 43
Akranes SC 43

INDIA
Churchill Brothers SC 292
Mohun Bagan AC 293
Kingfisher East Bengal 293
Dempo SC 293
Mumbai City FC 293
FC Goa 293

Delhi Dynamos FC 293

INDONESIA
Persebaya Surabaya 297
Persija Jakarta 297
Persib Bandung 297
Persipura Jayapura 297

IRAN
Esteghlal Tehran FC 288
Persépolis Tehran FC 288

IRAQ
Al-Quwa Al-Jawiya 288
Al-Zawra'a SC 288

ISRAEL
Maccabi Haïfa 148
Hapoël Tel Aviv FC 148
Hapoël Haïfa 148
Beitar Jerusalem 148
Maccabi Tel Aviv 149

ITALY
ACF Fiorentina 95
AS Roma 96
SS Lazio 97
Inter Milan 98-99
SSC Napoli 100-101
Juventus FC 102-105
AC Milan 106-109
Genoa CFC 110
Udinese 110
US Citta di Palermo 110
Vicenza Calcio 110
FC Pro Vercelli 1892 110
Hellas Verona 110
Torino FC 111
Atalanta Bergamsca 111
FC Bari 1908 111
Bologna FC 1909 111
Brescia Calcio 111
Parma FC 111
Cosenza 112
AS Livorno Calcio 112
Triestina 112
Cagliari Calcio 112
US Catanzaro 112
Chievo Verona 112
Calcio Catania 113
UC Sampdoria 113

IVORY COAST
Africa Sports National 258
ASEC Mimosas 258
Stella d'Adjamé 258
Séwé Sport 258

JAMAICA
Santos FC 184
Tivoli Gardens FC 184
Harbour View 184
Portmore United FC 184

JAPAN
Kashima Antlers 305
Nagoya Grampus 306
FC Tokyo 307
Sanfrecce Hiroshima 307
Kashiwa Reysol 307
JEF United Ichihara
    Chiba 307
Urawa Red Diamonds 307
Cerezo Osaka 307
Matsumoto Yamaga FC 308
Tokyo Verdy 308
Jubilo Iwata 308
Yokohama F. Marinos 308

Gamba Osaka 308
Shimizu S-Pulse 308

JORDAN
Al-Faisaly SC 285
Al-Wehdat SC 285

KAZAKHSTAN
FC Kairat 137
FC Shakhter Karagandy 137
Irtysh Pavlodar 137
FC Aktobe 137

KENYA
AFC Leopards 270
Gor Mahia FC 270
Tusker FC 270
Ulinzi Stars FC 270

KOSOVO
FC Prishtina 121
KF Besa Pejë 121

KUWAIT
Al-Arabi SC 285
Qadsia SC 285
Kuwait SC 286

KYRGYZSTAN
FC Alga Bishkek 289
FC Dordoi Bishkek 289

LAOS
Yothatikan FC 294
Lao Army FC 294

LATVIA
Skonto FC 137
FK Ventspils 137

LEBANON
Homenetmen Beirut FC 284
Al-Ansar SC 284

LESOTHO
Matlama FC 277
Lioli FC 277

LIBERIA
Invincible Eleven 258
Mighty Barolle 258

LIBYA
Al-Ittihad Club 248
Al-Ahli SC 248

LIECHTENSTEIN
FC Vaduz 83
USV Eschen/Mauren 83

LITHUANIA
Suduva Marijampole 49
FC Zalgiris 49
FBK Kaunas 49
FC Ekranas 49

LUXEMBOURG
CD Fola Esch 80
AS Jeunesse d'Esch 80
FC Avenir Beggen 80
F91 Dudelange 80

MACAU
CD Monte Carlo 298
GD Lam Pak 298

MACEDONIA
FK Vardar Skopje 121

FK Horizont Turnovo 121

MADAGASCAR
AS Adema 275
CNAPS Sport 275

MALAWI
Mighty Wanderers 273
Big Bullets FC 273

MALAYSIA
Selangor FA 296
Kelantan FA 296
Johor Darul Ta'zim FC 296
Pahang FA 296

MALI
Djoliba AC 253
Stade Malien 253
AS Real Bamako 254
Office du Niger Sports 254

MALTA
Floriana FC 113
Sliema Wanderers 113

MAURITANIA
ACS Ksar 251
FC Nouadhibou 251

MAURITIUS
AS Port-Louis 2000 275
Curepipe Starlight SC 275

MEXICO
CF América 189
CD Guadalajara 190
CF Pachuca 191
CD Albinegros de Orizaba 191
Club Atlas 191
CF Atlante 191
Deportivo Toluca FC 191
Club Necaxa 191
CA Monarcas Morelia 192
Cruz Azul FC 192
Club Leon FC 192
Tiburones Rojos
    de Veracruz 192
Puebla FC 192
CF Monterrey 192
Querétaro FC 193
Club Universidad
    Nacional 192
Tigres UANL 193
Club Santos Laguna 193
Chiapas FC 193
Club Tijuana 193

MOLDOVA
FC Zimbru Chisinau 136
FC Sheriff Tiraspol 136

MONGOLIA
Erchim FC 301
Khoromkhon FC 301

MONTENEGRO
FK Buducnost Podgorica 120
FK Sutjeska 120

MONTSERRAT
Royal Montserrat
    Police Force FC 185
Ideal SC 185

MOROCCO
Raja Club Athletic 252

Wydad AC 253
Maghreb AS Fès 253
Kawkab Marrakech 253
FAR Rabat 253

MOZAMBIQUE
CD Maxaquene 274
Grupo Desportivo
    de Maputo 274
Ferroviario de Maputo 274
CD Costa do Sol 274

NAMIBIA
Blue Waters FC 276
Orlando Pirates
    Windhoek 276
Civics FC 276
Black Africa SC 276

NEPAL
Three Star Club 290
Manang Marshyangdi
    Club 290

NETHERLANDS
AFC Ajax 68-71
PSV Eindhoven 72
Feyenoord Rotterdam 73
Sparta Rotterdam 74
SBV Vitesse 74
Willem II 74
MVV Maastricht 74
Ado Den Haag 7
NAC Breda 74
SC Heerenveen 75
Roda JC Kerkrade 75
FC Twente 75
AZ Alkmaar 75
FC Utrecht 75
FC Groningen 75

NEW CALEDONIA
Gaïtcha FCN 313
AS Magenta 313

NEW ZEALAND
University-Mount
    Wellington 312
Auckland City FC 312
Waitakere United 312
Wellington Phoenix FC 312

NICARAGUA
Diriangen FC 196
Real Esteli 196
Real Madriz 196
Deportivo
    Walter Ferretti 196

NIGER
Sahel SC 262
Olympic FC 262

NIGERIA
Shooting Stars SC 262
Enugu Rangers
    International 262
Bridge FC 262
Enyimba International 262
Heartland FC 263
Kano Pillars 263

NORTHERN IRELAND
Cliftonville FAC 42
Glentoran FC 42
Linfield FC 42
Crusaders FC 42

NORWAY
Odds Ballklubb 46
Viking FK 46
SK Brann 46
Molde FK 46
Valerenga Fotball 47
Lillestrom Sportsklubb 47
Rosenborg BK 47
Tromso IL 47

NORTH KOREA
April Twenty-Five SC 304
Pyongyang City SC 304

OMAN
Dhofar SCSC 287
Fanja SC 287

PAKISTAN
Wapda FC 290
KRL FC 290

PALESTINE
Hilal Al-Quds Club 284
Shabab Al-Dhahiriya SC 284

PANAMA
CD Plaza Amador 197
San Francisco FC 197
Tauro FC 197
CD Arabe Unido 197

PAPUA NEW GUINEA
Hekari United FC 309
Eastern Stars FC 309

PARAGUAY
Club Guarani 223
Club Nacional 223
Club Libertad 224
Sol de América 224
Cerro Porteno 224
Club Rubio Nu 224
12 de Octubre FC 224
CS Luqueno 224
Club Olimpia 225

PERU
Club Alianza Lima 216
Club Universitario
    de Deportes 216
Sporting Cristal 216
CDU San Martin
    de Porres 216

PHILIPPINES
Philippine Air Force FC 309
Global FC 309

POLAND
Wisla Krakow 126
RTS Widzew Lodz 126
Legia Warsaw 127
KS Ruch Chorzow 127
Lech Poznan 127
Gornik Zabrze 127

PORTUGAL
Associaçao Académica
    de Coimbra 165
Boavista FC 165
CS Maritimo 165
CD Nacional 165
SC Farense 166
Vitoria FC 166
CF OS Belenenses 166
SC Braga 166

SC Beira Mar 166
Vitoria SC 166
Sporting Clube
    de Portugal 167
SL Benfica 168-169
FC Porto 170-171

PUERTO RICO
Criollos de Caguas 183
Bayamon FC 183

QATAR
Lekhwiya SC 287
Al-Sadd SC 287

REPUBLIC OF IRELAND
Bohemian FC 41
Shelbourne FC 41
University College
    Dublin Association 41
Shamrock Rovers 41
Dundalk FC 42
Derry City FC 42

REPUBLIC OF THE CONGO
Étoile du Congo 268
AC Léopards 268

ROMANIA
Steaua Bucharest 114
CFR 1907 Cluj 115
FC Rapid Bucharest 115
FC Petrolul Ploiesti 115
FC Dinamo Bucharest 115
FC Universitatea Craiova 115
FC Otelul Galati 115

RUSSIA
FC Alania Vladikavkaz 127
Dynamo Moscow 127
FC Lokomotiv Moscow 128
FC Torpedo Moscow 128
FC Rotor Volgograd 128
FC Rostov 128
FC Rubin Kazan 128
FC Anzhi Makhachkala 128
Spartak Moscow 129
CSKA Moscow 130
FC Zenit Saint Petersburg 131

RWANDA
Rayon Sports FC 271
Armée Patriotique
    Rwandaise FC 271

SAINT KITTS AND NEVIS
Newtown United 185
Garden Hotspurs FC 185

SAINT LUCIA
Northern United All Stars 186
Big Players FC 186

SAMOA
Kiwi FC 315
Lupe o le Soaga 315

SAN MARINO
SP Tre Fiori 113
San Marino Calcio 113

SÃO TOMÉ AND PRÍNCIPE
SC do Principe 266
SC Praia Cruz 266

SAUDI ARABIA
Al-Ittihad FC 282
Al-Shabab FC 282

Al-Nassr FC 282
Al-Fateh FC 282
Al-Hilal FC 283

SCOTLAND
Glasgow Rangers FC 36-37
The Celtic FC 38-39
Kilmarnock FC 40
Hamilton Academical FC 40
Heart of Midlothian FC 40
Hibernian FC 40
Partick Thistle FC 40
Aberdeen FC 40
Dundee United FC 41
Inverness Caledonian
    Thistle FC 41

SENEGAL
ASC Jeanne d'Arc 254
ASC Diaraf 254
AS Douanes 254
Diambars FC 254

SERBIA
Red Star 116
OFK Belgrade 117
FK Vojvodina 117
FK Radnicki Nis 117
FK Obilic Belgrade 117
FK Partizan Belgrade 117
FK Spartak Subotica 117

SEYCHELLES
Saint Michel United FC 275
Saint Louis Suns United 275

SIERRA LEONE
Mighty Blackpool FC 255
East End Lions FC 255

SINGAPORE
Tampines Rovers FC 297
Warriors FC 297

SLOVAKIA
FC Petrzalka Akademia 125
MSK Zilina 125
SK Slovan Bratislava 126
FC Spartak Trnava 126
FK Inter Bratislava 126
FC VSS Kosice 126

SLOVENIA
NK Celje 119
FC Koper 119
NK Domzale 119
ND Gorica 119
NK Maribor 119
NK Olimpija Ljubljana 119

SOLOMON ISLANDS
Koloale FC 313
Western United 313

SOMALIA
Elman FC 271
Banadir SC 271

SOUTH AFRICA
AmaZulu FC 278
Orlando Pirates
    Johannesburg 278
Moroka Swallows FC 278
Bloemfontein Celtic FC 278
Kaizer Chiefs 278
Mamelodi Sundowns FC 278
Free State Stars FC 279
Santos FC 279

Jomo Cosmos FC 279
Supersport United FC 279
Platinum Stars FC 279
Ajax Cape Town FC 279

SOUTH KOREA
FC Seoul 302
Jeonbuk Hyundai
  Motors 303
Pohang Steelers FC 304
Busan Ipark FC 304
Seongnam FC 304
Suwon Samsung
  Bluewings FC 304

SOUTH SUDAN
Al-Malakia FC 269
Wau Salaam FC 269

SPAIN
Real Madrid 150-153
FC Barcelona 154-157
Atlético Madrid 158-159
Valencia CF 160
Athletic Bilbao 161
RC Recreativo de Huelva 162
RCD Espanol 162
Malaga CF 162
Real Sporting de Gijon 162
Seville FC 162
RC Deportivo La Coruna 162
Real Betis Balompié 163
Levante UD 163
Real Sociedad 163
Real Union 163
RCD Mallorca 163
CA Osasuna 163
Deportivo Alaves 164
RC Celta de Vigo 164
Villareal CF 164
Rayo Vallecano 164
Granada CF 164
Real Zaragoza 164
SD Eibar 165
Getafe CF 165

SRI LANKA
Saunders SC 291
Ratnam SC 291

SUDAN
Al-Merrikh SC 268
Al-Hilal Club 268

SURINAME
SV Robinhood 213
Inter Moengotapoe 213

SWAZILAND
Mbabane Swallows FC 277
Mbabane Highlanders FC 277

SWEDEN
Malmö FF 44
AIK Fotboll 45
Djurgardens IF 45
IFK Norrköping 45
IF Elfsborg 45
IFK Göteborg 45
Helsingborgs IF 45
Hammarby IF 46
Syrianska FC 46

SWITZERLAND
Grasshopper Club Zurich 81
FC St. Gallen 82
Servette FC 82
FC Basel 1893 82
FC Lausanne-Sport 82
FC Zurich 82
BSC Young Boys 82
FC Thun 83
FC Lugano 83
FC Sion 83
Neuchâtel Xamax FCS 83

SYRIA
Al-Karamah SC 284
Al-Jaish SC 284

TAJIKISTAN
Regar-TadAZ Tursunzoda 289
FC Istiklol 289

TAIWAN
Tatung FC 298
Taipower FC 298

TANZANIA
Young Africans SC 273
Simba SC 273

THAILAND
Air Force Central FC 295
Buriram United FC 295
Muangthong United FC 295
Chonburi FC 295

TOGO
Étoile Filante de Lomé 261
Dynamic Togolais 261
OC Agaza 261
AC Semassi 261

TONGA
LotoHa'apai United FC 314
Marist FC 314

TRINIDAD AND TOBAGO
Defence Force FC 187
W Connection FC 187

TUNISIA
Club Africain 248
Étoile Sportive du Sahel 248
CA Bizertin 248
CS Sfaxien 248
Espérence Sportive de
  Tunis 249

TURKEY
Altay SK 139
Kasımpaşa SK 139
Bursaspor 139
Trabzonspor 139
Galatasaray SK 140
Fenerbahçe SK 141
Besiktas JK 142

TURKMENISTAN
Balkan FK 288
FC ITTU 288

TURKS AND CAICOS ISLANDS
Cheshire Hall FC 181
AFC Academy 181

UGANDA
Kampala Capital
  City Authority FC 271
SC Villa 271

UKRAINE
Dynamo Kiev 132-133
FK Shakhtar Donetsk 134
FC Dnipro Dnipropetrovsk 135
FC Arsenal Kiev 135
FC Metalist Kharkiv 135
FC Chornomorets Odessa 135
SC Tavriya Simferopol 135
FC Karpaty Lviv 135

UNITED ARAB EMIRATES
Al-Ain FC 282
Al-Ahli Dubai FC 282

UNITED STATES OF AMERICA
LA Galaxy 174
DC United 175
New York Red Bulls 176
North Carolina
  Tar Heels 177
San José Earthquakes 178
Sporting Kansas City 178
New England
  Revolution 178
Seattle Sounders FC 178
Colorado Rapids 178
Chicago Fire 178
Real Salt Lake 179
Houston Dynamo 179
Portland Timbers 179
New York Cosmos 179
Orlando City SC 179
New York City FC 179

URUGUAY
CA Penarol 226-227
Club Nacional 228
Montevideo Wanderers 228
Central Espanol 228
Defensor SC 228
Liverpool FC 228
CA Bella Vista 228
Danubio FC 229
Tacuarembo FC 229

US VIRGIN ISLANDS
Helenites Soccer Club 183
Positive Vibes SCC 183

UZBEKISTAN
Pakhtakor Tachkent FK 289
FC Bunyodkor 289

VANUATU
Tafea FC 314
Amicale FC 314

VENEZUELA
Caracas FC 213
Deportivo Tachira FC 213

VIETNAM
Ho-Chi-Minh-City FC 295
Becamex Binh Duong FC 295

WALES
Wrexham FC 35
Cefn Druids AFC 35
Cardiff City FC 35
Swansea City 35

YEMEN
Al-Tilal SC 287
Al-Ahli Club Sana'a 287

ZAMBIA
Nkana FC 273
Zesco United 273

ZIMBABWE
Highlanders FC 277
Dynamos FC 277

PHOTO CREDITS

All photographs in this book appear courtesy Icon Sport picture agency,
except for pages: 11 (top); 81; 95; 104 (bottom); 114; 122; 220; 257; 259; 264; 286; 292 (rights reserved).
21 (bottom) (Evening Standard/Hulton Archive/Getty Images) and 177 (Will Mcintyre/The LIFE Images Collection/
Getty Images).